INSPIRE / PLAN / DISCOVER / EXPERIENCE

SLOVENIA

Date: 12/17/20

SLOVENIA

CONTENTS

DISCOVER 6

EXPERIENCE LJUBLJANA 58

EXPERIENCE SLOVENIA 124

NEED TO KNOW 218

Left: Gothic façade, Tartinijev trg, Piran
Previous page: Julian Alps, Triglav National Park
Front cover: The rooftops of the Old Town, Ljubljana

DISCOVER

Picturesque Piran on Slovenia's Adriatic coast

WELCOME TO
SLOVENIA

Epic mountain vistas and vibrant cities packed with art and culture. Luxurious spas, sun-soaked beaches and traditional festivals pulsing with colour. Fantastic food and lip-smackingly good wine – Slovenia has it all. Whatever your dream trip to this captivating country includes, this DK Eyewitness travel guide is the perfect companion.

1 The Church of St Primoz in Jamnik, Gorenjska.

2 Snowboarding in Vogel ski resort.

3 One of Slovenia's underground karst caves.

4 The Ljubljanica river flowing through Ljubljana.

Nestled in the heart of Europe, diminutive Slovenia is synonymous with awe-inspiring scenery and a seemingly limitless scope for outdoor adventure. Most famous for pictur-esque Lake Bled, the country is also home to the soaring peaks of the Julian Alps and other-worldly caves of the Karst plateau. Slovenia is wonderfully green, too, both literally and envi-ronmentally: over 60 per cent of the country's surface is blanketed by swathes of lush forests, and it has been hailed by the UN as one of the world's most sustainable countries.

It's not just natural beauty that draws the crowds, however: Slovenia also has culture in spades. Its rich history is evident everywhere you look, from the exquisite architecture and outstanding museums of its student-filled capital, Ljubljana, to its imposing hilltop castles and fiercesome fortresses. Lively festivals kick off throughout the year, with everything from spellbinding passion plays to acclaimed jazz programmes on offer. This is also the perfect place to feast, whether you're devouring deca-dent desserts or sampling outstanding wine from the country's lush vineyards.

Slovenia is filled with such a variety of sights that is can be hard to know where to start. We've broken the country down into easily navigable chapters, with detailed itineraries, expert local knowledge and colourful, comprehensive maps to help you plan the perfect trip. However long you plan to stay, this DK Eyewitness travel guide will ensure that you see the best of this spetac-ular country. Enjoy the book, and enjoy Slovenia.

REASONS TO LOVE
SLOVENIA

Magnificent natural scenery, an abundance of cultural riches, delectable wines and intriguing traditions – there are so many reasons to love Slovenia. Here, we pick a few of our favourites.

1 GORGEOUS LAKES

Lakes Bled and Bohinj are among Slovenia's most stunning scenery. Take a boat out to the island of Lake Bled *(p130)* or paddle across Lake Bohinj *(p134)* in a kayak.

PTUJ CARNIVAL 2

Time your visit to Ptuj *(p190)* to witness this colourful carnival. On the last Sunday before Lent, the iconic Kurenti romp through the streets, clanging cowbells to drive off evil winter spirits.

3 WORLD-CLASS ART

From folk art at the Museum of Apiculture *(p138)* to modern collections at the Museum of Contemporary Art *(p105)*, Slovenia's galleries are unique, eclectic and not to be missed.

WATERSPORTS 4

Whether it's kayaking the rapids of the Soča, testing the more serene waters of the Kolpa or sailing on the Adriatic, Slovenia has more than enough to keep fans of watersports happy.

HIKING 5

Few places in Europe rival Slovenia as a hiking destination, with over 10,000 km (6,200 miles) of marked hiking trails to choose from. Pull on your boots: soaring peaks and verdant valleys await you.

PREMURSKA GIBANICA 6

You can't visit Slovenia without sampling a slice of Premurska gibanica. Originally from the Prekmurje region, this tasty pastry has become something of a national dessert.

TRIGLAV NATIONAL PARK 7

Slovenia's Triglav National Park *(p132)* is a magnificent sprawl of mountain scenery and diverse flora. It's a wonderful place to hike, kayak or simply while away an afternoon.

LJUBLJANA'S ARCHITECTURE 8

Ljubljana *(p58)* is home to some fabulous architecture, and a walking tour is the perfect way to admire it – from the iconic Dragon Bridge to the legacy of Jože Plečnik *(p101)*.

9 ŠKOCJAN CAVES

Exploring the underground world of the Karst is an essential part of any trip to Slovenia – and nowhere is more jaw-droppingly impressive than the UNESCO-listed Škocjan Caves *(p160)*, home to the world's biggest underground river canyon.

10 THE SLOVENIAN COAST

Though often overshadowed by that of neighbouring Croatia, Slovenia's coastline is packed with things to see – visit bijou towns, golden beaches and historic salt pans.

FINE WINES 11

The Goriška Brda *(p180)* wine region is home to some of Slovenia's most celebrated vineyards. Along with the neighbouring Vipava Valley *(p156)*, this is the perfect place to taste local wines at small, family-run wineries.

THERMAL SPAS 12

Slovenia's rolling countryside is peppered with an extraordinary number of thermal spas *(p213)*. Seek out the nearest resort and get ready for a spot of relaxation and pampering.

EXPLORE
SLOVENIA

This guide divides Slovenia into five colour-coded sightseeing areas, as shown on this map. Find out more about each area on the following pages.

Wolfsberg

Klagenfurt

Villach

Tarvisio

Kranjska Gora

Jesenice

Bovec

Triglav National Park

Bled

THE ALPS
p126

Kranj

Domžale

Soča

Tolmin

Sora

ITALY

Udine

Ljubljana

Litija

Nova Gorica

Vrhnika

LJUBLJANA
p58

Gorizia

Ajdovščina

Logatec

Vipava

Monfalcone

COASTAL SLOVENIA AND THE KARST
p150

Cerknica

Postojna

Ribnica

Sežana

Trieste

Kočevje

Piran

Koper

Ilirska Bistrica

Umag

Rijecka

CROATIA

Opatija

Kraljevica

| 0 kilometres | 25 |
| 0 miles | 25 |

N
↑

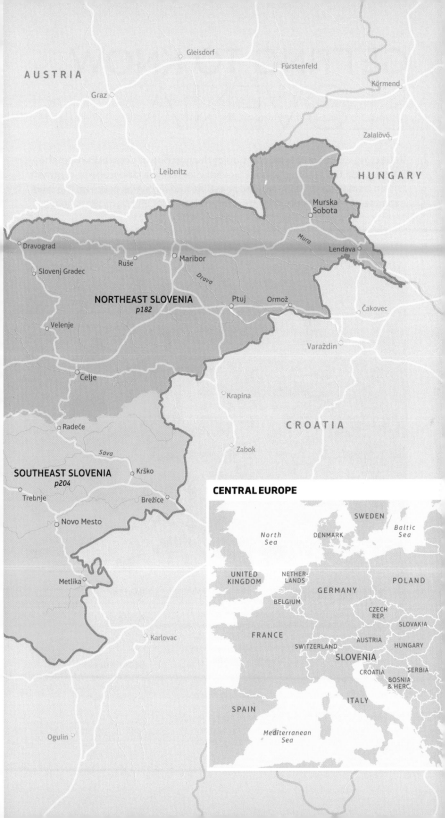

GETTING TO KNOW
SLOVENIA

Reflecting its geographical position at the junction of Central Europe, the Balkans and the Mediterranean, Slovenia serves up a landscape of contrasts within a small area. Palm-fringed coastline and high Alps make up the wild expanse of countryside, with the vibrant capital of Ljubljana at its heart.

LJUBLJANA

PAGE 58

Clustered along a stretch of the Ljubljanica river below an imposing castle, the Slovenian capital is a wonderfully captivating city that simply pulses with life. Known for its Secessionist architecture and in particular for the work of Slovenia's most famous architect, Jože Plečnik, Ljubljana is home to the country's finest museums and galleries, as well as some of its best festivals. The city's centre is largely pedestrianized, with cafés and bars spilling out on to the pavements of its riverside promenades. To escape the bustle, Tivoli Park offers a sprawling wedge of greenery that stretches right into the city centre.

Best for
Architecture and museums

Home to
Ljubljana Castle, National Gallery, Slovene Ethnographic Museum

Experience
A walking tour of the Old Town, which takes in many of the city's most famous sights

THE ALPS

Spectacular alpine scenery coupled with a rich history make northwest Slovenia the most acclaimed region in the country. Here, majestic mountains are studded with jewel-like lakes and slashed by breathtakingly beautiful river valleys. The Julian Alps form the bulk of Slovenia's mountain scenery, and are home to the picturesque Triglav National Park, while the Karavanke stretch along the northern border with Austria. Soaring above all is Mount Triglav, so iconic that it features on the national flag. Set within this amazing landscape are beautifully preserved medieval towns such as Radovljica, bustling ski resorts like Kranjska Gora, and irresistible lakeside havens such as Bled, Slovenia's visual trademark.

Best for
Outdoor activities, and taking in some of Slovenia's spectacular wildlife

Home to
Bled, Triglav National Park

Experience
A breathtaking hike through the wilderness of Triglav National Park

→

PAGE 150

COASTAL SLOVENIA AND THE KARST

In southwestern Slovenia, craggy ridges and highland meadows of the limestone plateau, known as the Karst, descend to meet a lush coastal strip rich in olive groves, palms and important historic towns. Koper, a bustling city with a well-preserved medieval Old Town at its heart, is the main centre of the region. Nearby Portorož is Slovenia's prime beach resort, offering boisterous nightlife in summer and soothing spa escapes the whole year round. Inland, the Karst region is riddled with gorges and caverns, of which the Škocjan and Postojna caves are Slovenia's most compelling.

Best for
Caves and gorgeous coastlines

Home to
Piran, Vipava Valley, Škocjan Caves, Postojna Caves, Predjama Castle

Experience
An unforgettable trip below ground at the Škocjan or Postojna caves

PAGE 182

NORTHEAST SLOVENIA

Slovenia's northeast region is incredibly diverse. The city of Maribor is a former European Capital of Culture, and home to some of Slovenia's most renowned festivals, while nearby Ptuj is one of the country's oldest recorded towns, and offers one of Slovenia's richest carnival traditions. The little-known Prekmurje region is a place of low-lying hills and riverside plains, where white storks nest in quiet villages and the country's most famous desert originated. Thanks to its vast green plains and idyllic vineyards, the northeast is also home to Slovenia's largest wine producers.

Best for
Wine-tasting and lively festivals

Home to
Celje, Maribor, Ptuj

Experience
Slovenia's colourful local culture during the Ptuj carnival

PAGE 204

SOUTHEAST SLOVENIA

While the southeast is the least visited part of Slovenia, it packs a punch with its spectacular castles, huge stretches of forest and rolling hills that make it a haven for outdoor adventurers. This is Slovenia's premier region for thermal spas, many of which come with several centuries of tradition behind them. Kočevlje is the most heavily forested part of Slovenia, an unspoilt area with UNESCO-listed pockets of primeval woodland and hiking trails. The River Kolpa, which forms the border with Croatia, is excellent for wild swimming.

Best for
Castles and thermal spas

Home to
The pleasant Posavje wine region and Podsreda Castle

Experience
A high-thrills kayak ride along the Kolpa river

←

① Ljubljana Town Hall in the city's Old Town.

② A funicular descending towards the red-roofed city.

③ Exhibits at Plečnik House.

④ The façade of Ljubljana's National Gallery.

Slovenia is a treasure trove of things to see and do, and its small size means that you can make your way around the country relatively easily. These itineraries will inspire you to make the most of your visit.

2 DAYS
in Ljubljana

Day 1

Morning Begin your day beneath the poet Prešeren's statue on the square of the same name *(p72)*; from here, stroll across the Triple Bridge *(p72)*, one of the famed architect Plečnik's ingenious designs, before perusing the produce from the city's colourful central market *(p74)*. Next, the funicular will whizz you up to the castle *(p70)*, where you can visit the Virtual Museum, climb the clock tower or just savour the views. Back down in the Old Town, pore over Baroque architecture, notably the Fountain of the Three Carniolan Rivers *(p73)* and Town Hall *(p74)*, before lunch at either Romeo *(www.caferomeo.si)* or Julija *(www.julijarestaurant.com)* – conveniently located opposite each other.

Afternoon Once refreshed, cross the Cobbler's Bridge and start exploring the left bank. Begin with Plečnik's extra-ordinary National and University Library *(p80)* – pop inside to view the Reading Room – then take a tour of the compelling City Museum *(p80)*, complete with its star exhibit: a 5,000 year-old wooden wheel. From here, wander past the neatly tended veg plots in the Krakovo suburb to Plečnik House *(p100)*, which looks much as it did while the great architect lived here.

Evening Have dinner at cosy Pri Škofu *(Rečna ulica 8)* before catching a live music performance in the atmospheric outdoor Križanke complex *(p81)*, another Plečnik masterpiece. Round off the evening with a glass of wine at the delightful Le Petit Café *(www.lepetit.si)*, just across the square.

Day 2

Morning Rise early and take a walk along Miklošičeva ulica, which bursts with eye-popping Secessionist architecture – you can't miss the Cooperative Bank building *(p82)*. Next, spend a couple of hours visiting the Slovenian Ethnographic Museum *(p94)*, where a superb range of artifacts from both Slovenia and beyond are showcased. You'll have worked up an appetite after all that walking, so treat yourself to a hearty, Balkan-style lunch at Sarajevo 84 *(Nazorjeva ulica 12)*.

Afternoon Get acquainted with Slovenia's greatest artists – including the much-loved Impressionists Jama, Jakopić, Grohar and Sternen – at the National Gallery *(p92)*. Afterwards, stop for a quick pick-me-up at the cool Moderna café inside the Museum of Modern Art *(p99)*. Round off the afternoon with a stroll around Tivoli Park *(p103)* or – if you're feeling particularly energetic – a brisk hike up through the wooded heights of Rožnik Hill *(p108)*.

Evening Make your way to Gostilna AS *(gostilnaas.si)*, located in one of the city's most vibrant neighbourhoods, for dinner; if you're visiting in summer, try to get a table on the elegant patio. Afterwards, head to Dvorni Bar *(www.dvornibar.net)* to sample some delicious local wines under the willow-lined Ljubljanica. Or, if you fancy something more upbeat, make tracks for Metelkova Mesto *(p104)*, the city's former army barracks turned alternative social and cultural centre.

→

1 A Vipava Valley vineyard.

2 Goregeous Lipizzaner horses at Lipica Stud Farm.

3 Piran's town square.

4 Ornate interior of the Church of St George in Piran's Old Town.

4 DAYS

around the Karst and Coast

Day 1

Morning Your first stop is the wondrous Postojna Cave complex *(p162)* to explore its spellbining subterranean caverns, filled with stalactites and stalagmites. From here it's a short drive to Predjama Castle *(p164)*, spectacularly – and improbably – sited in the mouth of a huge cavern, before a tasty lunch at nearby Proteus *(Titov trg 1)*.

Afternoon Continue northwest towards the wind-blown Vipava Valley *(p156)*, one of Slovenia's premier wine-growing regions. Any number of vineyards offer tours and tasting, but among the finest vintners are Batič and Rondić. Try to make time, too, to visit the fortified medieval village of Vipavski Križ *(p171)*.

Evening Seek out one of the Karst's many tourist farms for a restful overnight stay. You're likely to be very well fed – scrummy home-cooked food and home-harvested wine is usually the order of the day.

Day 2

Morning Set off early for Štanjel *(p172)*, the archetypal Karst village with crooked streets lined by brilliant bleached-white stone houses. Then continue to the world-famous Lipica Stud Farm *(p166)* for a closer glimpse of its magnificent horses and a presentation of the Classical Riding School.

Afternoon Admire the spectacular rock formations and underground waterways of the vast Škocjan Caves *(p160)*, one of Slovenia's greatest natural wonders. Back above ground, call in at the Church of the Holy Trinity in Hrastovlje *(p165)* to view its *Dance of Death* fresco, before the day's final stop in Koper *(p168)*.

Evening Wander the port city for an hour or two before kicking back at beachside Kroštola *(Kopališko nabrežje 1)*, where you can feast on the day's freshest catch while watching the sun go down.

Day 3

Morning Soak up Koper's Venetian streets and squares before continuing down the coast road to pretty Izola *(p169)*, which has an endearing Old Town core as well as one of the coast's best beaches at Simon's Bay.

Afternoon The highlight of the Slovenian coast, Piran *(p154)* features glorious Gothic-Venetian architecture. The Sergei Mašera Maritime Museum is a must-visit, shedding light on the town's rich seafaring history.

Evening Dine on squid and chips at the understated Fritolin pri Cantini *(Prvomajski trg 10)* before retiring to the Hotel Piran *(hotel-piran.si)*, whose stylish rooms offer sensational sea views.

Day 4

Morning Take an early morning walk along Piran's town walls, taking a look at the Church of St George along the way. Recharge with coffee and a pastry, in one of the many cheerful cafés on the marble-paved Tartinjev trg, Piran's main square.

Afternoon Set out for the eerily beautiful Šecovlje salt pans *(p170)*, where you can enjoy a demonstration of the salt-making process. Return to Piran via Portorož *(p170)*, stopping there for a beachfront cocktail.

Evening All that sea air will have you primed for a seafood supper along the waterfront Prešernovo nabrežje. Choose from one of the many restaurants here, before ending your night with an ice cream and a stroll along the promenade.

7 DAYS

in the Alps

Day 1

Head north from Ljubljana and spend an hour or so in delightful Kamnik *(p140)* before taking the cable car up to Velika Planina *(p142)*, a lush highland plateau spotted with shingle-roofed herdsmen's huts. You can buy local cheese here too, so rustle up a quick picnic or sample some cheese dumplings and *štruklji* on the terrace of the Zeleni Rob mountain hut. Next, drive to Logarska Dolina, an impossibly picturesque glacial valley pressed up against the Austrian border. Rent a bike and cycle to the end of the valley and the Rinka waterfall, before spending a relaxing evening in the fabulous Lenar tourist farm *(lenar.si)*.

Day 2

Get an early start for the drive west to Radovljica *(p138)*, whose attractive main square is framed by a raft of beautiful Gothic and Renaissance buildings, one of which is home to the engaging Museum of Apiculture *(p138)*. After lunch at Gostilna Lectar *(www.lectar.com)*, press on to Bled *(p130)*, Slovenia's star turn. Take a gondola or row across to Bled Island, where the Church of the Assumption sits in perfect isolation, then head up to the castle for a glorious, bird's-eye view of the lake. End the day with supper at the lakeside Villa Prešeren *(Veslaška promenada 14)*.

Day 3

From Bled it's not far to Triglav National Park *(p132)* and Lake Bohinj *(p134)*, even more serene than Bled itself. From the lake, make the short trek through verdant forest to the Savica Waterfall, a tumbling torrent that ends in a beautiful emerald pool. Next, take the cable car up to Vogel ski resort to enjoy awe-inspiring views over the lake and mountains. Nearby Studor, a beautifully preserved village renowned for its unique double hayracks (barn-like structures used for drying hay), is also worth a visit.

Day 4

Get your hiking boots on for a trek up to the Valley of the Triglav Lakes, arguably the park's most scenic walk and one that will occupy a good half a day. Leaving the

5

4

① Velika Planina plateau.
② The town of Radovljica.
③ The cable car to Vogel ski resort.
④ Kayaking the Soča river.
⑤ Most na Soči, at the edge of an emerald lake.

park behind, and after a brief diversion up the Vrata Valley to view Mount Triglav's massive north face, push on to Kranjska Gora *(p139)*, where you can marvel at the head-spinning Planica ski jumps. Test out your own ski-fly skills on the simulator at the exciting Planica Museum.

Day 5

Begin the dramatic ascent of the Vršič Pass *(p148)*, which climbs to 1,611 m (5,285 ft) over the course of 50 hairpin bends. Among the many attractions en route is the Russian Church, a poignant structure built to commemorate the deaths of over 300 Russian soldiers buried in an avalanche during the road's construction. Continue on through the Trenta Valley *(p135)*, stopping to see the source of the Soča river before spending the night at Pristava Lepena *(Lepena 2, 5232 Soča)*.

Day 6

It's thrill'n'spills time as you take to the magnificent and wild Soča river *(p137)* for a morning of adrenaline-fuelled activities

such as whitewater rafting or kayaking. After a well-deserved lunch at Letni vrt *(slo.letni-vrt.com)*, head down the imperious Soča Valley to Kobarid *(p145)* where the full horrors of World War I mountain warfare are relayed in the town's moving museum. Dine at Hiša Franko *(p145)*, arguably Slovenia's finest restaurant.

Day 7

Make the short drive to beautifully situated Tolmin *(p144)*. While this small town is of interest for its compelling archaeological museum, the area's real draw is the nearby Tolmin Gorge, which harbours the vertiginous Devil's Bridge and mysterious Dante's Cave. Also worth seeking out is Čadrg, Slovenia's first ecological village, where you can try the local speciality *frika* – a scrumptious fried-potato and cheese pie – at the welcoming Letni vrt Pr' Jakču *(Zadlaz - Čadrg 4)*. Complete your tour of the Alps in Most na Soči *(p144)*, one of Slovenia's most important prehistoric settlements – a well-conceived trail marks out the town's rich tapestry of natural and historical sights.

2 WEEKS

in Slovenia

Day 1

Kick off your tour in the cultural capital and head straight for the vast Ljubljana Castle (*p70*). Explore the quirky Museum of Puppetry inside and soak up glorious views of the distant Alps, then make your way down to the Old Town. After a tapas lunch at TaBar (*p74*), pop your head into St Nicholas's Cathedral (*p75*) to get your fill of its riot of frescoes. Spend the afternoon taking in the works of Slovenia's most enduringly popular Impressionist painters at the National Gallery (*p92*), a short stroll across Plečnik's cleverly designed Triple Bridge (*p72*). Later, enjoy dinner at the classy JB restaurant (*p32*) before retiring to the cosy Movia bar (*p77*) to sample some of Slovenia's exceptional wines.

Day 2

A short drive northwest of Ljubljana, Škofja Loka (*p114*) is one of Slovenia's oldest and loveliest towns; its focal point is medieval Mestni trg, centred on the Renaissance-style Homan House, where you can grab a coffee under the shade of a huge linden tree. Press on to Kropa, a comely one-street village bisected by the thrashing Kroparica, and whose formidable iron-mining and forging heritage is superbly relayed in the Iron Forging Museum. Your final stop on a busy day is Radovljica (*p138*), where you can acquaint yourself with all things apian in the marvellous Museum of Apiculture (*p138*).

Day 3

Arrive early in Bled (*p130*) – Slovenia's star attraction – and enjoy a relaxed stroll around the lake. Next, jump onto a *pletna* (canopied boat) found at the lake's edge to be rowed out to the famous island and its picture-postcard church. Following a leisurely lakeside lunch at Villa Prešeren, it's not far to Bohinj (*p134*), the pearl of the alpine lakes. Take your pick from any number of activities: a boat ride, a swim or a short hike to the photogenic Slap Waterfall. Time permitting, catch the cable car up to Vogel ski resort where you'll be rewarded with more sensational views – you may even see Mount Triglav itself.

1 Ljubljana's glass funicular ascends to the city's castle.

2 Traditional wooden *pletna* docked on Lake Bled.

3 Walking past huts in Bovec.

4 Canyoning in the Soča Valley.

5 The main square of Piran.

Day 4

Make a beeline for Kranjska Gora (p139) and its legendary Planica ski-jumps. Next up is the snaking Vršič Pass (p148), which, with its 50 hairpin bends, is Slovenia's most spectacular mountain drive; there are diversions aplenty, such as the poignant Russian Chapel and the source of the Soča. Head down through the beautiful Trenta Valley to Bovec (p143) for dinner and a good night's kip at Dobra Vila (www.dobra-vila-bovec.si).

Day 5

The magnificent Soča river beckons this morning for some adrenalin-fuelled activities, be it whitewater rafting or canyoning. Take a break for lunch, then make your way down the magisterial Soča Valley (p137) to Kobarid (p145), scene of some of the continent's most ferocious mountain warfare during World War I. The compelling Kobarid Museum and Kobarid Historical Walk can tell you more. End the day at Hiša Franko (www.hisafranko.com), likely the gastronomic highlight of your tour.

Day 6

Start the day in the Goriška Brda (p180), the country's most celebrated wine-growing region and a one-hour drive south. Wander around the fortified village of Šmartno (p118) then get back in the car (with a designated driver in tow) and make for the pretty village of Vipolže. Known for its lush vineyards, this is one of the best places to sample some of Slovenia's finest wines. Continue further south and bed down at one of the tourist farms in the Karst region.

Day 7

Your main activity this morning, and a highlight of the trip, is a guided tour of the unforgettable Škocjan Caves (p160). Leaving the Karst behind, make for the coast, pausing briefly in Koper (p168) for a stroll around its Venetian-inspired streets and squares. Press on to Piran (p154), the undisputed jewel in the coast's crown, where you can treat yourself to a seafood supper on the waterfront and a night in the classy Hotel Piran (www.hotel-piran.si).

Day 8

This morning, head to the fascinating Sečovlje salt pans *(p170)*, where you can learn all about the salt-making process. Then head back inland to the wind-blown Vipava Valley *(p156)*, one of Slovenia's most beautiful wine-growing regions; naturally, a tasting or two awaits. After a drop of Dutch courage, you might consider a tandem paraglide from the top of Nanos. End the day with a very special sleep at Majerija *(www.majerija.si).*

Day 9

There's more stunning cave action today at Postojna *(p162)*, where an underground train whizzes you to the start of a series of vast, stalactite and stalagmite infested chambers. Afterwards, pay a quick visit to Predjama Castle *(p164)*; you may even get to see some jousting. Nature reasserts itself in spectacular fashion at nearby Lake Cerknica *(p177)*, a seasonal body of water which drains away during the hotter summer months – that's why it's known as the disappearing lake!

Day 10

Kočevski Rog *(p208)* is home to some of Europe's last virgin forests, as well as the country's largest concentration of brown bears – indeed, the forest's many hiking trails are marked out, somewhat ominously, by bear paws. Continue south to the Kolpa Valley *(p210)* on the Croatian border, whose river rapids are perfect for canoeing. Travel eastwards to Novo Mesto *(p211)*, rich in archaeological treasures, before supper, and bed, at the homely Šeruga tourist farm *(Sela pri Ratežu 15).*

Day 11

Set off early for the longish drive northwest to Ptuj *(p190)*, Slovenia's oldest and most rewarding town. Two thousand years of history are manifest in a liberal sprinkling of Roman and medieval monuments, such as the remarkable Mithra shrines. Take an afternoon's excursion to the sun-kissed hills of the Jeruzalem wine-growing region *(p199)*, characterized by rolling, stepped vineyards. Return to Ptuj for an

1 The Secovlje Salina, one of Slovenia's most beautiful landscapes.

2 The interiors of the Postojna Caves, with truly incredible rock formations.

3 Rafters paddling slowly through the Kolpa Valley.

4 Scenic Ptuj, Slovenia's oldest town.

5 A hearty pot of traditional *bograč*.

6 Logarska Dolina, home to glorious alpine pastures and flora.

overnight stay at the wonderful MuziKafe (*www.muzikafe.si*), where you may even catch a concert.

Day 12

Spend the day pottering around Prekmurje, which is one of Slovenia's most unique landscapes; its flatness makes it ideal for cycling. Other places to explore nearby include the roadside churches at Bogojina (*p201*) and Martjanci (*p201*); the splash-tastic Terme 3000 resort in Moravske Toplice (*p200*); or Velika Polana (*p199*), where you can seek out the stork popu-lation. While in the region, make sure to sample some of the local cuisine, especially *bograč* (a goulash-type stew) and *gibanica*, an apple, walnut and poppy seed pie.

Day 13

Slovenia's second city, Maribor (*p188*), is wonderfully picturesque, thanks to its elegant confection of Baroque and Renaissance architecture – although its star attraction is the still-growing oldest

vine in the world, found in the riverside Lent District. Little-visited Koroška, on the other side of the Pohorje massif, merits a few hours of your time. Take in some breathtaking mountain scenery or set off on an exhilarating subterranean bike ride through the Peca Mine. The day's bicycle theme continues with a stopover at the Eco Hotel Koroš (*bikenomad.com*), Slovenia's first hotel for mountain bikers.

Day 14

Drive into the heart of the Kamniško-Savinjske Alps (*p146*) for yet more spectac-ular alpine scenery, this time in the shape of the twin glacial valleys, Logarska Dolina and Robanov kot. Hire a bike for a quick pedal down to the Rinka Waterfall, before rounding off this memorable trip with a cable car ride up to Velika Planina (*p142*), a verdant plateau sprinkled with eye-catching herdsmen's huts. Medieval Kamnik (*p140*) is your final stop. Explore its charm-ing castles, then look back on your trip with a freshly brewed pint at Korobač (*Šutna 76*), one of the town's cool microbreweries.

On Two Feet

With gorgeous mountain scenery and many miles of marked hiking trails, Slovenia is one of the finest hiking destinations anywhere in Europe. Hike hut-to hut through the breathtaking alpine landscapes of Triglav National Park *(p132)* or tackle one of Slovenia's longer trails – perhaps the 270-km (168-mile) Julian Alps Trail, or the Slovenian leg of the Alpe Adria Trail.

Trekking through the Julian Alps, with Lake Bled below

SLOVENIA FOR
OUTDOOR ADVENTURES

With an abundance of mountains, forests, hills, rivers and lakes, Slovenia offers unlimited potential for outdoor pursuits. Tackle the slopes of Mount Triglav, kayak down the Soča or cycle through the rolling hills of Dolenjska - there's something to suit every lover of the great outdoors.

TOP 4 WILD SWIMMING SPOTS

Podpeško Lake
C4
This popular spot is the deepest lake in Slovenia.

Lake Jasna
A3
The view from this pool, comprising two artificial lakes, is breathtaking.

River Kolpa
D6
Slovenia's warmest river is never too busy.

River Soča
A4
The outlet of the Soča Gorge is a welcoming spot to cool down in.

Biking Life

With mile upon mile of twisting mountain roads, off-road trails and quiet country lanes, Slovenia has more than enough to fill several cycling holidays. The magnificent Vršič Pass *(p148)* is both challenging and scenically rewarding, while the heavily forested Koroška region offers some wild rides. For a gentler trip, head for the wine-growing hills around Jeruzalem.

→

Bikers heading down the pebbled side of a steep mountain slope

Hit the Slopes

Skiing is by far the nation's number one sport, so it's little surprise that there are so many fantastic and affordable resorts. Family-friendly Kranjska Gora (p139) is Slovenia's largest resort, though Kanin offers the country's highest-altitude skiing and the largest skiing area. Snowboarders should make tracks for Vogel or Krvavec (p142); the former has glorious views, while the latter is popular with weekending Ljubljančani.

→

A busy piste within Slovenia's popular Vogel ski resort

Below Ground

Some of the finest underground systems in the world are found in Slovenia. Many spots offer classic tours through their main chambers, but there are also possibilities for longer and more immersive caving experiences. At Križna (p176), you'll don flashlights to cross a series of lakes. The more adventurous should head to the Pivka Cave in Postojna (p162), where one activity includes abseiling down a section of cave wall.

←

Exploring the otherworldly landscape of the famous Postojna Caves

Adrenaline Rush

Slovenia offers excellent adventure sports and activities, especially around its rivers. Here, the thrashing Soča (p137) comes into its own, with whitewater rafting, kayaking, canyoning and hydrospeed all high on the list for thrill-seekers. Or for bird's-eye views of Slovenia's natural scenery, why not try a tandem paraglide from the top of Mount Nanos in the Vipava Valley (p156)?

→

Canyoning in the Soča Valley through a narrow, pool-filled gorge

EAT

JB Restavracija
This outstanding spot offers one of the best fine-dining experiences in all of Slovenia.

C4 Miklošičeva 19, Ljubljana jb-slo.com

€€€

Hiša Denk
There is no menu at this countryside spot, where head chef Gregor Vračko serves seasonal, creative dishes.

E2 Zgornja Kungota 11a, Zgornja Kungota hisadenk.si

€€€

Vendors cooking up fresh dishes at Ljubljana's Open Kitchen ↑

SLOVENIA FOR
FOODIES

Slovenian cuisine is a deliciously earthy blend of different culinary cultures, particularly Austrian, Balkan and Mediterranean. Whether you decide to dine in the finest gourmet restaurant or a humble mountain hut, a wonderful gastronomic experience awaits.

Sweet Treats
There's no reason to feel guilty about the pleasures of Slovenian desserts. The best-known is *potica*, a tasty log-shaped cake filled with tarragon, hazelnuts and poppy seeds. Also popular is *gibanica*, a multi-layered sweet pie packed with poppy seeds, walnuts, cottage cheese and apple, originally from Prekmurje. And don't leave Bled without wolfing down a slice of *kremšnita*, a calorific puff pastry cake!

←

A slice of *potica*, revealing a perfect swirl inside

Ljubljana Festivals

The culinary capital packs a punch when it comes to food festivals. The Open Kitchen (*www.odprtakuhna.si*) takes place on Fridays in Ljubljana's main market square from early spring to late autumn. Around 60 stallholders (including some of Slovenia's top restaurants) serve up everything from street-food to fine-dining plates. The November Gourmet Festival, meanwhile, brings together traditional and modern dishes.

 INSIDER TIP
Think Vegan

If you're in the capital in August, check out Vegafest *(www.vega fest.si)* for a colourful and tasty celebration of all things vegan.

Heavenly Honey

Slovenia's remarkable beekeeping tradition goes hand in hand with the opportunity to taste some exceptionally good honey. Try the wonderfully rich Forest honey *(gozdni med)* from the Kočevje region *(p208)*, or reddish-brown chestnut honey *(kostanjo med)*, which has a slightly bitter taste due to its high concentration of pollen grains.

←

Golden jars of honey on sale
in a Ljubljana market

Traditional Cuisine

Most of the country's best-loved dishes are rooted in the past; the tenets of Slovenian cooking are simple, sturdy and meaty, and seasonal local produce is rightly celebrated. The two most traditional dishes are *jota* – a delicious soup made with sauerkraut – and *žganci*, a savoury buckwheat porridge that was once the staple diet of rural Slovenes. To sample these at their best, visit any *gostilna* or tourist farm. Most Slovenian dishes are finished off with a drop of deliciously nutty pumpkin seed oil.

→

A steaming bowl of *jota*, made with
sauerkraut and Carniolan sausage

Baroque Beauties

Through the 17th and 18th centuries, an influx of architects from Italy – including Andrea Pozzo and Francesco Robba – brought the best of Baroque to Slovenia's main towns. Ljubljana is the most obvious candidate, where the style is expressed most sublimely in buildings such as St Nicholas's *(p75)* Cathedral and the Fountain of the Three Rivers *(p73)*. But many other towns in Slovenia have well-preserved town centres, notably Maribor *(p188)* – whose Plague Column is an outstanding example of the Baroque form – and Škofja Loka *(p114)*, where buildings sporting colourful Baroque frescoes dot the picturesque main square.

→

The eye-catching gilded statue atop Maribor's Baroque Plague Column

SLOVENIA FOR
ARCHITECTURE

Flamboyant Baroque towns, medieval hilltop castles and Art Nouveau apartment blocks are just some of the exciting architectural styles to be found in Slovenia. Roam the cities and stroll through beautiful countryside to immerse yourself in the country's outstanding landscape.

Medieval Castles

For centuries Slovenia was a feudal society run by land-owning warlords, and their castles remain scattered across the landscape. Dramatically located castles at Ljubljana, Bled and Celje bear testament to the biggest and best of these, with all three having retained many of their original medieval features. Many castles were converted during the Renaissance and Baroque eras to serve as aristocratic dwellings, with those at Bogenšperk *(p116)* and Ptuj *(p190)* the greatest examples, though for sheer spectacle, Predjama Castle *(p164)* takes some beating.

←

The ruins of 12th-century Kamen Castle, near Begunje na Gorenjskem

Funky Folk

Folk architecture, with farmhouses and barns constructed from traditional materials, still survives in many rural areas. Travel around alpine Slovenia and you'll see timber housing with flower-bedecked verandahs everywhere, while in the Karst and along the Adriatic, houses are mostly made of white stone and grouped around narrow alleys. Perhaps the most distinctive examples of vernacular architecture, though, are hayracks, traditionally used for drying and storing hay. Most are single hayracks *(kozolec)*, but Slovenia is unique for its double hayracks *(toplars)*: two single racks joined by a double gabled roof. Head to the village of Studor near Lake Bohinj *(p134)* to view a wonderful grouping of these.

←

A *kozolec*, a traditional Slovenian hayrack structure

PICTURE PERFECT
Dragon Shot

The iconic dragons on Ljubljana's Dragon Bridge – with their swirly tails and spitting tongues – are among the country's most photographed architectural details.

Jože Plečnik in Ljubljana

No discussion of Slovenian architecture is complete without reference to Jože Plečnik, who single-handedly transformed Ljubljana between the 1920s and 1950s. From his iconic Triple Bridge *(p72)* to the conspicuously magnificent National and University Library *(p80)*, his contribution to Ljubljana was immense. Walking tours offer fascinating insight into his work, as does a visit to his old house *(p100)*.

→

The many-windowed façade of Plečnik's National and University Library

The Julian Alps

If one landscape defines Slovenia more than any other, it's the Julian Alps (Juliske Alpe) – a majestic range of jagged limestone summits, slashed by gorgeous valleys. Triglav (p132) is the country's highest (and most famous) peak, but there is almost unlimited scope for exploring further passes, valleys and views, most of it with far fewer visitors than the iconic Triglav itself. Try the southern route to the dizzying summit of Mala Mojstrovka from the Vršič Pass or the Koritnica Valley with its narrow gorge.

→

Looking out from the dramatic Triglav peak

 GREAT VIEW
Peak Views

Take the cable car up to the upper station of Vogel for superlative views of Mount Triglav.

SLOVENIA FOR
NATURAL
WONDERS

Slovenia's outstandingly beautiful and richly diverse scenery is one of the country's greatest attractions. Whether you're looking for epic mountain vistas, lush forest, jaw-dropping cave networks or shimmering lakes, there's a wealth of natural beauty to explore and enjoy.

From the Adriatic to Alpine Lakes

The Slovenian coast is short but exquisitely formed, with landscapes of salt pans melting into wildlife-rich reed beds and pebbly beaches. But it is arguably the lakes and rivers of inland Slovenia that really steal the show. There are plenty of photogenic mountain lakes, including Bled (p130), Bohinj (p134), and the artificial Jasna (p148), as well as dazzling ribbons of rushing mountain waters, such as the fabulous, foaming Soča river (p137).

←

Mountainous peaks reflected in the glass-like Lake Jasna

TOP
3
**UNMISSABLE
SMALL CAVES**

Križna
The only naturally preserved cave *(p176)* that can be visited in Slovenia, this water cavern is riddled with lakes, streams and passages.

Vilenica
View classic formations in Europe's oldest accessible cave *(p168)*, which is also the unlikely setting for a popular annual literary festival.

Kostanjevica
🅦 kostanjeviska-jama.com
Take a guided tour through this atmospheric cave, known for its horseshoe bats.

The Underground World of the Karst

The landforms of Slovenia's Karst region are extraordinary, and there are over 13,000 known caves in the country. The most famous is undoubtedly Postojna *(p162)*, whose vast chambers have been drawing punters since the early 19th century, but it is the UNESCO-listed Škocjan Cave *(p160)* that delivers the most heart-stopping views.

→

Walking through the spectacular Postojna Caves

Seeing the Forest for the Trees

Forests cover almost 60 per cent of the surface area of Slovenia, making it the third most forested country in Europe. Southeastern Kočevsko is Slovenia's most densely forested area, including tracts of ancient and primeval beech forest that form part of a UNESCO World Heritage Site. The country's forests are rich in wildlife, so hikers may spot a brown bear or two!

←

Dense virgin forest in the southeast of Slovenia

Liquers and Brandy

Alcohol distillation has a rich tradition in Slovenia, and this is manifest in some delicious – and often tremendously fiery – liquers and fruit brandies. The most common are *slivovka* (plum brandy), *viljamovka* (pear brandy) and *borovničevec* (made from blueberries). If you're down in the Karst region, you'll almost certainly be offered a drop of *brinjevec*, a spiky, juniper-based brandy. Another drink not to be missed is *medica*, mead distilled to the strength of brandy. Deceptively easy to drink, this smooth and sweet-tasting beverage is the perfect winter warmer.

→

Local Slovenian brandies bottled in the shape of the female form

SLOVENIA
RAISE A GLASS

You could happily spend weeks drinking your way around Slovenia, thanks to its abundance of world-class wineries and an ever-growing number of exciting micro-breweries – not to mention a centuries-old tradition of harvesting delicious and refreshing fruit brandies.

Getting Crafty

The Slovenian beer market has traditionally been dominated by the big two, Laško and Union, but these are now being given a serious run for their money thanks to an explosion of craft beer brewers. Seek out scrummy pale ales or flavoursome coffee stout at Human Fish in Vrhnika *(p118)*, Tektonik in Ljubljana *(p58)* or Reservoir Dogs in Nova Gorica *(p173)*.

Did You Know?

According to the first written records, beer brewing in Slovenia dates back to 1160.

↑ A bottle of Tektonik, one of Slovenia's leading craft beer brands

Wonderful Wine

Little known beyond its own borders, Slovenian wine is superb. The country has three very distinct wine-growing regions: Primorska in western Slovenia, Posavje in the southeast and Podravje – the largest region – in the northeast. Alongside the usual suspects, some excellent indigenous wines to look out for include Rebula from Brda *(p180)*, Pinela and Zelen from the Vipava Valley *(p156)*, and Refošk from the Karst *(p150)*. For something even more unusual, try a drop of Cviček, a light-bodied and slightly sour red from Dolenjska. Most towns in the region will have a cellar or *vinoteka* (wine shop) where you can sample a couple of wines and some nibbles for a few euros.

Well-stocked shelves of a *vinoteka* in wine-growing country

TOP 4 WINE ROUTES

Jeruzalem-Ljutomer
A sunny region *(p198)* that produces great white wines such as Beli Pinot and Traminec.

Vipava Valley
Wind-swept Vipava *(p156)* yields some stunning reds, notably Cabernet Sauvignon and Merlot.

Goriška Brda
Superlative reds and whites, including several sweet varieties, are harvested in this lush region *(p180)*.

Maribor
Some of Slovenia's finest vintners, such as Frešer and Gaube, can be sampled in the country's second-largest city *(p188)*.

Thirsty Festivals

Slovenia's impressive viticultural heritage is celebrated with numerous exciting events. Chief among these is Martinovanje (St Martin's Day) on 11 November, which honours the turning of must into wine. Elsewhere, the Old Vine Festival in Maribor *(p188)* entails the harvesting of the grapes from the world's oldest vine, while the lovely Days of Poetry and Wine in Ptuj *(p190)* each August offers a more cultural slant. To celebrate beer, head to Laško's *(p196)* booze-fuelled Beer and Flowers Festival.

Preparations under way for the annual Old Vine Festival in Maribor

Mountain Magic

Slovenia's great outdoors is a wonderland for children of all ages, with an abundance of accessible hiking and climbing opportunities dotted around the country. The riverside trail along the Soča (p137) is fantastic – think swing bridges, plenty of swimming spots and a stupendously deep gorge. Or for a safe introduction to rock climbing, check out the family-friendly courses around Bled (p130) and Bohinj (p134), where kids learn to climb with the help of experienced instructors.

INSIDER TIP

Family Skiing

Several of Slovenia's ski resorts are very well suited to families, with easy slopes for beginners, and good ski schools. Pohorje and Velika Planina are especially well equipped.

↑ Wooden suspension bridge across the emerald Soča river

SLOVENIA FOR
FAMILIES

Slovenia is a wonderful place to travel with kids. The gorgeously inspiring outdoor world promises hiking, swimming, and caving adventures, while inspiring museums and hands-on theatre performances will keep boredom at bay.

Splashing Around

There's plenty of scope for swimming, not least along Slovenia's (admittedly short) coast. Portorož (p170) is the most obvious destination, with loads of fun activities (tubes, jet-skis and so on) available, though the Blue Flag beach at Simon's Bay in Izola, with its huge water-slide, is also a great spot. If you'd rather retreat to the lakes, head to Bled's Castle Bathing Area, complete with two waterslides and fenced pools for fun (and safe) dips.

→ Making a splash from the massive waterslide at Simon's Bay in Izola

Marvellous Museums

Slovenia has some excellent child-friendly museums. The Slovene Ethnographic Museum *(p94)* in Ljubljana is a treat for curious kids, with hands-on exhibits, Slovenian artifacts and a host of organized tours and workshops just for them. Beyond the capital, you can keep the kids entertained for hours at Herman's Den in Celje *(p187)*, which has a delightful collection of more than 300 toys.

↑ Kids checking out the interactive exhibits at the Slovene Ethnographic Museum

Puppet Master

Puppetry is a much cherished art form in Slovenia – the first puppet show was performed in 1910 – and makes a perfect rainy day activity for kids and adults alike. There are two excellent theatres in Ljubljana and Maribor *(p188)*, while up in Ljubljana Castle *(p70)*, the wonderful Museum of Puppetry offers your little ones some hands-on fun with shadow puppets and marionettes.

←

Carefully preserved puppets at the Museum of Puppetry in Ljubljana

Over and Under

Slovenia's spectacular caves are an unforgettable experience for kids. Little ones can take a train ride into the underworld of Postojna *(p162)* or cross one of the underground lakes at Križna Cave *(p176)* by boat. Above ground, fun obstacle courses await in the adventure parks at Srnica and Celjska koča.

→

Using ropes to cross a narrow gorge at Srnica, near Bovec

Old Masters

Art flourished in the Baroque period, when artists such as Valentin Metzinger (1699-1759) enjoyed the support of patrons in the church and the Carniolan nobility, against a backdrop of greater political stability. Another great exponent of 18th-century church painting was Franc Jelovšek (1700-64), whose wall and ceiling frescoes adorn many Slovenian churches. To see some of their work, along with other masterpieces of the Baroque, Renaissance and Gothic periods in Slovenian art, make a beeline for the National Gallery *(p92)* in Ljubljana.

→

Spoved plemica by Valentin Metzinger at the National Gallery

SLOVENIA FOR
ART LOVERS

Though little known beyond its own borders, Slovenian art history is extremely rich. From the gilded altarpieces of the High Gothic to the much-loved Impressionist painters, along with some outstanding modern and contemporay works, there's much to savour here.

💬 INSIDER TIP
Street Art

Ljubljana has a vibrant street-art scene, with both clandestine and commissioned work. Two of the best spots to see street art in the capital are Metelkova mesto and the Rog factory.

The bold entrance to the
↓ Museum of Contemporary
Art Metelkova

Modernism and Contemporary

Key figures in modern Slovenian art include Zoran Mušič (1941-2005), much of whose work can be viewed at Dobrovo Castle in Goriška Brda *(p180)*, and Metka Krašovec (1941-2018), who was the first female artist to be given a full retrospective at the Museum of Modern Art *(p99)*. The latter museum is the pick of Slovenia's modern galleries, though the Museum of Contemporary Art Metelkova and MoTA (Museum of Transitory Art) are also well worth a visit.

Folk Art

Slovenia has a rich heritage of folk art, the most cherished form of which is the painting of beehive panels *(p138)*. First emerging in the mid-18th century, these highly decorative panels typically portray biblical or historical scenes. Not dissimilar was the work of the naive artists – essentially untrained peasant painters whose work was usually characterized by vivid, almost childlike scenes and images. The Gallery of Naive Artists *(p214)* in Trebnje holds a wonderful selection of paintings by both Slovenian artists and those from other countries of the former Yugoslavia. Otherwise, look out for ceramics – especially black pottery – from Prekmurje, items produced by the lace-makers of Idrija *(p172)* and painted Easter eggs.

← Delicately patterned Idrija lace, a local speciality

The Slovenian Impressionists

Slovenia's most revered group of artists are the Impressionists, in particular a group of four outstanding painters: Rihard Jakopič (1869-1943), Ivan Grohar (1867-1911), Matej Sternen (1870-1949) and Matija Jama (1872-1947). Their landscapes and genre scenes brought a new approach to light and colour in the early years of the 20th century, and the National Gallery *(p92)* in Ljubljana holds the greatest collection of works by this quartet. The must-see pieces to tick off the bucket list here are *The Sower* by Grohar and Jakopič's *The Green Veil*.

→ *The Green Veil* (1915), an oil painting by Rihard Jakopič

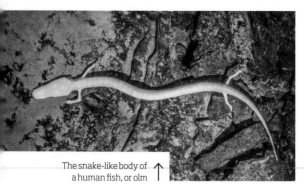

The Human Fish

Slovenia's Karst underworld is home to a remarkably rich fauna, though none is as revered – or as enigmatic – as *Proteus anguinus*, or human fish *(p163)*. Officially called an olm, this remarkable amphibian is totally blind, can go years without food and lives until around the age of 100. It's highly unlikely that you'll see one in the wild, but you can view them up close in the Vivarium at Postojna *(p175)*.

The snake-like body of a human fish, or olm ↑

SLOVENIA FOR
WILDLIFE
ENCOUNTERS

For such a small country, Slovenia's biodiversity is truly remarkable. Track down large carnivores, seek out mysterious subterranean species, spot birds and butterflies, or explore Slovenia's wonderful endemic fauna – it will prove to be a rewarding part of any visit.

Bear Watching

There are between 800 and 900 brown bears in Slovenia, the majority in the remote forests of the southeast (Kočevje), but human-bear encounters are very rare. For a chance to see these carnivores in the wild, take a four-hour trip with the Loška Dolina tourist office *(www.loskadolina.info)*.

→

Brown bears, found in Slovenia's thick, remote forests

INSIDER TIP
Wildlife Photos

Pick your season according to what you want to photograph. Alpine flora is its most colourful in the summer, while the autumn sees brown bears frequenting the forests. Always head into the wilderness with a local wildlife-watching agency.

Stork Villages in Prekmurje

The villages of Mala and Velika Polana (p199) form part of the European Stork Villages initiative, set up by EuroNatur in response to the stork's ongoing habitat loss. Located near the Mura and Drava rivers, close to extensive areas of wet meadows and alder forest, they provide an ideal environment for the white storks. They're easy enough to spot, either in their tangled-looking nests or pacing across meadows while foraging for food.

↑ Stork's nest built atop a brick chimney

Native Flora

Slovenia is home to impressive flora. The best place to see some of the country's beautiful wildflowers is Triglav National Park (p132), where Zois' bellflower, Hawksbeard and Christmas rose are just some of the many plant species to be encountered. If you're visiting in the summer months, Bohinj's Wildflower Festival is an excellent opportunity to learn more about the country's native flora.

Pretty purple Zois' bellflower, growing in a crevice on a limestone cliff face

TOP 4 NATIVE ANIMALS TO LOOK OUT FOR

Alpine ibex
Easily identifiable by their long horns, these creatures are mainly found in the Julian Alps.

European otter
These semi-aquatic animals can be seen year-round within the Goričko Landscape Park.

Ural owl
This light-coloured bird is shy, but widely found within the Notranjska Regional Park.

Alpine salamander
A shiny black amphibian generally found in areas above 800m (2,600 ft).

Carnival Crazy

The most uniquely Slovenian celebration is that of the Shrovetide Carnival, or *Pust*. Both a fertility rite and celebration of the coming of spring, this boisterous event sees spooky-looking masked figures travel from house to house warding off the evil winter spirits. The most important of these events is Ptuj's Kurentovanje, or Kurent *(p191)*. No less entertaining is the Laufarija in Cerkno *(p174)*, central to which is the horned *Pust*, who is hauled up before a court while the Laufari, distinguished by their brilliantly distinctive masks, look on.

→

Fantastically dressed figures celebrating Shrovetide

SLOVENIA FOR
FESTIVALS

Slovenia is a country that loves to celebrate. There are strongly rooted folklore events and colourful summer shindigs, and these jostle alongside a host of exciting food and wine-based festivals. Whatever your mood, you'll always find something going on.

Glorious Food and Wine

The country abounds in some wonderfully idiosyncratic culinary events that cater to all tastes and preferences, whether you're a dedicated oenophile or simply keen to sample some local specialities. Two of the most enjoyable are the Salt pans Fest in Sečovlje *(p170)* and the Žlikrofi Festival in Idrija *(p172)*; the sweet-toothed won't want to miss the Radovljica Chocolate Festival. The most prestigious wine-related events are Maribor's Old Vine Festival in September and St Martin's Day on 11 November, when Slovenian wineries celebrate the turning of must into wine.

←

A chef preparing a dish at Idrija's Žlikrofi Festival

TOP 4 **MUSIC FESTIVALS**

Druga Godba (May)
Top-class, world music gathering in Ljubljana and Maribor.

Ljubljana Jazz Festival (Jun)
Big names perform in the wonderful open-air Križanke Theatre.

Sevicqc Brežice Festival (Jun)
Prestigious festival of Baroque music.

Metaldays (Aug)
Week-long rock fest in a great setting down near the Soča river.

Religious Festivals

As a predominantly Catholic country, Slovenia's most atmospheric festivals are religious. The Škofja Loka Passion Play, a retelling of Christ's suffering, is one of the most enduring events. Involving over 600 amateur actors, it is only performed every six years. The largest annual pilgrimage, meanwhile, sees 40,000 people descend upon Brezje's Basilica of St Mary Help - Slovenia's national shrine.

$\rightarrow$

Local people taking on roles in Škofja Loka's celebrated Passion Play

Traditional Slovenian costumes in Kamnik

$\uparrow$

Traditional Festivals

If you're looking for a taste of local life, you'll find it at one of Slovenia's long-established festivals. One of the oldest events is the Kravji Bal, or Cow's Ball, which takes place around Lake Bohinj and celebrates the return of the herdsmen and their cattle from the higher pastures. Other colourful events include Kamnik's Traditional Costumes Festival, which celebrates the nation's dress, and the King Matjaž Snow Sculpture Festival in January.

Responsible Transport

Slovenia's central European location makes it very easy to reach by train instead of plane. Within Slovenia itself, public transport is excellent, and there has been a concerted effort to reduce traffic in its inner-city areas by introducing low emission buses and increasing pedestrianized zones – Ljubljana continues to lead the way here. Slovenia is also a fantastic cycling destination, with oodles of dedicated trails and widely available bike hire.

$\rightarrow$

Cycling a scenic route through the vineyards in Jeruzalem

SLOVENIA
THINK GREEN

Slovenia is one of Europe's greenest and most environmentally sound destinations. The opportunities for hiking, cycling and wildlife watching are vast, and plenty of farmsteads offer slow food and locally sourced produce, allowing you to travel sustainably and leave no trace in this beautiful land.

Sustainable Shopping

Most Slovenian towns will have a market offering local produce, while Ljubljana has become a mecca for green shopping, promoting minimal waste and eco-friendly packaging. Beyond food, visit 3Muhe, Slovenia's first Fair Trade shop, many of whose products are supplied by innovative local company Smetumet – an art collective that makes stylish gifts from recycled materials.

$\rightarrow$

An overflowing fruit stall at Ljubljana's Open Market

Did You Know?

———

Ljubljana was voted European Green Capital in 2016.

The Green Scheme

When planning your trip or booking accommodation, look out for hotels, guesthouses and destinations carrying the Slovenia Green certificate. This nationwide initiative is awarded to businesses that observe a high standard of environmental protection regulations and standards, and place an emphasis on sustainable tourism. Rural, family-run farm stays also offer one of the most authentic visitor experiences in Slovenia, with homely lodgings and tasty home-cooked meals, often from organic gardens.

← Hotel in Rogaška Slatina, a Green destination

EAT

Avokado

Fabulous bistro in Koper serving vegan fast food, including breakfasts and a daily changing menu of lunches and more substantial meals.

 A6 🏠 Gortanov trg 4, Koper 📞 (05) 148 6704

€€€

Café Cokl

This Ljubljana café uses only Fair Trade coffee, which it roasts itself.

C4 🏠 Krekov trg 8, Ljubljana 📞 (0)41 837 556

€€€

The Trail Less Travelled

The Juliana or Julian Alps Trail *(p135)*, which opened in 2019, is a long-distance trekking route that encourages hikers to explore beyond Slovenia's iconic but overcrowded Triglav *(p132)*. Instead of visiting Triglav itself, this trail swings in a loop through the Julian Alps, taking in scenery that is just as stunning as the more trodden route. All stages of the trail are accessible by public transport, so you can leave your car at home.

↑ Breathtaking views from the Julian Alps Trail

A YEAR IN
SLOVENIA

JANUARY

BIO – Ljubljana Design Biennial *(mid-Nov–late Feb)*. Ljubljana's renowned international platform for new approaches in product, graphic and information design.

△ **Ice Trophy** *(late Jan)*. Amateur and ex-pro ice-hockey players compete on frozen Lake Jasna.

FEBRUARY

MENT *(early Feb)*. Small music festival held in Ljubljana, featuring rock, pop and electronica.

△ **Kurentovanje** *(last weekend before Lent, Feb/Mar)*. Traditional Shrovetide carnival in Ptuj, featuring the colourful, sheepskin-clad Kurenti.

Laufarija *(last weekend before Lent, Feb/Mar)*. Crkno's traditional Shrovetide carnival, at which the Laufari wear distinctive masks.

MAY

Druga Godba *(mid-May)*. One of Central Europe's greatest world music festivals, held in Ljubljana and Maribor.

△ **World Bee Day** *(20 May)*. Inaugurated in 2018 and held widely across the country, to highlight the role played by honeybees in the food chain.

Wildflower Festival *(last week May–first week Jun)*. Bohinj celebrates the spectacular native flora of Triglav National Park.

JUNE

Idrija Lace Festival *(mid-Jun)*. A celebration of this town's intricate lace-making tradition.

△ **Pride Parade Festival** *(mid-Jun)*. Ljubljana's Pride Parade has been taking place since 2001 and includes a full programme of events in celebration of LGBT+ culture.

Jurjevanje *(late Jun)*. Held in Bela Krajina, this is the oldest folklore festival in Slovenia.

SEPTEMBER

Festival of Slovenian Film *(mid-Sep)*. Held in Portorož, this is Slovenia's premier festival of home-grown film-making.

Pikin Festival *(mid-Sep)*. A children's festival celebrating Pippi Longstocking, held in Velenje.

△ **Maribor Festival** *(late Sep)*. Maribor's leading festival of chamber and orchestral music, which was founded in 1964.

OCTOBER

△ **City of Women** *(mid-Sep–mid-Oct)*. An award-winning international festival of contemporary arts in Ljubljana, featuring between 40 and 60 women artists and theorists each year.

Maribor Theatre Festival *(late Oct)*. The country's longest-running and most prominent theatre festival.

MARCH

Chilli and Chocolate Festival *(mid-Mar)*. Maribor's celebration of all things sweet and spicy, with delicious products on offer from 40 different chocolate artisans.

△ **Ski Flying World Championships** *(late Mar)*. FIS Ski Jumping World Cup, held in Planica.

APRIL

Asparagus Festival *(early Apr)*. Every year during the wild asparagus season, the villagers of Brestovica pri Komnu set up stalls offering tempting dishes using this fresh local vegetable.

△ **Radovljica Chocolate Festival** *(mid-Apr)*. Slovenia's largest chocolate festival, with live music, entertainment and plenty of tasting opportunities.

Easter Hike to Mala Gora *(Easter Monday)*. A traditional hike from the village of Kamnje to Mala Gora, in the Vipava Valley.

JULY

Ljubljana Festival *(Jul–Aug)*. Ljubljana's summer festival of classical music and the arts, which runs for two months.

△ **Ana Desetnica** *(early Jul)*. International street theatre festival in Ljubljana.

Beer and Flower Festival *(mid-Jul)*. A large, popular music festival, held in Laško.

Metaldays *(late Jul)*. Slovenia's heavy-metal music festival, held in Tolmin.

Okarina *(late Jul)*. World music festival in Bled.

AUGUST

Summer Puppet Pier *(Aug)*. An international puppet festival in Maribor.

Seviqc Brežice *(late Aug)*. Festival of early music, held at castles and other sites across southeast Slovenia.

△ **Tartini Festival** *(late Aug–early Sep)*. International classical music festival in Piran, which celebrates the works of Piran-born composer Giuseppe Tartini and sees locals dress up in traditional clothes.

NOVEMBER

△ **Old Vine Festival** *(11 Nov)*. Annual wine festival, held on St Martin's Day (which is celebrated across the country) and ending with a grape harvest in front of the Old Vine House.

LIFFE *(late Nov)*. The capital's popular International Film Festival.

DECEMBER

△ **Christmas Markets** *(Dec)*. Festive markets are held in Ljubljana, Bled, Maribor and other towns, with plenty of mulled wine and entertainment.

1

A BRIEF
HISTORY

Slovenia's history is incredibly complex. Ruled by a succession of invaders and occupiers, from Celts and Romans to the Habsburgs, Slovenia then spent much of the 20th century entangled within a fraught Yugoslav federation, before finally becoming an independent state in 1992.

Prehistoric Slovenia

Some remarkable archaeological treasures suggest that present-day Slovenia was already settled in the Paleolithic era; Neolithic pile-dwellings, meanwhile, have been found in the marshes south of Ljubljana. A more sophisticated culture emerged with the Halstatt (late Bronze/early Iron ages), which were centred around Most na Soči and the Dolenjska region.

The Celts and Romans

The Halstatt cultures were superseded by migrating Celts around 300 BC, who carved out several states, of which the most

Did You Know?

Migrating Celts brought the horse-drawn chariot and the potter's wheel to Slovenia in 300 BC.

Timeline of events

300 BC
The Celts establish the state of Noricum in the eastern Alps.

181 BC
Beginning of Roman occupation on Slovene lands.

900 BC
Magyars settle in the Pannonian region of eastern Slovenia.

550–600 BC
Slav tribes settle on Slovene lands leading to the creation of the Duchy of Karantanija.

1130
The dynastic line of the Counts of Celje begins with Gebhard I de Saun.

powerful was Noricum in northern Slovenia. Roman expansion towards present-day Slovenia in 2 BC was a largely peaceful process, and it was under Emperor Augustus that the region was fully absorbed into the Roman state. The key settlements were Emona (Ljubljana), Celeia (Celje) and Poetovio (Ptuj). The disintegration of the Roman Empire in the fifth century paved the way for other warring tribes, such as the Huns, to assume power.

From the Slavs to the Habsburgs

During the great migration in the 6th century, Slav tribes settled in what is now Slovenia and southern Austria, resulting in the Duchy of Karantanija, the first Slav political entity. A brief period of autonomy ensued before the Slavs were gradually absorbed into the Frankish Empire. After Frankish rule was shaken after raids by the Magyars, a German-speaking aristocracy held sway throughout Slovene lands until the end of the 19th century. This process of Germanization intensified further under the Habsburgs, whose only serious rivals were the aristocratic dynasty of the Counts of Celje; elsewhere, small pockets of land were governed by Venice and Hungary.

1. A map of Slovenia as it looked in 1570.

2. Glass beads were part of the sophisticated Halstatt cultures.

3. This funerary stele was found in Celje.

4. An illustrated depiction of a Žiče charterhouse in the 18th century.

1160
Žiče becomes the first Carthusian monastery to be established outside of France or Italy.

1470
Ottoman Turks advance on Slovenia but are repelled by the Habsburgs.

1550
The first books in the Slovene language are published.

1144
First recorded mention of Ljubljana (then called Laibach).

1280
Habsburgs establish feudal holdings on Slovene lands.

18th-Century Reform and Enlightenment

After the publication of natural historian Janez Vajkard Valvasor's topography *The Glory of the Duchy of Carniola* in 1689, there was a renewed interest in Slovenia's history and culture. Intellectual life in Ljubljana began to take off at the turn of the 18th century, with increased importance placed on the Slovene language, and the founding of learned societies such as the Academia Operosorum and the Academia Filharmonicorum.

By the end of the century, the concept of Yugoslavism – the idea that south Slav people who shared similar languages (Serbs, Croats and Slovenes) should form a common state – was fast gaining ground.

World War I and the Kingdom of Yugoslavia

During the early stages of World War I, Slovenes fought on several fronts on behalf of the Austrians. When Italy declared war on the Austro-Hungarians in 1915, so began three years of brutal mountain warfare along the Soča (Isonzo) Front. The Italians were eventually defeated in October 1917, though not before more than a million soldiers and civilians had lost their

VALENTIN VODNIK (1758-1819)

One of the founding fathers of Slovenian literary culture, Vodnik wrote some of the first poems ever to be published in Slovenian. He also edited the first Slovenian newspaper, and his work became a rallying cry for late 19th-century Slovenian patriots.

Timeline of events

1689
Janez Vajkard Valvasor publishes *The Glory of the Duchy of Carniola.*

1760–1820
Period of Slovene Enlightenment.

1800
Birth of France Prešeren, Slovenia's greatest poet.

1809–1813
Ljubljana is designated the capital of the Illyrian provinces.

1813
Following Napoleon's defeat, Slovenia is once again incorporated into the Austria Empire.

lives during this conflict. With the defeat of the Austro-Hungarians in October 1918, Slovene leaders rushed to declare a union with their south Slav neighbours, creating the Kingdom of Serbs, Croats and Slovenes (which included Bosnia, Macedonia and Montenegro). While Slovenians thought that the south-Slav state would be a loose federation in which they would enjoy some autonomy, the 1920 Treaty of Rapallo and the 1921 Vidovan Constitution quashed these aspirations. With a royal dictatorship in place, the state was renamed the Kingdom of Yugoslavia.

World War II

The German blitzing of Belgrade in 1941 brought an end to the Kingdom of Yugoslavia, and Slovenia itself was divided between Germany, Italy and Hungary. In response, a number of pan-Yugoslav resistance groups emerged. In Slovenia this was the Liberation Front, or Osvobodilna Fronta (OF), which was born out of the Communist Party of Slovenia. Despite strong anti-Communist resistance, most prominently in the form of the Home Guard (Domobranci), by May 1945, all remaining occupiers had been swept out of Slovenia by the Communists.

[1] The Seminary Palace Library was founded in 1701, in connection with the Academia Operosorum.

[2] Italian troops were defeated on the Isonzo Front in 1917.

[3] Serbian negotiators signed German peace conditions in Belgrade in 1941.

[4] A memorial dedicated to anti-Communists, many of whom were executed in 1945.

1864
Founding of the Slovene Society marks a period of significant cultural progression.

1915–1917
Fighting on the Soča Front leaves more than a million dead.

1918
Kingdom of Serbs, Croats and Slovenes established.

1929
The official name of the state is changed to the Kingdom of Yugoslavia.

1941
Slovenia occupied by Germans, Italians and Hungarians, causing a rise of resistance groups.

1

2

3

Tito and Socialism

Elections in 1945 resulted in victory for the Communist-led Liberation Front and, led by the Communist revolutionary Josip Broz Tito, the Federal People's Republic of Yugoslavia was proclaimed, still comprising the original six republics. A 1948 rift between Yugoslavia and the USSR resulted in the former's expulsion from Cominform, the Soviet-controlled organization of European Communist countries, paving the way for Tito to fashion his own form of socialism. The 1950s and 60s saw a rise in living standards and a boom in consumerism, particularly for Slovenes. However, as the most economically advanced of the six republics, Slovenia often felt short-changed by a system that channelled funds into projects in the poorer south. In 1972, Communist leader Stane Kavčić was forced out of power by Tito's vassals for defending Slovene interests. The 1974 constitution gave more autonomy to the republics, but problems endured.

The Road to Independence and the Ten-Day War

Following Tito's death in 1980, republic relations worsened. In 1990, at the final congress of the Yugoslav League of

THE TEN-DAY WAR

As Slovenia declared its independence, Yugoslav army (JNA) tanks were approaching Ljubljana airport and Slovenian border posts for what was to become the briefest of conflicts. Most clashes were small-scale affairs, but the Serb-dominated JNA hadn't reckoned on such stubborn Slovene resistance. They surrendered 10 days later, and the Brioni Accord ended the conflict.

Timeline of events

1948
Leader Tito splits with Russia and Yugoslavia is expelled from the Cominform.

1972
Liberal leader Stane Kavčič forced to resign by conservatives.

1945
Slovenia becomes a republic within the Federal People's Republic of Yugoslavia.

1980
Tito dies and Yugoslavia begins to fracture.

1990
The first multi-party elections see Milan Kučan elected president.

Communists, the Slovene delegation walked out, a move that effectively precipitated Slovenian independence. The country's first multi-party elections took place a few months later and Slovenia declared independence on 25 June 1991. This triggered a Ten-Day War, at the end of which the Yugoslav army (JNA) was ejected from Slovene territory. Slovenian independence was finally recognized by the European Union nations in 1992. In 2004 Slovenia joined both NATO and the EU, and in 2007 it was the first of the new EU member states to adopt the Euro.

Slovenia Today

Without doubt, Slovenia has established itself as one of the economic and political successes of post-Communist Europe. Its reputation as a safe, clean and welcoming country means that Slovenia's stock as a tourist destination continues to rise, while its sustainable tourism principles are even more impressive. With nearly 60 percent of the land forested (Europe's third most forested country), it's little surprise that Slovenia is currently one of the world's most sustainable countries, with Ljubljana named European Green Capital in 2016.

1 Josep Broz Tito led the People's Front party.

2 Army trucks were used in the Ten-Day War.

3 Slovenia joined the European Union in 2004.

4 Pedestrianized walkways in Ljubljana.

Did You Know?

France Prešeren's *A Toast* (Zdravljica) was adopted as the Slovenian national anthem in 1989.

1991
Slovenes declare independence, heralding the start of the Ten-Day War.

2004
Slovenia joins both NATO and the EU.

2007
Slovenia becomes the first of the new EU member states/former Communist states to adopt the Euro.

1992
Slovenia officially recognized as an independent country.

2016
Ljubljana named European Green Capital.

EXPERIENCE
LJUBLJANA

Triple Bridge leading to Prešernov trg, Old Town

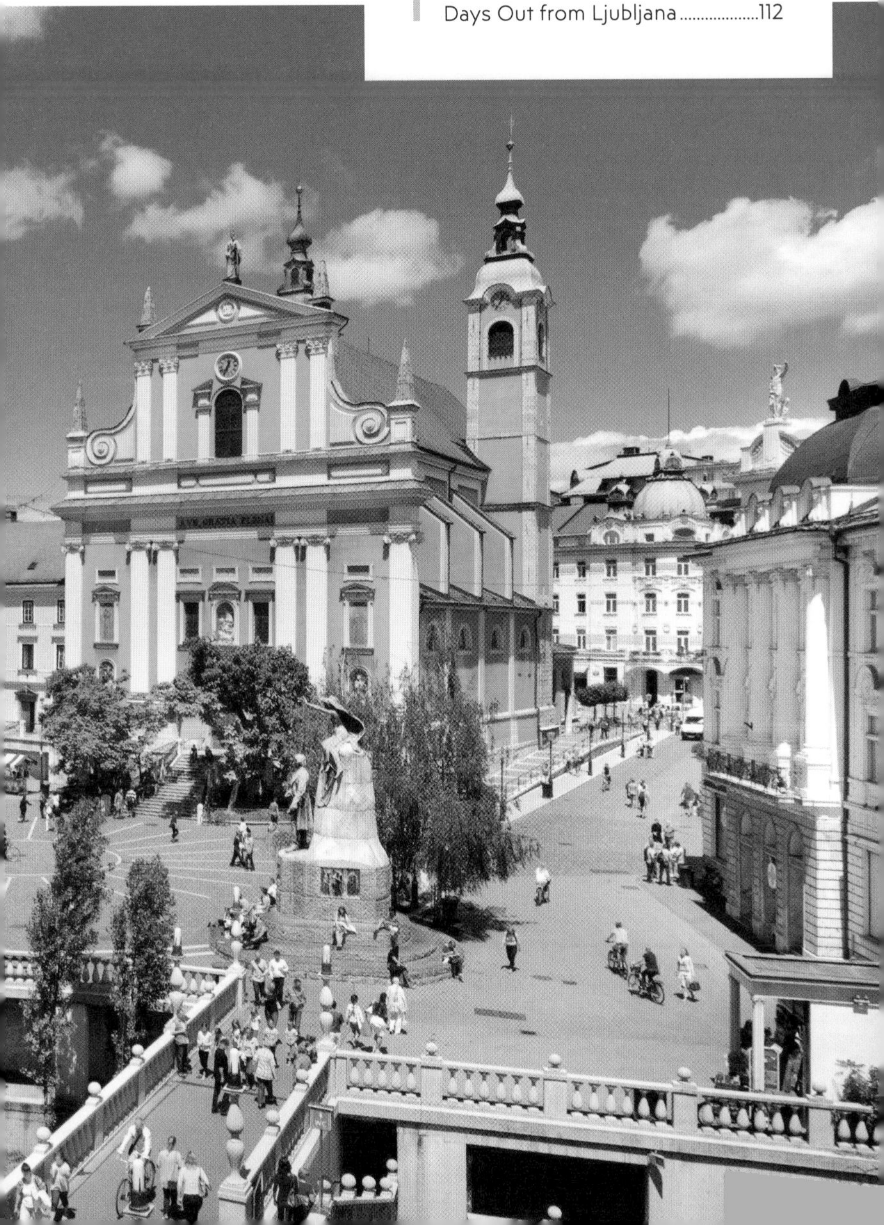

EXPLORE
LJUBLJANA

This guide divides Ljubljana into two sightseeing areas, as shown on this map, plus two areas beyond the city. Find out more about each area on the following pages.

Union Experience

Slovene Museum of Contemporary History

CELOVŠKA CESTA

Tivoli Park

Tivoli Mansion

Orthodox Church of Sts Cyril and Methodius

National Gallery

Opera House

National Museum of Slovenia

CESTA 27 APRILA

CESTA

CESTA

TRG REPUBLIKE

KONGRESNI TRG

BLEIWEISOVA

PREŠERNOVA

University of Ljubljana

Tobacco Factory

National and University Library

Roman Wall

KRAKOVO

MIRJE

TRŽAŠKA CESTA

St John's Church

BARJANSKA CESTA

GERBIČEVA CESTA

0 metres 500

0 yards 500

N

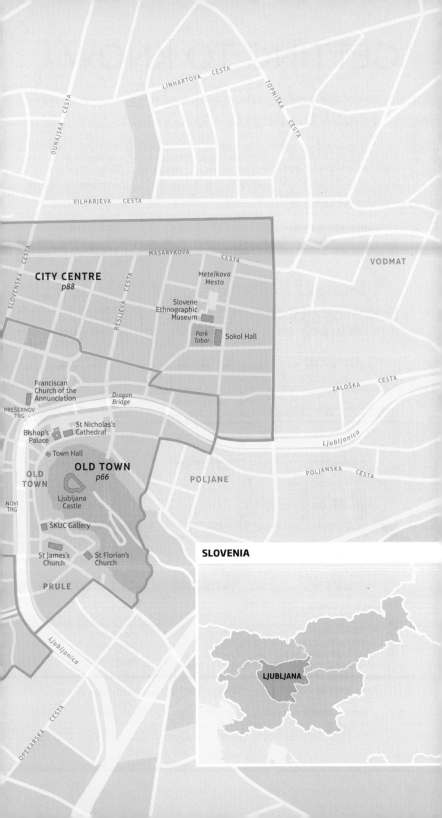

GETTING TO KNOW
LJUBLJANA

Small and uncrowded, yet crackling with energy, Ljubljana is one of Europe's most picturesque capitals. At its heart is the Ljubljanica river and the photogenic Old Town, which is overlooked by the imposing hilltop castle. Outside the centre, an array of cultural sights await exploration.

OLD TOWN

PAGE 66

Ljubljana's beautiful Old Town centre lies below Castle Hill along the banks of the Ljubljanica river, which is spanned by a succession of bridges. Big on atmosphere, from the colourful bustle of its market to the vibrant buzz of riverside eateries, and largely pedestrianized, this part of the city is home to some of its most iconic landmarks – including the Dragon Bridge, Prešeren Square and Ljubljana Castle. Make sure to squeeze in a trip to the last of these, which provides the ultimate vantage point over the city below.

Best for
Architecture, cafés and bars

Home to
Ljubljana Castle

Experience
Great views from the funicular as it climbs to Ljubljana Castle – or if you're feeling particularly active, make the journey on foot

CITY CENTRE

West of Castle Hill on the opposite bank of the Ljubljanica, the busy cafés and bars of the riverside promenade give way to elegant façades punctuated with neatly arranged parks and gardens. This area of the city centre provides the setting for most of Ljubljana's major museums and galleries, from the excellent National Gallery to the fascinating Plečnik House Museum. It's also the place to see some of the city's most impressive Art Nouveau architecture, in particular along Miklošičeva cesta. Tivoli Park provides an oasis of calm, while Metelkovo – housed in a former army barracks that became a squat in the 1990s – has developed into a vibrant centre of alternative culture, and is the best place in Ljubljana to see street art.

Best for
Museum-hopping and good food and drink

Home to
The National Gallery, Slovene Ethnographic Museum

Experience
Stunning works by the Slovenian Impressionists at the National Gallery of Slovenia

→

BEYOND THE CENTRE

Venturing beyond the fringes of the Old Town and city centre certainly doesn't mean that you'll run out of things to see and do. Some of Plečnik's greatest architectural works can be found in this area; walk beyond the main railway station to see the Cemetery at Žale, or along the riverside terraces at Trnovo for some of his most understated works. Near the edge of Tivoli Park, pleasant St Bartholomew's Church is one of the oldest surviving churches in Ljubljana, while Tovarna Rog is a social and cultural centre and squat, housed in an old bicycle factory. There are also plenty of green spaces – go for a stroll on Rožnik Hill, or visit the Botanical Garden with its 4,500 species and sub-species of plants.

Best for
Green spaces and getting off the beaten track

Home to
Rožnik Hill and the imposing Žale Cemetery

Experience
A ramble up Rožnik Hill first thing in the morning, when you're likely to miss most of the crowds

DAYS OUT FROM LJUBLJANA

Slovenia is small enough that visitors to Ljubljana are almost spoilt for choice when it comes to possible days out from the capital. The Ljubljana Marshes, to the southwest of the city, are a unique landscape and rich in wildlife and rare plants, while the town of Škofja Loka has a beautifully preserved medieval core and every few years enacts a vast Passion Play involving the town's entire population. There are also a whole slew of castles in the area, dating from the 13th to the 17th century – the one at Bogenšperk is arguably the most impressive, while the 15th-century manor in the tiny village of Polhov Gradec is a hidden gem. There are some excellent museums to seek out, too, such as the Ljubljanica River Exhibition in Vrhnika.

Best for
History and dramatic castles

Home to
Škofja Loka, Bogenšperk Castle

Experience
A bike ride across Ljubljana Marshes, stopping at rural farmsteads to sample delicious local foods

OLD TOWN

Ljubljana's Castle Hill is believed to have been settled since as early as 1200 BC, but the city's historic core – as we know it today – really began life as the Roman settlement of Emona, which was founded some 2,000 years ago near the banks of the Ljubljanica. The earliest reference to a castle existing on the hill appears in the 12th century, when it was the seat of the Counts of Spanheim. By the 13th century, the core of medieval Laibach (as the city was then known), including Stari trg, Mestni trg and Novi trg, was laid out below the castle, and in the 14th century, as part of the Duchy of Carniola, the city became part of the Habsburg Empire, and remained so until 1797.

Ljubljana's historic centre received two facelifts due to major earthquakes. The first came in 1511, after which the city was rebuilt in Renaissance style. Another quake came in 1895, and Ljubljana was then rebuilt in Secessionist style under the direction of the city's mayor Ivan Hribar.

OLD TOWN

Must See

1 Ljubljana Castle

Experience More

2 Prešernov trg
3 Franciscan Church of the Annunciation
4 Triple Bridge
5 Fountain of the Three Rivers
6 Market
7 Town Hall
8 St Nicholas's Cathedral
9 Bishop's Palace
10 Stari trg
11 Seminary
12 ŠKUC Gallery
13 Dragon Bridge
14 Gruber Palace
15 St Florian's Church
16 St James's Church
17 National and University Library
18 Ljubljana City Museum
19 University of Ljubljana
20 Križanke
21 Kongresni trg
22 Cooperative Bank
23 Philharmonic Hall

Eat

① EK Bistro
② Barbarella Arkade Bistro
③ TaBar
④ Špajza

Drink

⑤ Pritličje
⑥ Movia
⑦ Tozd
⑧ Čajna Hisa
⑨ Le Petit Café

Stay

⑩ Hotel Cubo
⑪ Lesar Hotel Angel
⑫ Antiq Palace Hotel
⑬ Adora Hotel

Shop

⑭ Ika
⑮ 3 Muhe
⑯ Kraševka

National Gallery

Opera House

Nebotičnik

Slovene Parliament

TRG REPUBLIKE

CITY CENTRE
p88

Hauptman House

Kongresni Trg **21**

Philharmonic **23** Hall

University of Ljubljana **19**

12

Čevljars mo

NOVI TRG

National and University Library **17**

9

Ljubljana City Museum **18**

Križanke **20**

KRAKOVO

St John's Church

Plečnik House

GOSPOSVETSKA ULICA
CESTA
ŽUPANČIČEVA ULICA
SLOVENSKA CESTA
NAZORJEVA ULICA
ČOPOVA ULICA
CANKARJEVA CESTA
TOMŠIČEVA
ULICA
ŠUBIČEVA ULICA
WOLFOVA UL
KONGRESNI TRG
SLOVENSKA CESTA
NABREŽIC
IGRIŠKA ULICA
VEGOVA ULICA
GOSPOSKA
DVORNI TRG
HRIBARJEVO
GREGORČIČEVA UL.
TURJAŠKA UL.
RIMSKA CESTA
RIMSKA C.
TRG FRANCOSKE REVOLUCIJE
EMONSKA CESTA
KRIZEVNISKA UL.
BREG
ZOISOVA CESTA
CESTA
KRAKOVSKI
BARJANSKA ULICA
MIRJE
KRAKOVSKA ULICA
GRADAŠKA
EMONSKA ULICA
GRADAŠKA ULICA
Gradaščica
EIPPROVA ULICA
KOLEZIJSKA ULICA

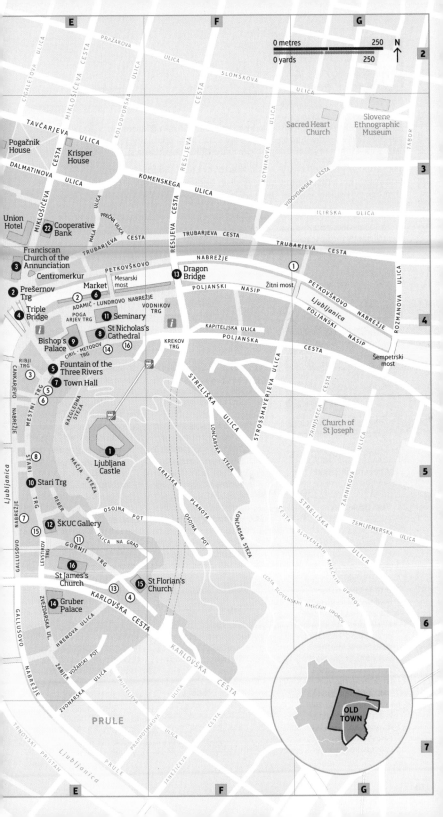

ULICA

PRAŽAKOVA

ULICA

ULICA

SLOMŠKOVA

ULICA

Sacred Heart
Church

Slovene
Ethnographic
Museum

TAVČARJEVA   ULICA

Pogačnik
House

Krisper
House

DALMATINOVA   ULICA

KOMENSKEGA   ULICA

ILIRSKA   ULICA

Union
Hotel

Cooperative
Bank

22

TRUBARJEVA   CESTA

TRUBARJEVA   CESTA

Franciscan
Church of the
Annunciation

3

Centromerkur

Market

Mesarski
most

NABREŽJE

Dragon
Bridge

13

PETKOVŠKOVO

Ljubljanica

**Prešernov
Trg**

2

2

6

ADAMIČ - LUNDROVO NABREŽJE

POLJANSKI   NASIP

Žitni most

PETKOVŠKOVO   NABREŽJE

**Triple
Bridge**

4

POGA
ARJEV TRG

11

Seminary

VODNIKOV
TRG

POLJANSKI   NASIP

Bishop's
Palace

9

8

St Nicholas's
Cathedral

KAPITELJSKA   ULICA

POLJANSKA

Šempetrski
most

CIRIL - METODOV
TRG

14

16

KREKOV
TRG

RIBJI
TRG

5

Fountain of the
Three Rivers

3

7

Town Hall

STRELIŠKA   ULICA

STROSSMAYERJEVA   ULICA

Church of
St Joseph

5

6

RAZGLEDNA   STEZA

1

Ljubljana
Castle

8

LONČARSKA   STEZA

ZARNIKOVA   ULICA

STRELIŠKA   ULICA

ZEMLJEMERSKA   ULICA

10

Stari Trg

MAČJA   STEZA

OSOJNA   POT

GRAJSKA   PLANOTA

LONČARSKA   STEZA

7

12

ŠKUC Gallery

15

11

GORNJI   TRG

ULICA   NA   GRAD

OSOJNA   POT

CESTA   SLOVENSKIH   KMEČKIH   UPOROV

St James's
Church

16

13

15

St Florian's
Church

4

CESTA   SLOVENSKIH   KMEČKIH   UPOROV

Gruber
Palace

14

KARLOVŠKA   CESTA

HRENOVA   ULICA

KARLOVŠKA   CESTA

ŽABJEK   VOŽARSKI   POT   ULICA

ZVONARSKA   ULICA

PRIJATELJEVA   ULICA

PRULE

OLD
TOWN

❶ ⊘ ⊘ 🍴 🍽 🛍

LJUBLJANA CASTLE
LJUBLJANSKI GRAD

📍 E5 **🚪 Grajska planota** **🚌 From Krekov trg; every 10 min** **🕐 Grounds:
Jan–Mar & Nov: 10am–8pm daily; Apr, May & Oct: 9am–9pm daily; Jun–
Sep: 9am–11pm daily; Dec: 10am–10pm daily** **🌐 ljubljanskigrad.si**

This imposingly sited castle has looked over Ljubljana for around
900 years. It's a fascinating place to visit, due to the historical rooms
that can be toured and the spectacular city views on offer.

Perched atop a cone-shaped hill, Ljubljana
Castle looms above the Old Town. The city's
most instantly recognizable landmark originally dates from the 11th century, when the
Spannheims adopted Ljubljana as their feudal
power base. Following the city's absorption by

Austria in 1355, the castle became the
property of the Habsburg family, before going
on to serve as a barracks, and then as a refuge
for the poor and a prison. The castle is now a
popular tourist destination, with many attractions around its irregular courtyard.

↑ The ornately frescoed
ceiling of the castle's
Chapel of St George

THE DRAGON

There is no more
immediately recog-
nizable symbol of the
Slovenian capital than
the dragon. Legend has
it that while returning
to Greece with the
Golden Fleece, Jason and
the Argonauts stopped
at a lake near Ljubljana
and slew a dragon that
lived there. Another
story is that the dragon
symbol was adopted
from St George, the
patron of the castle's
medieval chapel. Today,
the city's most famous
dragons are the sculp-
tures that guard the
Dragon Bridge (p77).

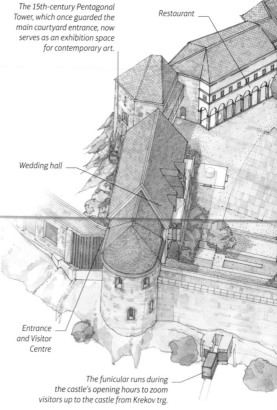

The 15th-century Pentagonal
Tower, which once guarded the
main courtyard entrance, now
serves as an exhibition space
for contemporary art.

Restaurant

Wedding hall

Entrance
and Visitor
Centre

The funicular runs during
the castle's opening hours to zoom
visitors up to the castle from Krekov trg.

INSIDER TIP
Save the Dragon

If you're looking for an adventure, take part in the Escape Castle game. Starting at the Visitor Centre, you'll have just one hour to complete five fun tests in order to rescue the city's famous dragon.

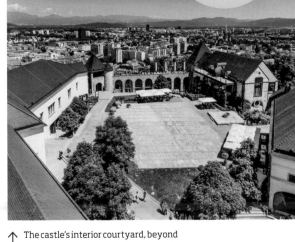

↑ The castle's interior courtyard, beyond which the city can be seen laid out below

The clock tower provides a wonderful panorama of the city.

Virtual Museum

The Chapel of St George, a 15th-century Gothic chapel, may have been dedicated to St George, the legendary dragon slayer. It is decorated with the coats of arms of the noble families of Carniola, and those of Habsburg emperors Rudolf I and Charles IV.

The courtyard is now used for music and drama performances on summer evenings.

Estate Hall

Casemates

↑ Ljubljana Castle, which sprawls across the top of the city's Castle Hill

Did You Know?

The castle has its own vineyard, with a cutting from the world's oldest grape-bearing vine from Maribor.

71

EXPERIENCE MORE

Prešernov trg

E4

Located between Ljubljana's Old Town and the 19th-century districts on the west bank of the Ljubljanica river, Prešernov trg is the symbolic heart of the city. It is named after France Prešeren, the Slovenian poet whose patriotic verses were central to the development of a Slovenian national consciousness. The poet is immortalized by a monument in the centre of the square, accompanied by a scantily clad muse wielding a sprig of laurel. The unveiling of the statue in 1905 was a major political event, bringing thousands of patriotic Slovenians out on to the street at a time when the city was still ruled by the Habsburg Empire.

Around the square are some of the finest Art Nouveau structures in Ljubljana. The Urbanc House (also known as Centromerkur), on the northeastern corner, was built in 1903 by Austrian architect Friedrich Sigismundt to serve as a department store. Crowning the building is a statue of Mercury, the Roman god of trade. Now occupied by the fashion store Galerija Emporium, the interior retains some stunning Art Nouveau details, with carved female heads at the bottom of the Y-shaped staircase and some ornate light fittings above.

On the opposite side of the square is the mid-19th-century Hauptman House, renovated in 1904 by the city's leading Art Nouveau architect, Ciril Metod Koch. Edged with green and turquoise tiles, it is an outstanding example of the Viennese-inspired decorative style of the age.

Just behind it, the building at Wolfova No 4 features a relief of the 19th-century beauty Julija Primic peering from a mock first-floor window. Primic was the object of Prešeren's unrequited love, an obsession that inspired the air of romantic melancholy that characterized much of his work.

Franciscan Church of the Annunciation

Frančiškanska Cerkev Marijinega Oznanjenja

E4 **Prešernov trg**
9am–noon & 3–7pm daily

Dominating the northeast corner of Prešernov trg is the lavish, Baroque 17th-century Franciscan Church.

The main attraction is the high altar by Francesco Robba, the Venetian sculptor who spent most of his adult life in Ljubljana. Expressive statuettes on either side of the altar showcase Robba's work at its graceful best. The ceiling frescoes were painted by Slovenian artist Matevž Langus in the mid-19th century, and reworked by Slovenian Impressionist Matej Sternen following damage during the 1895 earthquake.

FRANCE PREŠEREN (1800–49)

The Romantic poet France Prešeren was the first to demonstrate that Slovenian – hitherto considered a peasant language – could serve as the vehicle for great literature. His verse contained a strong patriotic undercurrent, spurring the development of a modern national consciousness. His fine collection, *Crown of Sonnets* (1834), used the author's own sense of a lack of fulfilment as a metaphor for the country's position in the Habsburg Empire. More optimistic, though, is *Zdravljica* (1844), the wine-drinking song, part of which became the text for Slovenia's national anthem. A lifelong drinker himself, Prešeren did not live long enough to enjoy the fame his works ultimately generated.

Triple Bridge

Tromostovje

E4

If the capital city has one immediately recognizable

The Triple Bridge leading to the Franciscan Church of the Annunciation and *(inset)* the church's high altar

5
Fountain of the Three Rivers

Vodnjak treh kranjskih rek

E4 Mestni trg

Rising above the cobblestoned Mestni trg, this tall triangular obelisk is the most celebrated work of Francesco Robba. The fountain gets its name from the three pitcher-wielding giants at its base, thought to symbolize the Ljubljanica, Sava and Krka, the three main rivers of the historical duchy Carniola. The fountain was commissioned in 1743, but it was another eight years before the project reached comple-tion. Probable inspiration for the work was Bernini's Fountain of the Four Rivers in Rome's Piazza Navona. What visitors see today is actually a replica – the original fountain was moved to the National Gallery *(p92)* in 2008, where a glass-covered atrium protects it from the elements.

landmark, it is probably this three-lane crossing designed in 1929 by the city's most prolific architect, Jože Plečnik *(p101)*. Faced with the problem of how to widen the city's main crossing point to accommodate increasing traffic levels, Plečnik decided to retain the 19th-century bridge in the middle, adding two angled side bridges for pedestrians. It was an inspired piece of town planning, turning Prešernov trg into the focal point of the city and bringing life to both banks of the river.

The bridge is embellished with the kind of decorations typical of Plečnik, with stone baubles sprouting from the parapets alongside curvy lampstands tipped with buds of milk-coloured glass. The elegant balustrades bring a Venetian sense of style to the whole ensemble.

STAY

Hotel Cubo
This outstanding hotel in a converted Art Deco apartment building offers stylish rooms and impeccable service. It also has a great modern restaurant.

D5 Slovenska cesta 15 hotelcubo.com

€€€

Lesar Hotel Angel
Art and antiques fill this elegant boutique hotel, housed in an early 19th-century building. The rooms are bright and spacious and there is a gorgeous garden from which there are views of Ljubljana Castle just above.

E5 Gornji trg 7 angelhotel.si

€€€

Antiq Palace Hotel
Housed in a beautifully renovated 16th-century palace, this excellent venue is a member of the Small Luxury Hotels of the World. The individually styled rooms combine the latest amenities with period details.

D5 Gosposka ulica 10 antiqpalace.com

€€€

Adora Hotel
This cosy, family-run hotel, on the edge of the Old Town, is located in a renovated old townhouse.

E6 Rožna ulica 7 adorahotel.si

€€€

EAT

EK Bistro

Head here for tasty breakfast or lunch options, which are served up beneath a vaulted brick ceiling.

G4 Petkovškovo nabrežje 65 (051) 624 061

€€€

Barbarella Arkade Bistro

This humble café has a tiny menu and just a few tables, but it serves some of the best vegan and vegetarian food in the capital, including tasty vegan and gluten-free desserts.

E4 Adamič Lundrovo nabrežje 3 barbarella-arkade.si

€€€

TaBar

The seasonal menu at this fashionable bar offers a variety of cold and warm tapas and cheeses. There's also an extensive list of Slovenian wines.

E4 Riblji trg 6 tabar.si

€€€

Špajza

A cluster of elegant small rooms decorated with folksy bric-a-brac form a homely setting here. The fine restaurant also serves up expertly cooked Mediterranean and seafood dishes.

E6 Gornji trg 28 spajza-restaurant.si

€€€

Market

Glavna tržnica

E4/5 Vodnikov trg
Market Colonnade: 7am-4pm Mon-Fri, 7am-2pm Sat

The northern end of the city's Old Town is largely taken up by Ljubljana's sprawling market. Apart from being the local fruit and vegetable market, the place also has numerous stalls selling herbs, speciality foods and souvenirs.

Dominating the market's northern side is the Market Colonnade, a gently curving riverside structure that looks like an elongated Graeco-Roman temple. It was designed by Jože Plečnik (*p101*) in 1942 to provide shelter for a row of food stalls. Staircases descend to the colonnade's lower storey, home to a fish market filled with piles of Adriatic octopus, squid and lobster.

Plečnik initially planned to build a covered bridge linking the eastern end of the colonnade to the opposite bank of Ljubljanica river – a project that did not take off due to lack of funds. The original plan was partly carried out with the construction of the Butchers' Bridge (Mesarski most) in 2010. Guarding the approaches to the bridge are statues of Adam, Eve and Prometheus, by local sculptor Jakov Brdar. To the east of the colonnade is the main fruit and vegetable market, and presiding over the southern end of the square is a statue of Valentin Vodnik. A priest and poet, Vodnik was one of the founding fathers of Slovenian literary culture and an inspiration to 19th-century patriots. He edited the country's first newspaper, and his works helped to shape the modern Slovenian language.

Immediately east of Vodnikov trg is the so-called Flat Iron (Peglezen), a four-storey apartment built by Jože Plečnik in 1932. Named after its narrow wedge shape and flat roof, the building is a typical example of Plečnik's architectural style – a mix of Modernist, Renaissance and Classical – with an arcaded ground floor and geometrical window frames further up.

Town Hall

Mestna hiša

E4 Mestni trg 1

Adding an air of distinction to Mestni trg's western side is Ljubljana's 18th-century Town Hall, a Renaissance-influenced structure with an arcaded ground floor and a hexagonal

↑ Umbrellas offering shade to shoppers by the edge of Ljubljana's market

The stunning interior and intricately painted ceiling of St Nicholas's Cathedral ↑

clock tower. Just inside the entrance is a 17th-century statue of Hercules preparing to batter a wild beast. According to local myth, Hercules visited Ljubljana in the company of Jason and the Argonauts who, having sailed up the Danube and Sava rivers, had to pull their boat overland in order to secure passage to the Adriatic Sea.

Beyond the statue lies a trio of arcaded inner courtyards – the central one is decorated with a sgraffito frieze featuring horn-blowing cherubs and frolicking unicorns. Slightly hidden in one corner is a fountain overlooked by a statue of Narcissus, attributed to Francesco Robba's workshop. Guided tours of the Town Hall itself take place every Saturday at 1pm.

St Nicholas's Cathedral
Stolna Cerkev sv Nikolaja

📍 E4 🏛 Dolničarjeva 1
📞 (01) 234 2690 🕒 6am-
noon & 3-7pm daily

Towering above the market are the twin towers of the Baroque St Nicholas's Cathedral. Built on the site of an earlier church by leading Jesuit architect Andrea Pozzo in 1707, the church has a relatively plain exterior, enlivened by the two bronze sculptured doors made to commemorate Pope John Paul II's visit to Slovenia in 1996. The (main) west door depicts scenes from 1,250 years of Slovenian Christianity – the top of the door portrays Pope John Paul II peering from a window, while towards the bottom is an illustration of the baptism of the Slovenian nation. The south door shows the mitred profiles of six of Slovenia's 20th-century bishops praying at Christ's tomb.

Inside, the cathedral has a richly decorated sequence of side chapels as well as a nave dominated by an Illusionist

Did You Know?

St Nicholas is patron saint of fishermen and sailors.

ceiling painting of the Crucifixion by Giulio Quaglio the Elder (1610–58). There is also a Corpus Christi altar (1752) by the Italian sculptor Francesco Robba, which is flanked by statuettes of angels. Niches in the transept hold four statues of the bishops of Roman-era Emona carved by the 17th-century sculptor Angelo Putti.

Bishop's Palace
Škofijski dvorec

📍 E4 🏛 Ciril Metodov trg 4
📞 (01) 234 2600 🕒 Mon-Fri

Connected to the cathedral by a covered pedestrian bridge is the Bishop's Palace, a distinguished building facing the Ljubljanica river. It was originally built for Bishop Ravbar in 1512. The beautiful arcaded courtyard and loggia, added in the 18th century, gives the building its charm.

Napoleon Bonaparte stayed here after routing Austrian armies in 1797. The palace also served as the official residence of the Governor-General of the French-ruled Illyrian Provinces between 1808 and 1813.

Stari trg

 E5

The main thoroughfare of the Old Town is Stari trg, a narrow cobbled street overlooked by well-preserved Baroque and Neo-Renaissance houses. Once inhabited by Ljubljana's wealthier merchant families, the street is now lined with designer clothes boutiques, craft shops and restaurants. A lattice of alleyways connects Stari trg to Cankarjevo nabrežje, the café-lined promenade that runs along the riverbank to the west.

The 18th-century Schweiger House (Schweigerjeva hiša), at No 11, has a portal overlooked by a stone figure of a man holding his finger up to his lips – a witty allusion to the building's original owner, Franz Karl Schweiger von Lerchenfeld; in German

Schweiger means "Silent One". A bust mounted on the wall beside the doorway honours one of the house's most famous residents, the poet Lili Novy (1885–1958).

Seminary

Semenišče

E4 Dolničarjeva ulica 4
(01) 306 1215

Immediately northeast of the cathedral (p75) is the Seminary, a grand Baroque structure built by the architect Carlo Martinuzzi between 1708 and 1714. The most impressive feature on the exterior is the south portal, an arched doorway flanked by a pair of stone Titans carved by Angelo Putti. The Seminary's library on the first floor was the first public library in Ljubljana and its Baroque interior is still

preserved today. The ceiling vaults are filled with frescoes by Giulio Quaglio. Books are stored in ornate wooden cases made by local cabinet-maker Josip Wergant. The library can only be visited by prior arrangement. The Ljubljana Tourist Information Centre organizes visits.

ŠKUC Gallery

Galerija ŠKUC

E5 Stari trg 21
Noon-8pm Tue-Sun
skuc.org

Occupying the front half of a corner house at the junction of Stari trg and Gornji trg, ŠKUC Gallery has been Ljubljana's primary venue for contemporary art ever since it opened its doors in 1978.

Founded as a student cultural centre (Študentski kulturni center, hence the acronym), ŠKUC soon became the focus of radical activity. It has promoted artists from all over "the former" Yugoslavia, released punk-rock records under its own label, supported

> **The main thoroughfare of the Old Town is Stari trg, a narrow cobbled street overlooked by well-preserved Baroque and Neo-Renaissance houses.**

↑ Pretty, pastel Neo-Renaissance houses lining Stari trg

minority rights groups and organized intellectual discussions. Most of the civil rights activists who shaped the Slovene Spring of the 1980s were part of ŠKUC at some stage in their lives.

The centre organizes several excellent festivals, including Living Literature (Živa književnost) in June, when authors give book readings in front of the gallery; and Let's Meet at ŠKUC (Dobimo se pred Škucem) in July, a series of outdoor concerts.

The ŠKUC Gallery still looks like an alternative cultural space, with black doorways and darkened windows eloquently conveying the message that this is not a mainstream art gallery. A full programme of exhibitions presents a great opportunity to see artists from Slovenia as well as from other countries.

13

Dragon Bridge
Zmajski most

⚑ F4

Located just beyond the market's eastern boundary, the Dragon Bridge was the first major Art Nouveau project to be built in the city. Designed by the architect Jurij Zaninovič, it was built in 1901 to mark the 60th birthday of Austro-Hungarian Emperor Franz Josef I. The bridge gets its name from the bronze dragons that stand guard over its ends. It is said that the legendary voyagers, Jason and the Argonauts, fought with and killed a dragon in the marshes south of Ljubljana before continuing on their journey towards the Adriatic.

Rising from the bridge's parapet is a line of Art Nouveau lampposts, decorated with griffin motifs and crowned with fruit-like clusters of glass globes. A plaque halfway along the bridge honours Ivan Hribar (1851–1941), the mayor of Ljubljana who oversaw the bridge's construction. The western end of the bridge provides a fine view of Ljubljana's market halls, with the twin towers and dome of the cathedral rising in the distance.

←

One of the intricate bronze dragon statues that adorns the Dragon Bridge

DRINK

Pritličje
This dynamic hipster café-bar also functions as a cultural centre, hosting live music and other events. There's even a comic book store.

⚑ E4 🏠 Mestni trg 5 🌐 pritlicje.si

Movia
Choose from a terrific selection of wines from throughout Slovenia at this small but sophisticated bar.

⚑ E5 🏠 Mestni trg 2 🌐 movia.si

Tozd
Whether you're after coffee or craft beer, this little hangout is sure to deliver. It includes a bring-and-take library: you can take away a book for free if you leave one of your own behind.

⚑ E5 🏠 Gallusovo nabrežje 27 🌐 tozd.eu

Čajna Hisa
Slow things down and kick back with a cuppa at this bijou teahouse. It's the cosiest spot in town – perfect for when the temperatures take a dive in winter.

⚑ E5 🏠 Stari trg 3 🌐 cha.si

Le Petit Café
Whether it's serving up early morning coffee and a pastry, or a glass of red wine as the sun sets, this street corner café remains one of the city's most enduring.

⚑ D5 🏠 Trg Francoske revolucije 4 🌐 lepetit.si

14

Gruber Palace
Gruberjeva palača

🗺 E6 🏠 Zvezdarska 1
📞 (01) 241 4200 🕐 By appt

Marking the southern extent of the Old Town is Gruber Palace, a stately yellow building that now houses the State Archives. The palace was built in Baroque and Rococo style in the 1770s on the initiative of Jesuit priest and engineer Gabriel Gruber (1740–1805), and it originally served as a school of hydrology and navigation. It was one of the best-equipped schools of the era, with facilities such as

↑ The impressive yellow façade of Gruber Palace, which dates from the 18th century

manufacturing workshops, a chemistry laboratory and an astronomical observatory.

A relief just left of the main door shows the school's founder holding a varied collection of scientific instruments. The interior, visits to which can be arranged through Ljubljana's Tourist Information Centre, contains a chapel decorated with paintings by the late-Baroque Austrian artist Kremser Schmidt (1718–1801). There is also a stuccoed oval staircase overlooked by frescoes of figures symbolizing scientific endeavour.

The other great contribution made by Gruber to Ljubljana was the construction of the canal that runs south of Castle Hill, diverting seasonal floodwaters away from the city centre.

Old Town. The church was restored by Jože Plečnik (p101) between 1933 and 1934.

The church is rarely open to the public, but there are plenty of interesting details on the exterior, such as the faded 18th-century fresco of Our Lady of Mercy, high above the main door. Occupying a niche on the street-facing side of the church is Francesco Robba's (1698–1757) lively sculpture of the Czech martyr St John of Nepomuk. Here, the saint is portrayed being thrown into the Vltava river as cherubs cling to his robes.

SHOP

Ika
Showcasing gorgeous, handmade products by local designers, such as art, clothes and pottery, this is a souvenir shop par excellence.

🗺 E4 🏠 Ciril Metodov trg 13 🌐 trgovinaika.si

---

3 Muhe
The colourful "Three Flies" is a superb fair trade enterprise. It sells a wonderful array of goodies, from jewellery to ceramics.

🗺 E5 🏠 Stari trg 30 🕐 Sun 🌐 pravicna-trgovina.si

Kraševka
Treat yourself to delicious Slovenian delicacies at this local produce outlet – there's wine, goat's cheese, *pršut* and pumpkin-seed oil, to name just a few.

🗺 E4 🏠 Vodnikov trg 4 🕐 Sun 🌐 krasevka.si

15

St Florian's Church
Cerkev sv Florjana

🗺 E6 🏠 Gornji trg

Presiding over the mansard-roofed Baroque houses on the picturesque Gornji trg is onion-domed St Florian's Church, which is dedicated to the patron saint of firefighters. The dedication took place after the church, a 17th-century structure, was damaged by a fire in 1774 that ripped through much of the

> **The interior of St James's Church remains one of Ljubljana's most outstanding displays of Baroque religious art, with Francesco Robba contributing a great deal to the design.**

St James's Church
Cerkev sv Jakoba

📍 E6 🏠 Gornji trg 18
📞 (01) 252 1727

Rising to the south of Stari trg (*p76*) are the lemon-yellow walls of St James's Church, a church of Gothic origins that received a Baroque makeover when the Jesuits adopted it as their base in 1598. The basilica was damaged in the 1895 earthquake. A subsequent second wave of rebuilding resulted in the addition of the Neo-Gothic spire that is the church's focal point today. The church's name is occasionally mistranslated as St Jacob's, as Slovene uses the same word for both James and Jacob.

The interior remains one of Ljubljana's most outstanding displays of Baroque religious art, with Francesco Robba, who lived in the vicinity of the church, contributing a great deal to the design. There are parallel rows of altars that are filled with extravagant statuary, including Robba's high altar (1732), which is flanked by a graceful pair of angels depicted with their hands clasped in prayer.

The octagonal St Francis Xavier Chapel (1709) is found on the northern side of the church, and features more angels sculpted by Paolo Groppelli (1677–1751) and female figures by Jacopo Contieri personifying the continents of Europe and Africa – the latter lavishly clad in grasses and feathers.

→ St James's Church, with its Neo-Gothic spire soaring above the Old Town

TOP 4 **ALTERNATIVE TOURS OF LJUBLJANA**

From Ljubljana With Love
🌐 curiocity.si
Visit shops, restaurants, and businesses that have a strong community focus.

Ljubljana Feminist Tour
🌐 ljubljanaurbantours.com
This tour highlights some of the many women whose roles in local history have been overlooked.

The Punk Poet's Tour
🌐 ljubljanaurbantours.com
A cycling tour through the city's former socialist punk scene.

Ljubljana Alternative Tour
🌐 visitljubljana.com
An off-beat tour of the city's counter-culture, taking in street art, alternative venues and the survival of the city's largest squat.

17

National and University Library
Narodna in univerzitetna knjižnica

📍D5 🏛Turjaška 1 🕐8am-8pm Mon-Fri, 9am-2pm Sat �🌐nuk-uni-lj.si

Located off the west bank of the Ljubljanica river, the National and University Library is considered the greatest masterpiece in Slovenia of architect Jože Plečnik (p101). Completed in 1940, the building is characteristic of Plečnik's work, combining the straight lines of modern architecture with organic surfaces and inspired decorative details. The striking exterior features a patchwork of different hues, mixing grey hunks of Slovenian granite with terracotta-coloured brickwork. Upon entering through the main door (on Turjaška ulica), visitors find themselves in a dark stairway of polished black limestone. This leads to the brightly lit first-floor reading rooms, with the light increasing as you move further into the library, symbolizing the transition from ignorance to knowledge. Interior details, such as the doorknobs, window fittings and wooden beamed ceilings were all designed by Plečnik himself, fusing Art Deco with folk-influenced motifs to create a highly personalized style. During regular library opening hours the famous reading rooms, furnished with ornate desk lamps and chandeliers, are open only to students, but for a glimpse visitors are free to enter the lobby; at the weekend, tours can be booked in advance. There is also a good café in the library basement.

> **Located off the west bank of the Ljubljanica river, the National and University Library is considered the greatest masterpiece in Slovenia of architect Jože Plečnik.**

18

Ljubljana City Museum
Mestni muzej Ljubljana

📍D5 🏛Gosposka ulica 15 🕐10am-6pm Tue-Sun (to 9pm Thu) �🌐mgml.si

At the eastern end of Trg Francoske revolucije stands the superb 17th-century Auersperg Palace, home to the Turjak counts for some 300 years. Subsequently acquired by the city authorities, the building was spectacularly renovated to accommodate the City Museum. The site now includes a curved glass atrium, along with a spiral walkway that links the building's basement to the upper floors. Archaeological finds, such as bits of Roman road and medieval brickwork, unearthed during renovation, are on display in the basement.

The museum's permanent collection features a variety of artifacts illustrating the daily life of the city dwellers in the past. The museum's most prestigious exhibit by far is a wooden wheel discovered in the Ljubljana Marshes in 2002 (p121). Analysis suggests that it is over 5,000 years old, which makes it the oldest such specimen in the world. There is also a vast collection of art on display, with pieces including an 18th-century bust of Emperor Charles VI by Francesco Robba as well as 15th-century statues of Adam and Eve that once stood in niches on the façade of the Town Hall (p74).

←

The National and University Library's reading room and (inset) main stairway

One of the inner courtyards of Križanke, which was once a monastery ↑

 19

University of Ljubljana

Univerza v Ljubljani

D5 **Kongresni trg 12** **uni-lj.si**

The most prominent building on the southern side of Kongresni trg is the Neo-Renaissance palace that serves as the main headquarters of the University of Ljubljana. Built in 1902 to provide the Duchy of Carniola with a prestigious venue for meetings and receptions, the palace is adorned with ornate corner towers and spires.

Arranged in a semicircle in front of the entrance are sculptures and busts of noteworthy academic figures, including that of Ivan Hribar (1851–1941), the long-serving mayor of Ljubljana who was instrumental in getting the university off the ground. Mooted by leading Slovenian politicians in the 1890s, the university did not come into being until 1919. It is now has a significant student population of over 65,000.

 20

Križanke

D5 **Trg francoske revolucije**

South of the National and University Library lies Križanke, a former monastery complex that now serves as a concert venue. It is also where orchestral events are held during the Ljubljana Festival (p51) as well as major rock, jazz and world music concerts from spring through to autumn. Classical music concerts are held in the indoor Knight's Hall throughout the year.

Križanke dates from the 13th century, when Duke Ulrich III of Spannheim invited the Teutonic Knights to Ljubljana to develop schools and hospitals for the poor. The complex of ceremonial halls and interlocking courtyards dates from the 16th and 18th centuries. The monastery fell into disrepair after the Communists moved the monks out in 1945; Plečnik was given the task of restoring it as a cultural centre.

The main courtyard is usually open only to concert-goers, although visitors are free to explore the entrance courtyard (Malo dvorišče), where a bust of Plečnik adorns a balustrade. The courtyard is lined by arcades on three sides, with bold sgraffito decorations conveying an air of Renaissance gaiety. The occasional outdoor chamber concerts held in the Peklensko dvorišče, an intimate quadrangular courtyard, are worth buying tickets for.

 INSIDER TIP
Those Summer Nights

If attending a summer concert at Križanke's wonderful covered outdoor venue, be sure to bring a blanket and a flask of hot tea – it can get quite chilly here in the evening!

㉑ Kongresni trg

⑨ D4

The gently sloping rectangle of grass and trees known as Kongresni trg, or Congress Square, takes its name from the Congress of the Holy Alliance – Russia, Austria and Prussia – held in Ljubljana in 1821. Hosted by Emperor Francis I of Austria and attended by dignitaries from all over Europe, most notably Tsar Alexander I of Russia, the Congress aimed to bring stability to the pan-European political system agreed upon at the Congress of Vienna in 1815. With four months of negotiations accompanied by an endless round of dinners, large firework displays and glamorous masked balls, it was the biggest party in Ljubljana's history.

The event involved a major overhaul of the city's infrastructure. The square, which was already occupied by a smaller plaza during the Baroque period, was levelled and expanded to host the daily military parades, while roads were repaved and street lighting was installed. The square also played an important role in the Slovene Spring – mass demonstrations demanding the release of the Ljubljana Four were held here in June 1988.

The most appealing of the buildings surrounding the square is the Baroque Ursuline Church at the western end. Most of the other buildings on the square, including the pink-hued Neo-Classical palace (Kazina) on the northern side, are from the 19th century. Originally a club for Ljubljana's wealthier citizens, the Kazina was briefly the seat of the Slovenian parliament in the years following World War II.

At the centre of the square is the lovely Zvezda Park (Star Park), which is popular with locals and families. The square itself now hosts regular music concerts and national festivities.

Did You Know?

Ljubljana's river has seven names, changing each time it goes underground and re-emerges.

㉒ Cooperative Bank

Zadružna gospodarska banka

⑨ E3 ⌂ Miklošičeva 8

The most decorative building in downtown Ljubljana, the Cooperative Bank was created by Ivan Vurnik (1884–1971) and his wife Helena Vurnik. Ivan was a Radovljica-born architect who studied under Otto Wagner, the doyen of Viennese Art Nouveau.

Begun in 1921, it represents a unique mixture of ethnographic detail and Art Nouveau, with jazzy chevrons and zigzags weaving around the oriel windows on the façade. Rich in blues, yellows and brickreds, the decorative scheme is inspired by the embroidery of rural Slovenia. Vurnik, clearly, was also influenced by folk-art patterns found throughout Slavic Europe.

The Cooperative Bank now houses the Ljubljana Land Registry Office; you can peek into the extravagantly decorated lobby during working hours. Geometrical patterns frame frescoes extolling the beauty of the Slovenian landscape and the virtues of its hard-working countrymen and women.

↑ Kongresni trg encircled by grand buildings, including the Philharmonic Hall

 23

Philharmonic Hall

Filharmonija

📍 **D4** 🏛 **Kongresni trg 10**
🌐 **filharmonija.si**

Sitting on the southeastern corner of Kongresni trg is the Philharmonic Hall, Ljubljana's main venue for classical music, which was built in 1891. The "1701" inscription on the façade refers to the date of the foundation of Academia Filharmonicorum, Ljubljana's first musical society. The academy's members performed only at state occasions and society funerals, and it was not until the formation of the Philharmonic Society in 1794 that Ljubljana gained a regularly performing orchestra. During his tenure as conductor at Ljubljana's Provincial Theatre, Gustav Mahler, then 21 years old, was invited by the society to play piano at their concerts in 1882.

Ljubljana did not have a full symphony orchestra in the years following World War I until 1947, when the Slovene Philharmonic was refounded and this building became the company's permanent home.

ART NOUVEAU

Ljubljana experienced a building boom in the early 20th century, when an array of apartments and office blocks were built just north of Prešernov trg. The Art Nouveau style of these buildings was influenced by the Austrian Secessionist movement as well as traditional Slovenian design motifs.

The most eye-catching of Ljubljana's Art Nouveau buildings is the Cooperative Bank. Its architect, Vurnik, was keen to develop a Slovenian national style by blending folk motifs with the best of modern design; this building is his ideological statement. Also worth looking out for is the Centromerkur building on Prešernov trg *(p72)*. Now a department store, it was built in 1903 and among its original features are a petal-shaped canopy and a beautiful Y-shaped staircase. Just across the square is the Hauptman House, a charming wedge-shaped building decorated with geometric shapes and floral swirls.

↑ The cast-iron canopy of the Centromerkur building

A SHORT WALK
LJUBLJANA OLD TOWN

Distance 1.5 km (1 mile) **Walking time** 20 minutes
Nearest station Ljubljana

Located between the medieval castle and the leafy banks of the Ljubljanica river, Ljubljana's Old Town contains some of the best-preserved Baroque buildings in southeastern Europe. Arcaded 18th-century houses, domed churches, fountain-studded piazzas and narrow cobbled alleys lined with cafés and shops add to the Old Town's elegant character.

Ljubljana's lively **outdoor market** *(p74) is known for its fresh herbs and dried mushrooms.*

VODNIKOV TRG

Dragon Bridge *(p77) is an example of the Art Nouveau style.*

Butchers' Bridge *was opened to the public in 2010. Couples in love come here to affix engraved padlocks to the parapet.*

Created by Giulio Quaglio in 1706, the ceiling of **St Nicholas's Cathedral** *(p75) is a fine example of Baroque illusionist painting.*

Franciscan Church of the Annunciation *(p72) is the city's most attractive Baroque church, with an 18th-century altar by Italian sculptor Francesco Robba.*

START

The Prešeren Statue, *one of Ljubljana's best-known landmarks, honours Romantic poet and national icon France Prešeren (p72).*

Designed by Jože Plečnik in 1929, the three-lane **Triple Bridge** *(p72) was part of the renovation of the riverbank.*

← Riding the scenic funicular railway up to Ljubljana Castle

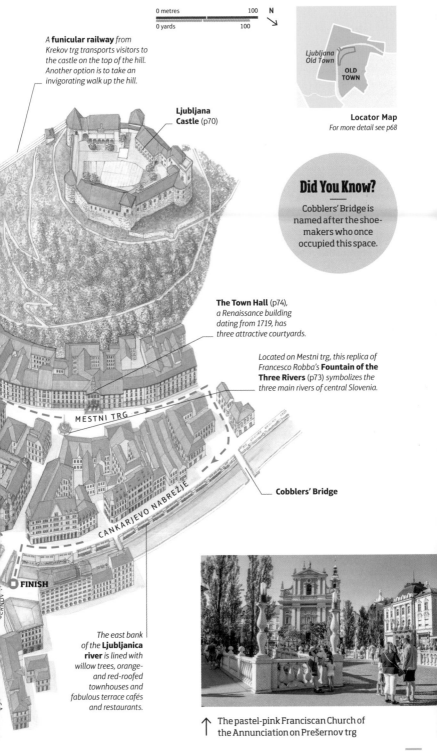

A **funicular railway** from Krekov trg transports visitors to the castle on the top of the hill. Another option is to take an invigorating walk up the hill.

Ljubljana Castle (p70)

Did You Know?

Cobblers' Bridge is named after the shoe-makers who once occupied this space.

The Town Hall (p74), a Renaissance building dating from 1719, has three attractive courtyards.

Located on Mestni trg, this replica of Francesco Robba's **Fountain of the Three Rivers** (p73) symbolizes the three main rivers of central Slovenia.

MESTNI TRG

Cobblers' Bridge

CANKARJEVO NABREŽJE

FINISH

The east bank of the **Ljubljanica river** is lined with willow trees, orange- and red-roofed townhouses and fabulous terrace cafés and restaurants.

↑ The pastel-pink Franciscan Church of the Annunciation on Prešernov trg

A SHORT WALK

LJUBLJANA UNIVERSITY DISTRICT

Distance 1 km (0.5 miles)   **Walking time** 15 minutes
Nearest station Ljubljana Tivoli

Ljubljana University District contains many examples of the city's finest 19th-century architecture, much of it laid out around the leafy expanse of Kongresni trg. The area resonates with history, its buildings occupied by many of Slovenia's most important cultural and educational institutions. This part of the city is closely associated with 20th-century architect Jože Plečnik, who designed the impressive National and University Library and renovated the courtyards of the Križanke monastery.

↑ Cycling past a row of fine buildings in the historic University District

Drama Theatre

START

VEGOVA ULICA

TURJAŠKA ULICA

FINISH

GOSPOSKA

The most famous of Jože Plečnik's buildings in Ljubljana, the **National and University Library** (p80) *features a rough-and-smooth façade of stone and brick. Its bay windows are in the shape of open books.*

The **Illyrian Monument** *recalls Ljubljana's role as the capital of the French-run Illyrian Provinces from 1809 to 1813. Reliefs of Napoleon Bonaparte and female heads adorn it.*

Renaissance arcades and Postmodern lamp fittings mark the former monastery of **Križanke** (p81) *as one of Jože Plečnik's foremost restoration projects. The courtyards now host major outdoor concerts.*

Ljubljana City Museum (p80)

ZOISOVA CESTA

Zois House, *home of Baron Žiga Zois (1747–1819), was a meeting point for Slovenian intellectuals.*

The **University of Ljubljana** (p81) has witnessed many historical events, including Tito speaking from the balcony in May 1945 and political reformers addressing large crowds in June 1988.

Locator Map
For more detail see p68

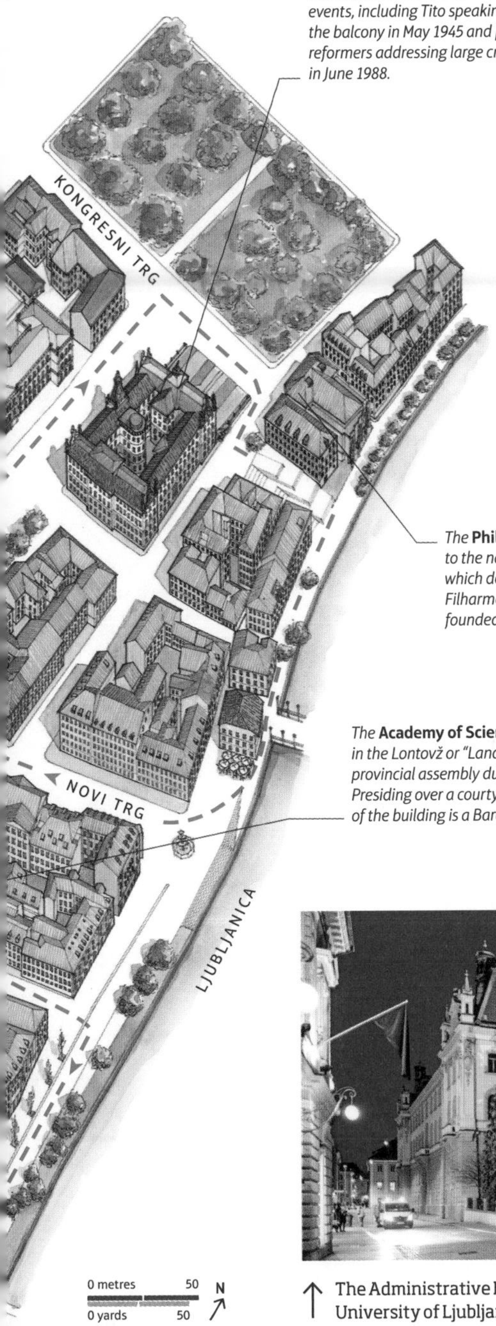

OLD TOWN

Ljubljana University District

Did You Know?

The University of Ljubljana is one of the biggest universities in Central Europe.

The **Philharmonic Hall** (p83) is home to the nation's leading orchestra, which descended from the Academia Filharmonicorum, a cultural society founded in 1701.

The **Academy of Sciences and Arts** is located in the Lontovž or "Landhaus", home to the provincial assembly during the Habsburg era. Presiding over a courtyard on the eastern side of the building is a Baroque statue of Neptune.

KONGRESNI TRG

NOVI TRG

LJUBLJANICA

0 metres 50
0 yards 50
N

↑ The Administrative Building of the University of Ljubljana lit up at night

CITY CENTRE

The walls of Roman Emona were built between AD 14 and 15, enclosing a rectangle on the left bank of the Ljubljanica, where the city stood until it was sacked by the Huns in 452. Most traces of Ljubljana's Roman past have vanished, although Jože Plečnik restored one section of the walls in 1926. From the 11th century the early medieval settlement of Laibach developed into a town, expanding to include the left bank of the river as well, with medieval walls strong enough to withstand a Turkish siege in the 15th century.

The city gained a Baroque appearance in the 16th and 17th centuries, expanding westwards when the medieval walls were pulled down in the 17th century. Following the devastating earthquake of 1895, Ljubljana's city centre was rebuilt in Secessionist style, under the direction of the architect Max Fabiani. In the 1920s and 1930s, Jože Plečnik added his distinctive, visionary touches to the city's architecture.

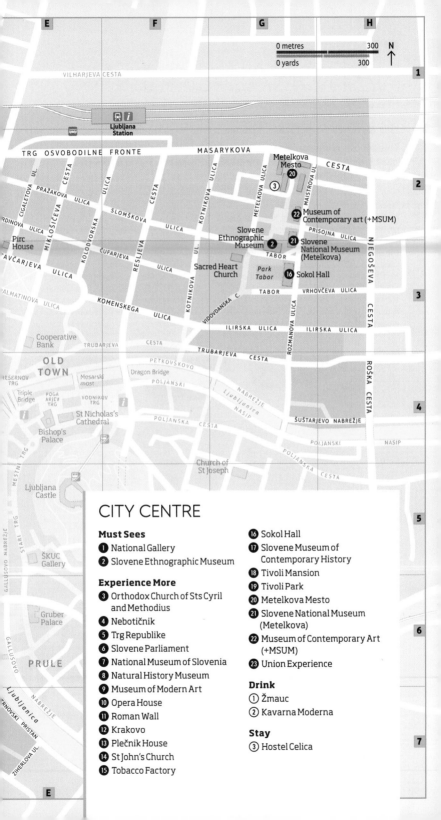

CITY CENTRE

Must Sees

① National Gallery
② Slovene Ethnographic Museum

Experience More

③ Orthodox Church of Sts Cyril and Methodius
④ Nebotičnik
⑤ Trg Republike
⑥ Slovene Parliament
⑦ National Museum of Slovenia
⑧ Natural History Museum
⑨ Museum of Modern Art
⑩ Opera House
⑪ Roman Wall
⑫ Krakovo
⑬ Plečnik House
⑭ St John's Church
⑮ Tobacco Factory
⑯ Sokol Hall
⑰ Slovene Museum of Contemporary History
⑱ Tivoli Mansion
⑲ Tivoli Park
⑳ Metelkova Mesto
㉑ Slovene National Museum (Metelkova)
㉒ Museum of Contemporary Art (+MSUM)
㉓ Union Experience

Drink

① Žmauc
② Kavarna Moderna

Stay

③ Hostel Celica

NATIONAL GALLERY
NARODNA GALERIJA

⊙ C3 ⌂ Prešernova 24 ⏰ 10am–6pm Tue–Sun (to 8pm Thu) ⊕ ng-slo.si

This imposing, cream-coloured building holds Slovenia's largest and most important collection of fine art, comprising nearly 600 works by both national and international artists.

Slovenia's national art collection occupies an elegant 19th-century building full of stucco ceilings and ornate chandeliers. Erected in 1896 to serve as the Slovene Cultural Centre, the building became home to the National Gallery in 1925. A modern annexe was opened in 2001, with a glass-fronted atrium at the junction of the old and new buildings holding the collection's pride and joy – Francesco Robba's Fountain of the Three Rivers, which was moved here from its original location on Mestni trg in 2009. Temporary exhibitions are also held in the atrium, while the original 19th-century wing contains the national collection of Slovenian art, from Gothic to the early 20th century. The museum's collection is particularly rich in Gothic statuary and Baroque religious paintings. Space is also devoted to the Slovenian Impressionists: Rihard Jakopič, Matija Jama, Ivan Grohar and Matej Sternen, all four of whom were committed landscape painters. Also displayed are works by Slovenia's most acclaimed female painter, Ivana Kobilica.

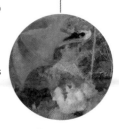

Solomon's Verdict, Franc Kavčič

▽ The Vienna-educated Kavčič (1755-1828) was Slovenia's greatest exponent of Neo-Classicism, and painted a series of large-scale mythological or biblical subjects.

Red Parasol, Matej Sternen

▽ Painted in 1904, this is arguably the best-loved canvas by Sternen (1870-1949), an artist known for his female portraits.

Fountain of the Three Rivers

△ Robba's 18th-century sculpture is surrounded by balconied walkways, providing wonderful viewpoints. At its base, three Tritons symbolize Slovenia's main rivers.

The Krakovo Madonna

Correctly entitled *The Madonna on Solomon's Throne*, this delicate 13th-century relief was the work of an anonymous mason known as the Master of Solčava.

THE SLOVENIAN IMPRESSIONISTS

Pre-World War I, Rihard Jakopič, Ivan Grohar, Matija Jama and Matej Sternen energized the local art scene by painting Slovenian subjects with the kind of style previously associated with French artists such as Renoir. Initially snubbed by conservative critics, today they are regarded as the high point of the nation's art.

← An airy interior room of the National Gallery, housed within an ornate pillared building *(inset)*

2 🤿 Ⓜ️ 💻 🛍️

SLOVENE ETHNOGRAPHIC MUSEUM

SLOCENSKI ETNOGRAFSKI MUZEJ

📍 G2 🏛️ Metelkova 2 🕐 10am–6pm Tue–Sun 🌐 etno-muzej.si

The Slovene Ethnographic Museum is one of the most imaginative of its kind in Europe, exhibiting artifacts from Slovenia and around the globe in a series of visually captivating displays.

The museum's collection is brought to life with the help of documentary films, sound recordings and a computer lounge allowing visitors to access audiovisual content. The setting is itself impressive, occupying a 19th-century barracks to which a futuristic glass-and-steel façade has been added. The museum is particularly suited to younger visitors, with interactive toys on the top floor, an ethno alphabet display and a merry-go-round and see-saw that stand on the lawn outside the café.

The permanent collection begins on the second floor with a display, "I, We and Others", which looks at ethnography globally. The third floor showcases Slovene life and culture through the ages.

Museum Highlights

Objects of Life, Objects of Desire

This room on the third floor sheds light on the industrious and creative side of human society, with traditional trades such as shoe-making and clock-making displayed alongside wonderful examples of folk costume, painting and wood sculpture.

Čupa

▷ This dug out canoe, carved out of a log, dominates the Water and Earth section, which is devoted to local agriculture and trade. It was used for fishing by Slovenians living on the Adriatic coast north of Trieste (now in Italy).

Folk Costumes

▽ The display includes costumes from all regions of Slovenia and the fine clothes worn by 19th-century town dwellers. There is also a fascinating collection of bonnets, which were important symbols of regional and national identity.

↑ An attention-grabbing display in one of the museum's rooms

💬 INSIDER TIP
Craft Workshops

Artisans in the museum's ground-floor workshops are on hand to demonstrate traditional pottery and weaving techniques. Visitors can buy textiles, including contemporary accessories such as ponchos, bags and scarves with folk motifs.

Painted Beehive Panels

These hand-painted panels are a typically Slovenian form of popular art. As well as scenes of daily life, they frequently portray parades of animals dressed in human clothes.

Painted Furniture

Children's cradles and chests are among the most popular pieces of painted furniture displayed on the third floor.

West African Ritual Masks

▷ Brought to Slovenia by Anton Petkovšek, who toured Africa as a trade representative, these masks shed light on the role of private collectors in shaping the Slovenian public's vision of the wider world. Nearby are Javanese puppets collected by Slovenian diplomat Aleš Bebler.

↑ Exterior of the Slovene Ethnographic Museum

EXPERIENCE MORE

Orthodox Church of Sts Cyril and Methodius

Pravoslavna cerkev sv Cirila in Metoda

🅠 C3 🅐 Prešernova cesta
📞 (01) 252 4002

Built in 1932 for Ljubljana's Serbian community, this church is inspired by the medieval monastery churches of southern Serbia, with a cluster of bulbous cupolas mounted on a high cross-shaped nave. Covering every inch of the spacious interior are frescoes by contemporary artist Dragomir Jašović. The frescoes follow centuries-old Serbian models, with scenes from the New Testament juxtaposed with friezes of Serbian saints.

Presiding over the park in front of the church is a bust of the Reformation preacher Primož Trubar, who published the first books in Slovenian.

Nebotičnik

🅠 D3 🅐 Cnr of Štefanova and Slovenska ulica

Adding a dash of Art Deco elegance to Ljubljana's main shopping street is Nebotičnik (Skyscraper), an upmarket residential block designed by Vladimir Šubic in 1933. Though modest in comparison with the skyscrapers of today, this 13-storey structure was the tallest in Yugoslavia when it was constructed.

In contrast to the building's stern façade are the round porthole-style windows on the ground floor and the arched window frames. An angelic figure sculpted by Lojze Dolinar occupies a plinth on the sixth floor, watching over the pedestrians on the pavement below. You can enter the lobby from Štefanova ulica to admire the faux marble walls. The spiral staircase is accessible only to residents, but tourists

GREAT VIEW
Coffee with a View

Enjoy a coffee at Kavarna Nebotičnik, which occupies the top three floors of the building with its café, bar and restaurant. From the café's terrace there are superb views of the cityscape.

← The stunningly frescoed interior of the Orthodox Church of Sts Cyril and Methodius and *(inset)* its Serbo-Byzantine exterior

Modernist tower blocks, designed by architect Edvard Ravnikar, on Trg Republike ↑

can take the lift up to Kavarna Nebotičnik, a cafe, bar and restaurant at the top that is open until late.

⑤ Trg Republike

 C4

Stretching south of the Parliament building, Trg Republike (formerly named Trg Revolucije) was developed in the 1960s to provide a modern focal point to the capital's New Town. With the Maximarket department store on the eastern side, and two large office blocks, originally owned by Ljubljanska banka and the Iskra telecommunications company, to the south, the whole unit was intended as a powerful expression of socialist progress. Today, a major part of the square serves as a car park.

Located behind the two office blocks is Cankar Hall (Cankarjev dom), a prestigious cultural centre. Opened in 1982, it was designed by Slovenia's leading postwar architect Edvard Ravnikar and named after Slovenia's greatest novelist and playwright, Ivan Cankar (p119). Covered with slabs of Carrara marble, the building contains a concert hall with seating for 1,500 people, three smaller multipurpose halls and an exhibition gallery.

Outside the main entrance is the cube-shaped monument to Ivan Cankar by the Slovenian sculptor Slavko Tihec (1928–93). At first glance it looks rather like a rusty box, although an image of Cankar's face, formed by the dark fissures covering the monument's surface, is visible.

⑥ Slovene Parliament
Parlament Slovenije

 C4 🏠 Šubičeva 4
📞 (01) 478 9400

A Modernist block designed by Vinko Glanz in 1960, the political heart of Slovenia resembles an office building. However, the Slovene and European Union flags near the entrance hint at its importance. The sculpted figures on the building's façade are one of former Communist Europe's more artistic statements. The work of 20th-century sculptors Zdenko Kalin and Karel Putrih, they offer a utopian vision of socialism – a collective striving to create a beautiful new society.

> Stretching south of the Parliament building, Trg Republike (formerly Trg Revolucije) was developed in the 1960s to provide a modern focal point to the capital's New Town.

A Roman bronze statue on display in the National Museum of Slovenia

National Museum of Slovenia
Narodni muzej Slovenije

C4 Prešernova cesta 20 Jun-Sep: 10am-6pm Mon-Wed, Fri & Sun, 8am-10pm Thu & Sat; Oct-May: 10am-6pm daily (to 8pm Thu) nms.si

Occupying one wing of an imposing Neo-Renaissance pile dating from the 1880s, the main branch of the National Museum of Slovenia concentrates on the country's archaeological heritage. The collection of applied art is on display in a separate branch of the museum located on Metelkova ulica (p104).

The ground floor of the museum contains an extensive collection of expressively carved funerary monuments from the Roman settlement of Emona, together with a gilded bronze statue of a young male aristocrat. Ancient Egypt is represented by a 6th-century BC coffin of the priest Isahta, decorated with brightly painted hieroglyphics.

Without question the museum's star exhibit is a 55,000-year-old Neanderthal bone flute, discovered at Divje Babe Cabe near Cerkno in 1995. The femur of a young cave bear perforated with four small holes, it is claimed to be the world's oldest known musical instrument. Another superb specimen is the 6th-century BC Vače Situla, a 30-cm- (12-inch-) high bronze bucket decorated with some beautifully crafted reliefs, variously depicting a parade of horsemen, a drinking party and a row of antelopes.

Dominating the park in front of the museum is a monument dedicated to Janez Vajkard Valvasor (p117), 17th-century antiquarian and publisher who pioneered the documenting of history in Slovenia.

Natural History Museum
Prirodoslovni muzej

C4 Prešernova cesta 20 Jun-Sep: 10am-6pm Mon-Wed, Fri & Sun, 8am-10pm Thu & Sat; Oct-May: 10am-6pm daily (to 8pm Thu) pms-lj.si

Located in the same building as the National Museum of Slovenia, the Natural History Museum offers informative insight into the flora, fauna and geology of Slovenia.

A highlight of the exhibits is an almost complete skeleton of a mammoth found near Kamnik (p140). The museum also has an audiovisual

Admiring a mammoth skeleton at the Natural History Museum ↓

display devoted to *Proteus anguinus* or the human fish, a salamander-like denizen of Slovenia's karst caves.

Museum of Modern Art
Moderna galerija

C3 **Cankarjeva cesta 15** **10am–6pm Tue–Sun** **mg-lj.si**

Housed in a low grey building designed in 1947 by Edvard Ravnikar, the Museum of Modern Art comprises the national collection of post-World War II art.

Despite the imposition of Communist ideology in the late 1940s, Slovene art was remarkably free and varied from the mid-1950s onwards. Ample evidence of this is provided by the surreal figurative paintings of Gabriel Stupica (1913–90) and the abstract works of Janez Bernik (1933–2016). More perplexing is the work of the 1960s art collective OHO, whose ambiguous conceptual performances (most famously, dressing up in a huge dark gown to resemble Slovenia's highest mountain, Triglav) are documented in a series of black-and-white photographs. Representing the turbulent changes of the 1980s are works by IRWIN, a group of artists who mixed avant-garde art and extreme political symbolism to produce some ironic statements on national identity.

INSIDER TIP
On Your Bike

Take advantage of Ljubljana's excellent Bicikelj bike-sharing scheme *(www.bicikelj. si)*, which entitles users to the first hour free of charge. There are 60 stations dotted around the city, including one on the same street as the Museum of Modern Art.

↑ The semicircular Opera House, with numerous statues adorning its walls

Standing on the lawn of the gallery are several notable sculptures, including Drago Tršar's abstract *Manifestants* (1959) and France Rotar's *Dissected Sphere* (1975).

Opera House
Operna

C3 **Župančičeva ulica 1** **opera.si**

The home of Slovenia's national opera and ballet companies was built in 1892 by Czech architects Jan Vladimir Hrasky and Anton Hruby. Ljubljana's cultural centre has elements of Neo-Classical, Neo-Renaissance and Neo-Baroque styles, all apparent on the building's semicircular façade.

Sculptor Alojz Gangl (1859–1935) was responsible for much of the exterior decoration, which features statues of griffins, cherubs and scantily clad nymphs on the pediment and in niches on either side of the main entrance. Above the building's pediment is the sculpture of an androgynous figure wielding a torch – a symbol of artistic inspiration.

The Opera House stages a wide repertoire of classical and modern operas, ballets and concerts.

DRINK

Žmauc
Beyond the colourful, graffiti-daubed exterior of this café-bar is an equally exuberant interior, plus a buzzy terrace. A favourite of locals and tourists alike.

C5 **Rimska cesta 21** **barzmauc.sqwiz.si**

Kavarna Moderna
After exploring the Museum of Modern Art, head to its café. Expect Scandi-style furnishings and excellent freshly roasted coffee.

C3 **Cankarjeva cesta 15** **Mon** **kavarnamoderna.si**

STAY

Hostel Celica
The cells of this former prison have been converted into stylish double rooms.

G2 **Metelkova ulica 8** **hostelcelica.com**

A section of Ljubljana's Roman Wall, which was reconstructed by Jože Plečnik ↑

 11

Roman Wall
Rimski zid

📍 C6 🚌 Mirje

The long straight street of Mirje marks the southern end of the original Roman settlement of Emona (modern-day Ljubljana), founded between AD 14 and 25 as a legionary base and subsequently a major mercantile city. Parallel to the street, a 300-m (985-ft) stretch of the Roman Wall that bordered the settlement has been partially rebuilt, and offers an evocative indication of what Emona's boundaries once looked like. The architect Jože Plečnik was responsible for the reconstruction. He added decorative details of his own – notably the brick pyramid above an arched gateway halfway along the wall.

Behind the house at No 4 Mirje is the Emona House, the remains of which date from around the turn of the 5th century. Consisting of four separate apartments grouped around an entrance hall, the most impressive features are two well-preserved black-and-white floor mosaics and an elaborate underfloor heating system, which indicate that the owner was very wealthy.

The Jakopič garden gets its name from the Impressionist painter Rihard Jakopič (1869–1943), who had a studio in the adjacent house. The garden, which contains the remains of a Roman house built in the 1st century AD, can be visited by appointment through the Ljubljana City Museum (p80).

12

Krakovo

📍 D6

Despite its location on the fringes of central Ljubljana, the suburb of Krakovo is famous for having preserved its medieval street plan and rustic appearance. Narrow streets such as Krakovska, Kladezna and Rečna feature rows of houses standing with their backs to the road in typical village style, many

> ### Did You Know?
> Much of the produce sold at the market on Vodnikov trg comes from the plots in Krakovo.

featuring three windows on the street-facing gable – a surviving relic of medieval edicts that specified how many and what kind of windows each house was permitted to have.

Krakovo originally served as the quarter for boatmen and fishermen, although, from the mid-19th century, locals increasingly turned towards vegetable growing and market trading. Krakovo's vegetable plots are still a major feature of the suburb, providing a refreshingly bucolic contrast to the relatively dense urbanization on show elsewhere in the city.

13

Plečnik House
Plečnikova hiša

📍 D7 🏠 Karunova 4
🕐 10am–6pm Tue–Sun
🌐 mgml.si

The architecture of Jože Plečnik is visible at every step in Ljubljana, and a visit to his former home, where he was resident for almost 40 years, provides an ideal introduction to his life and work.

After studying in Vienna and enjoying early success in Prague, Plečnik returned to

Ljubljana in 1922 and set about transforming this property into a home and studio. The two traditional-style houses that came with the plot accommodated Plečnik's housemaid and gardener. Behind these, he built a modern two-storey house for himself and his brother, Andrej.

Today the house is a small but extremely intriguing museum, with the interiors left largely as they were during Plečnik's lifetime. Hourly guided tours of the property begin with the light-filled entrance lobby, decorated with some of the stubby Classical columns left over from Plečnik's building projects. Also on the ground floor is Plečnik's study, a circular room whose curving windows admit light whatever the time of day. On a corner of Plečnik's desk, a sleek black trophy in the shape of an eagle – made for the Orel or Eagle gymnastics society – demonstrates Plečnik's artistry as a designer. Elsewhere are plans, models and photographs of his major works. Most famous among his unfinished projects is the Slovene Acropolis, a monumental parliament building in the form of a huge cone, originally intended for Ljubljana's Castle Hill. A more down-to-earth aspect of his taste is revealed by the rustic wood-panelled meeting room, filled with folksy ornaments brought from Czechoslovakia. Also of interest is the kitchen, which still contains a special chair that allowed Plečnik to eat and work at the same time.

Looking out on to the rectangular vegetable garden is the sunny conservatory, accommodating a handful of palm and fig trees.

→

St John's Church, standing on the edge of a willow-lined stream

14

St John's Church
Cerkev sv Janeza Krstnika

D7 **Kolezijska 1**
(01) 283 5060

With its Neo-Romanesque twin towers, St John's Church is one of the most inspiring sights in southern Ljubljana. According to local legend, it was here that the Romantic poet France Prešeren (p72) first set eyes on Julija Primic, his unrequited love, who provided the inspiration for many of his poems.

Renovation of the church's interior in the 1950s was entrusted to architect Jože Plečnik, who added several characteristic details such as the small lamps that hang from the ceiling and pillars.

In front of the church is the Trnovo Bridge (Trnovski most), a Plečnik-designed single-arch bridge with obelisks in the shape of pyramids protruding from the parapet. Standing between the obelisks is sculptor Nikolaj Pirnat's statue of St John the Baptist, his face turned towards the church.

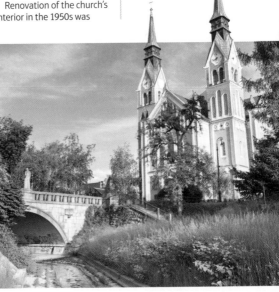

Tobacco Factory

Tobačna tovarna

A5 **Tobačna** **11am-5pm Tue-Fri** **mgml.si**

Founded in 1871, Ljubljana's Tobacco Factory was a major regional cigarette manufacturer until 2004, when production at this site ceased. Although Imperial Tobacco still has an administrative office here, plans are afoot to convert the rest of the complex into a residential and business quarter.

One restored building houses the Tobačna 001 Cultural Centre, home to a gallery of contemporary art and the Tobacco Museum. The museum covers the history of smoking, along with that of cigarette production in the capital. Sepia pictures show life on the factory floor, with its mainly female workforce, known as the cigar ladies.

Sokol Hall

Sokolski dom

G3 **Tabor 13** **sportnodrustvo-tabor.si**

This sports hall was one of the most unconventional buildings to emerge from the Slovenian Modernist movement of the 1920s. Designed for the Sokol (Falcon) Sports Club by Ivan Vurnik, architect of the Cooperative Bank (p82), it features rows of Graeco-Egyptian columns decorated with zig-zags, chevrons and other geometric shapes inspired by Slavic folk art.

Originally founded in Prague in 1862, the Sokol movement sought to encourage solidarity among the Slavs of the Habsburg Empire by promoting physical exercise, especially gymnastics. Like its Czech counterpart, the Slovenian branch of the Sokol used sport as a means to nurture national values among the youth by organizing gymnastic displays that were rousingly patriotic as well as spectacular to watch. Now the property of the Tabor Sports Association (Športno društvo Tabor), the hall retains its social importance for the locals, offering sporting and fitness programmes for all ages.

Slovene Museum of Contemporary History

Muzej novejše zgodovine Slovenije

B1 **Celovška cesta 23** **10am-6pm Tue-Sun (Jun-Aug: to 8pm Thu)** **muzej-nz.si**

Located behind Tivoli Hall is a stately pink-coloured mansion built in 1752 for Count Leopold Karl Lamberg. The building was adapted to house the Museum of the Revolution in 1952 and became the Slovene Museum of Contemporary History following the end of the Communist regime in 1991.

Parked in front of the building is an ex-Yugoslav army (JLA) tank commandeered by the Slovenian territorial defence forces during the Ten-Day War of June/July 1991. Inside, the museum tells the story of 20th-century Slovenia using film footage and sound

recordings to bring each period to life. The 30-minute film (with English subtitles) documenting the impact of World War I on Slovenia is well worth a watch; you can ask the curator if you wish to see it. There is also a recreation of World War I trenches and a display of World War II uniforms and weaponry.

Other exhibits reveal both good and bad sides of Tito's Yugoslavia – a collection of posters and products pays tribute to social progress under Communism, while a side room commemorates the anti-Communist activists who were imprisoned during the same period.

← An old army tank, on display outside the Slovene Museum of Contemporary History

↑ Tivoli Mansion, with a grand stone staircase leading down to the flower-filled gardens

Tivoli Mansion
Tivolski grad

📍B3 🏠Pod turnom 3
🕐10am–6pm Tue–Sun
🌐mglc-lj.si

Built in the 18th century as a villa for the local Jesuit hierarchy, Tivoli Mansion stands at the top of a stone staircase guarded by sculptures of fierce-looking tongueless dogs created by Austro-German sculptor Anton Fernkorn around 1870. The mansion subsequently served as the summer residence of the Ljubljana archbishops before it was presented in 1852 to the 86-year-old hero of Habsburg military campaigns, Field Marshal Josef Radetzky, a much-loved symbol of Austrian patriotism.

The mansion now houses the International Graphic Arts Centre (Mednarodni grafični likovni center), which hosts the prestigious Ljubljana Biennial of Graphic Arts, the world's longest-running graphic arts exposition. The centre also holds high-quality exhibitions of posters, prints and drawings.

Tivoli Park
Tark Tivoli

📍B2

Stretching to the west of the city centre is Tivoli Park, a leafy expanse much loved by strollers, joggers and dog-walkers who come here to escape the city bustle. Named after the Jardins de Tivoli in Paris, it was first laid out during the period of Napoleonic rule in the early 19th century.

> 💬 INSIDER TIP
> **Autumn in Tivoli Park**
>
> The best time to visit leafy Tivoli Park is in the autumn when it explodes into a riot of vibrant colour – you're quite likely to see a few red squirrels here too.

Today, it offers an appealing mix of order and wilderness, with well-tended lawns and trimmed shrubs alternating with wildflower meadows and thickets of trees. The park's main avenue, Jakopičevo sprehajališče, is lined with display stands where outdoor exhibitions of art and photography are held.

The northern end of the park is dominated by the Tivoli Hall (Hala Tivoli), Ljubljana's main venue for ice hockey, basketball, and big rock and pop concerts. Designed by architect Marjan Božič (b 1932), this grey-brown rectangular building was a widely admired example of architectural Modernism when it first opened in 1965.

At the same end there is also the popular indoor swimming pool **Kopalisce Tivoli**, as well as some tennis courts and a playground for children.

Kopalisce Tivoli
 🏠Celovška cesta 25 📞(01) 430 6668 🕐Sep–Jun: daily

20

Metelkova Mesto

📍 G2 🏛 Cnr of Masarykova cesta and Metelkova ulica
🌐 metelkovamesto.org

Metelkova's buildings, covered in colourful murals and splashes of mosaic, house a number of bars, clubs, artists' workshops and NGOs, driving home the nonconformist message.

Visitors looking for a glimpse into contemporary Ljubljana will enjoy spending time in Metelkova Mesto, the city's alternative social centre that occupies one half of a large area of old army barracks to the east of Ljubljana Railway Station. Built by the Habsburgs and subsequently used by the Yugoslav People's Army (JLA), the abandoned barracks were encroached upon by a varied group of musicians and artists in the early 1990s. The city authorities initially wanted them evicted, but ultimately let them stay, allowing Metelkova to develop into one of the most vibrant alternative communities in Central Europe. Metelkova's buildings, covered in colourful murals and splashes of mosaic, house a number of bars, clubs, artists' workshops and NGOs, driving home the nonconformist message.

In many ways Metelkova is the natural successor to the post-punk alternative culture of the 1980s, from which Slovenia's civil rights movement was born. Providing a fascinating link to the past is **Hostel Celica**, which occupies a former military prison at No 8. It was here that the Ljubljana Four were incarcerated in 1988 sparking the political demonstrations that ultimately led to Slovenia's independence. The rooms in the former cells have been redesigned by contemporary artists.

Beyond its interesting history, Metelkova Mesto is a popular night-time attraction – there is a large central courtyard here that is usually filled with revellers attracted by the numerous bars and live music venues.

↑ One of Metelkova Mesto's buildings, completely covered in bright graffiti

Hostel Celica

  Metelkova 8

For tours at 2pm daily

hostelcelica.com

21

Slovene National Museum (Metelkova)

Narodni muzej Slovenije (Metelkova)

G2 Maistrova 1

10am–6pm Tue–Sun

nms.si

The grand-looking trio of Habsburg-era barrack buildings, at the southern end of Metelkova ulica, form a museum complex known as the Museum Quarter, comprising the Ethnographic Museum (p94) and the National Museum (Metelkova).

> **POLITICAL ART COLLECTIVE**
>
> NSK (Neue Slowenische Kunst or New Slovene Art), formed in 1984, was the most controversial and influential of the alternative movements to come out of the former Yugoslavia in the 1980s. Addressing issues of culture and national identity, NSK consisted of several groups: the rock band, Laibach, which is also credited as its founder; a theatre collective called the Scipion Nasice Sisters; and the visual arts collective, Irwin, some of whose work is on display at the Museum of Contemporary Art (+MSUM) and the Museum of Modern Art (p99).

Occupying the eastern and southern side of the complex's central plaza is the Metelkova branch of the National Museum of Slovenia (p98). It displays over 2,500 objects, including costumes, toys and applied art showing a rich diversity of styles from the 14th century to the present day. The notable furniture collection includes ornate medieval storage chests and opulent Baroque wardrobes, as well as the mass-produced plywood furniture eagerly purchased by Slovenian households in the 1960s. Temporary historical exhibitions take place on the ground floor of the building.

22

Museum of Contemporary Art (+MSUM)

Muzej Sobodne Umetnosti Metelkova

G2 Maistrova 3

10am–6pm Tue–Sun

mg-lj.si

Standing adjacent to the Slovene National Museum, on Maistrova ulica, is the Museum of Contemporary Art (+MSUM), which opened in the renovated building of a former barracks complex in 2011. Its permanent collection focuses on contemporary works by Eastern European avant-garde artists , especially important pieces from the 1990s, and includes exhibits from its sister institution, the Museum of Modern Art (p99).

It also hosts temporary exhibitions and houses Slovenia's largest research library for modern and contemporary art.

23

Union Experience

Pivovarski muzej

C1 Celovška 22

For tours Mon–Sat

union-experience.si

Dominating the horizon just north of Tivoli Park is the tall grey façade of the Union Brewery (Pivovarna Union), Slovenia's second-largest beer producer. Tours begin in the museum, which is housed in an old malting house. It documents the brewery's history through a fabulous collection of old beer signs and plates, wooden crates, and a horse-drawn cart that once used to deliver the brew around the city. Following a visit to the factory floor, a welcome pint awaits in the convivial bar.

The brewery was founded by Kočevje-born Germans Ivan and Peter Kosler in 1864; the latter used the wealth he amassed from beer brewing to purchase the Lamberg Mansion in Tivoli Park, which is today the Slovene Museum of Contemporary History (p102). Popular legend maintains that Kosler had beer delivered from the brewery to his palatial home via an underground pipe, enabling him to test the quality of the brew whenever he wanted to.

BEYOND THE CENTRE

Experience

Ljubljana expanded beyond its medieval and Renaissance core in the 17th century with the pulling down of the city walls, and then again with the urban planning and rebuilding that followed the 1895 earthquake. The Botanical Garden was laid to the southeast of the centre in 1810, and Jože Plečnik built his unconventional Church of St Francis of Assisi north of Tivoli Park in 1925–27, and redesigned Žale Cemetery in the 1930s.

During World War II, Ljubljana was under Italian and then German occupation, and surrounded by some 30 km (18 miles) of barbed-wire fence as a deterrent to the Partisan resistance movement. This fence ran through outlying areas such as Žale, Bežigrad, Vič and Šiška, and its former course now forms the Path of Comradeship and Remembrance, a walking and cycling path around the city.

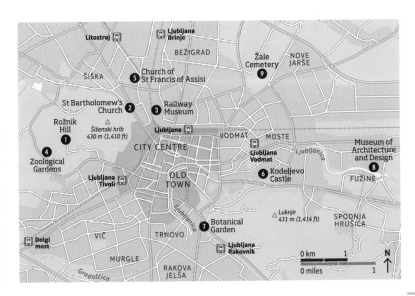

EXPERIENCE

①

Rožnik Hill

Rising above the western end of charming Tivoli Park are a series of small wooded hills grouped around the 390-m- (1,285-ft-) high Rožnik Hill, a popular destination for local weekend walkers. The main route to the hill begins just south of the Slovene Museum of Contemporary History, looping around the 430-m- (1,410-ft-) high peak of Šišenski hrib before following a pleasant, undulating trail on towards Rožnik.

Occupying the ridge just below the summit is the

> **INSIDER TIP**
> **Early Bird**
>
> To make the most of a trip up Rožnik Hill, set out at the break of dawn. At this time you'll be able to avoid the ramblers and runners; it's quite possible that you'll have the wonderful citywide views all to yourself.

Gostilna Rožnik inn, where novelist and playwright Ivan Cankar *(p119)* lived from 1910 to 1917. The innkeeper's wife, Štefanija Franzotova, was a childhood friend of Cankar's, and offered the writer free use of an attic room in the hope that his presence at the inn would bring in added custom. The impoverished Cankar's appetite for free food and drink soon took its toll on his friendship with the innkeeper's family, however, and the writer was eventually persuaded to move out. Occupying the former barn opposite the inn, the **Ivan Cankar Memorial Room** (Spominska soba Ivana Cankarja) preserves his writing desk and other possessions.

Just uphill from the inn is the 18th-century Church of the Visitation (Cerkev Marijinega obiskanja), a rose-coloured Baroque building that contains a painting of the *Visitation* by the highly esteemed Slovenian artist Jurij Šubic (1855–90). The church is rarely open outside Sunday mass times but its picturesque exterior and Neo-Classical façade are worth the walk. The meadow below the church is the scene of an all-night bonfire party on 30 April, an annual celebration of spring that involves much drinking and feasting.

Ivan Cankar
Memorial Room
🅰Rožnik ⏱Apr-Oct: 11am-6pm Sat & Sun mgml.si

---

②

St Bartholomew's Church
Cerkev sv Jerneja

🅰**Celovška cesta**

A grey-brown edifice that looks more like a village church, St Bartholomew's dates from around the 1370s. Known to locals simply as the "Old Church", it is thought to be the oldest surviving place of worship in the city. The

↓ The Church of the Visitation, standing on Rožnik Hill

An antique locomotive on display in Slovenia's popular Railway Museum

Zoological Gardens
Zivalski vrt

Večna pot 70 **May–Sep: 23 Daily; Feb–Mar & Nov: 9am–5pm; Apr–Sep: 9am–7pm; Oct: 9am–6pm; Dec–Jan: 9am–4:30pm** **zoo.si**

Spread across the densely wooded southern slopes of Rožnik Hill, within a protected nature park surrounded by meadows, is Ljubljana's zoo, which houses a wide variety of creatures from around the world with a focus on animals from the alpine, Pannonian and Mediterranean habitats. Near the entrance is a selection of animals that might be found on the average Slovenian farm. A recreated thatch-roofed farm cottage displays the kind of insects and rodents that traditionally live in proximity to humans. Further on is a varied collection of more exotic animals such as giraffes, Siberian tigers and an energetic family of gibbons that can be seen leaping from branch to branch in their enclosure. The zoo extends quite a long way up the hillside, with wooded paths leading to large enclosures housing wild cats and bears.

Did You Know?

St Bartholomew's Church was added to the Slovenian Cultural Heritage List in 2009.

---

church was extensively refurbished in the 1930s by Jože Plečnik (*p101*), who added colonnaded porches to the front and back of the building.

Standing at the bottom of the staircase beside the church is another example of Plečnik's creative architectural style – a lampstand made up of bubble-like forms mounted one on top of the other.

Railway Museum
Zelezniški muzej

Parmova 35
10am–6pm Tue–Sun
slo-zeleznice.si

The history of railways in Slovenia began with the Südbahn, the line southwest from Vienna that reached Maribor in 1844 and Ljubljana in 1849. Many of the locomotives that plied this route are on display in the Railway Museum's main exhibition space – a crescent-shaped engine shed packed with vintage rolling stock. The oldest locomotive on show is the sleek SB 718, which was built in Vienna by Scottish engineer John Haswell in 1861 and was in use in Yugoslavia until 70 years later. More elegant still is the SB 17c, an express locomotive built in 1896, which rattled along at a speed of 80 kmph (50 mph). Particularly delightful are the squat locomotives with funnel chimneys; these were once used on Slovenia's numerous narrow-gauge railways.

The above collection was the only part open to the public when the museum was inaugurated in 1981, but today a hall across the road from the shed displays the museum's second permanent exhibition, which focuses on antiquated signalling equipment. There is also a recreated station-master's office from the 1920s. A room full of railway uniforms reveals the different styles adopted by the various states to have ruled over the region. These range from the Ruritanian finery of the Habsburg era to the black overalls and red-star insignia adopted during the early years of the Communist rule.

→
Giraffe, one of the many species that can be observed in the Zoological Gardens

The wooden interior
of the Church of
St Francis of Assisi ↑

French rule. The linden tree planted by French governor Marshal Marmont still presides over a tree-strewn park, while paths weave their way through shrubs and flowers indigenous to Central Europe. A palm house at the southern end of the garden has displays of more exotic flora.

⑤
Church of St Francis of Assisi
Cerkev sv Frančiška Asiškega

◘ Černetova ulica 20
☎ (01) 583 7270 🚌 1, 3, 5
(to Šiška)

Located in the suburb of Šiška and begun in 1924, the Church of St Francis of Assisi was one of the first major projects by Jože Plečnik (p101) in Ljubljana and contains many elements associated with his style.

As you approach it from the east, the church looks like a Classical temple, with a façade supported by four columns. Adorning the pediment is a contemplative statue of St Francis, while the most bizarre part of the structure is the hollow belfry, with two tiers of colonnades topped by the greenish cone of a spire.

The main entrance to the church is on the southern side, where a small courtyard is illuminated by large, egg-shaped lamps. The interior features equally inventive touches; the central chandelier is made up of small dangling lanterns and the tall main altar is shaped like a pyramid.

⑥
Kodeljevo Castle
Grad Kodeljevo

◘ Koblarjeva ulica 34

Built in the early 17th century by the Thurn family, this castle is one of Ljubljana's best-preserved Renaissance residences. It gets its name from the Codelli family, who bought it in 1700 and added the Baroque chapel to the western wing. Lavishly decorated with frescoes by France Jelovšek (1700–64), the chapel is rarely open to the public. A plaque on the castle wall honours its most famous resident, Baron Anton Codelli von Fahnrenfeld (1875–1954), the first man to drive an automobile on the streets of Ljubljana.

Several of the castle's atmospheric rooms are occupied by the Grad Kodeljevo restaurant and pizzeria.

⑦
Botanical Garden
Botanični vrt

◘ Ižanska cesta 15 🕐 Apr-Jun, Sep & Oct: 7am-7pm daily; Jul & Aug: 7am-8pm daily; Nov-Mar: 7:30am-5pm daily 🌐 botanic-gardens-ljubljana.com

Located to the southeast of the Old Town, Ljubljana's Botanical Garden was founded in 1810 during

---

🔍 HIDDEN GEM
Botanical Glasshouse

Not so much hidden but certainly a gem, this imposing tropical glasshouse was built for the garden's 200th anniversary, and harbours over 400 plant species.

Museum of Architecture and Design
Muzej za arhitekturo in oblikovanje

◘ Pot na Fužine 2 🚌 20
🕐 10am-6pm Tue-Sun
🌐 mao.si

Occupying an attractive riverside site on the city's eastern outskirts, this museum makes for a rewarding excursion, not least because of its setting in Fužine Castle (Grad Fužine). The castle was originally built in the mid-16th century; restored in the 1990s, it is a fine example of a Renaissance chateau, with cylindrical corner towers and an arcaded central courtyard.

As well as hosting the Biennial of Design, the museum is the permanent home of the Plečnik

Exhibition, a collection of plans, models and furniture first shown at Paris's Centre Pompidou in 1986. You can enjoy scale models of Plečnik's most famous buildings as well as maquettes of projects that were never built. The most famous of these designs is the Slovenian Acropolis, a magnificent parliament house that sadly never left the drawing board.

9

Žale Cemetery

Pokopališče Žale

 Med hmeljniki 2   2
Apr-Sep: 7am-9pm daily;
Oct-Mar: 7am-7pm daily
zale.si

Žale Cemetery is another of the iconic sights associated with architect Jože Plečnik.

The cemetery has been the city's main burial ground since 1906, but it was in 1937 that Plečnik – then at the height of his career – was given carte blanche to redesign the site. The graveyard is entered via an archway flanked by two-tiered colonnades, intended by Plečnik to mark the transition from the world of the living to that of the dead.

Immediately beyond the gateway lies the All Saints' Gardens (Vrt vseh svetih) with a cluster of Plečnik-designed chapels, executed in radically differing styles to express humanity's religious and cultural diversity.

In contrast to many of the Classical structures seen at the cemetery are the Chapel of St Agathius (kapela sv Ahaca), a cone inspired by Etruscan grave mounds, and the octagonal Chapel of St Peter (kapela sv Petra), which recalls the Moorish styles of southern Spain.

To the north of the chapel lies the graveyard proper, a

grid of plots edged by trimmed hedges and shrubs. Plečnik himself is buried here; his typically modest grave is in Plot 6, to the left as you enter. To the east is the Ossuary of Victims of World War I, an impressive rotunda designed by Plečnik's student, Edvard Ravnikar, in 1939. It commemorates the Slovenians who served in the ranks of the Austro-Hungarian army. The entrance to the ossuary is via a stepped bridge watched over by Lojze Dolinar's (1893–1970) statue of a soldier.

Running between the central part of the cemetery and the newer plots to the north is the Path of Remembrance and Comradeship (Pot spominov in tovarištva), a 33-km- (21-mile-) long walking and cycling route. This path follows the barbed-wire fence that was built around Ljubljana by Fascist Italian occupiers in 1942.

The imposing arched entrance and (inset) memorial chapels of Žale Cemetery ↓

DAYS OUT FROM LJUBLJANA

Must Sees

1 Škofja Loka
2 Bogenšperk Castle

Experience More

3 Šmarna Gora
4 Lake Zbilje
5 Polhov Gradec Castle
6 Vrhnika
7 Bistra Castle
8 Iški Gorge
9 Ljubljana Marshes
10 Arboretum Volčji Potok
11 Turjak Castle
12 Stična Monastery

Beyond Ljubljana's suburbs lies an area of low hills and farmland, which holds a wealth of potential for day trips. Immediately south of the city are the flatlands of the Ljubljana Marshes (Ljubljansko barje), crisscrossed with tracks that provide the perfect terrain for cyclists. Enthusiastic hikers can tackle the Šmarna Gora hill, located just north of the capital, or venture into the forest-shrouded Iški Gorge that lies to the south. Historical attractions include the Slovene Technical Museum at Bistra Castle and the Cistercian monastery at Stična to the south, as well as the splendours of 17th-century Bogenšperk Castle to the east. To the northwest, huddled beneath its Baroque castle, well-preserved Škofja Loka offers the perfect taste of small-town Slovenia.

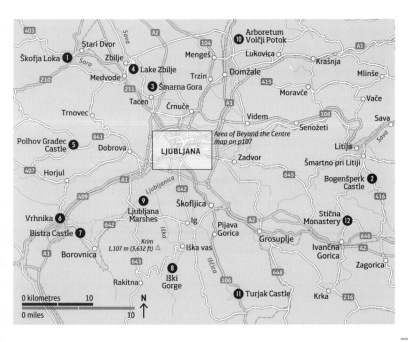

← The Old Town of Škofja Loka, backed by scenic wooded ridges

❶

ŠKOFJA LOKA

🅰C4 🚗23 km (15 miles) NW of Ljubljana 🚆🚌From Ljubljana 🛈Mestni trg 42; www.visitskofjaloka.si

Located at the confluence of two branches of the Sora river, Škofja Loka (Bishop's Meadow) is one of the most attractively situated towns in Slovenia. A major trade and craft centre throughout the Middle Ages, the town was hit by an earthquake in 1511 and rebuilt in an early Baroque style. Today Škofja Loka is most famous for its Passion Play, written in 1721 and enacted by hundreds of costumed locals every six years at Easter.

① 🖼

Mestni trg

Central Škofja Loka consists of a warren of streets woven tightly around this medieval market square. Dominating the square's northern end is the 16th-century Homan House (Homanova hiša), whose lively façade features jutting oriel windows, sgraffito patterns and a larger-than-life painting of St Christopher. Occupying the building's ground floor is the Café Homan, long the centre of the town's social life and once the favoured sketching spot of Impressionist painter Ivan Grohar (1867–1911).

Midway along the square is the former Town Hall (Mestna hiša), its façade enlivened by the fragmented remains of 17th-century frescoes. These are unexpectedly exotic, depicting friendly-looking sphinxes squatting on pillars. Diagonally opposite the Town Hall is the Plague Column, topped by a serene statue of the Virgin and Child. The column was erected in 1751 to ensure divine protection from disease and natural disasters.

②

St James's Church

🅰Cankarjev trg 13

Built in 1471, St James's Church (Cerkev sv Jakoba) has preserved much of its late-Gothic appearance. Of note is the delicate stone relief above the main entrance showing Judas grasping a bag of money, watched expectantly by Herod's soldiers. After an earthquake hit the town in the early 16th century, the church's belfry was remodelled, when it acquired a characteristically bulbous Baroque spire.

Inside, the ceiling is a masterpiece of Gothic vaulting, with brightly coloured floral designs filling the spaces between the stone ribs. Hovering above the pews is a forest of brass chandeliers and lanterns, added by 20th-century architect Jože Plečnik (p101). Behind the church stands a sturdy 16th-century schoolhouse, which has a plaque honouring its founder Michael Papler, who was the lord of Škofja Loka Castle (Grad Škofja Loka).

③ Castle Museum

🏛 Grajska pot 13 🕐 Apr–Sep: 10am–6pm Tue–Sun; Nov–Mar: 10am–5pm Tue–Sun 🌐 loski-muzej.si

Škofja Loka's Baroque castle served as the seasonal residence for the bishops of Freising, after whom the town is named, and was the seat of their administration when the prelates were away. Easily reached via a winding pathway from Mestni trg, the building now houses the extensive collections of the Town Museum (Mestni muzej).

Highlights here include the brightly decorated pottery used in Loka households

> **GREAT VIEW**
> **From Above**
>
> Standing within the grounds of the town castle, you'll be able to take in superlative views of the Old Town below, with its flutter of red roofs and - in the distance - the lush Škofja Loka Hills.

through the ages, as well as original wares from the lace- and hat-making workshops that once figured prominently in the local economy. The corridors are filled with canvases by local painters, including several works by Ivan Grohar.

④ Mihelič Gallery

🏛 Spodnji trg 1 🕐 By appt 🌐 loski-muzej.si

Dominating Spodnji trg is a severe-looking, 15th-century granary. This was once one of the most important buildings in town, housing the food supply as well as the citizens' tax records. Today, the granary's timber-beamed upper storeys accommodate the Mihelič Gallery (Galerija Mihelič), devoted to artist France Mihelič (1907–98), who was born in Škofja Loka.

Mihelič is primarily known for his distinctively surreal graphic works, in which human forms were made to resemble twig-like creatures and insects. Among his most striking works are the series of lithographs

depicting the Kurenti, masked men who lead the Kurentovanje revels in Ptuj.

⑤ Nace's House

🏛 Puštal 74 ☎ (04) 050 0791 🕐 By appt

Southeast of the centre, on the opposite bank of the Poljanska Sora, spreads the pleasant suburb of Puštal. The oldest of the surviving dwellings in this part of town is the 16th-century Nace's House (Nacetova hiša), a beautifully preserved, largely timber building. Named after its early 19th-century owner Ignac "Nace" Homan, the house served as an inn until 1907. The interior is packed with traditional furnishings and original features. One of these is the archaic "black kitchen", so called because it did not have a standard chimney – smoke from the fire escaped upwards through the rafters, drying the household's grain and curing sausages as it went.

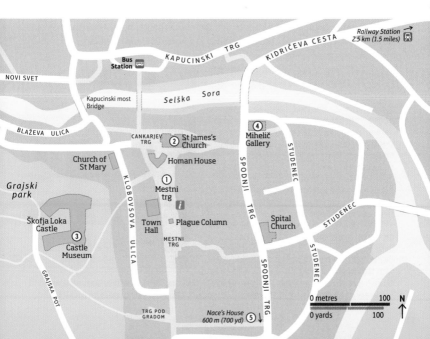

The wide façade and imposing round tower of Bogenšperk Castle

2 ⑤ ⑬

BOGENŠPERK CASTLE
GRAD BOGENŠPERK

🅰 D4 📍 41 km (26 miles) E of Ljubljana 🕒 Times vary, check website 🌐 bogensperk.si

Considered to be one of the country's most attractive castles, Bogenšperk is best known as the former home of Slovenian historian Janez Valvasor.

Lying on the northern slopes of the Lower Carniola, the Renaissance castle of Bogenšperk was built for the Wagen family in the early 16th century. Its place in Slovene history is due to Janez Valvasor, the antiquarian and author who bought the castle in 1672 and turned it into his printing workshop. Here, he produced the copper-plate engravings subsequently published as part of his magnum opus, *The Glory of the Duchy of Carniola*. Printing debts forced Valvasor to sell his books and artifacts, but his castle survives as a popular tourist attraction.

Today Bogenšperk Castle is home to an intriguing museum. Many of the exhibits are dedicated to the castle's most famous former owner, but there are also displays concerned with folk dress, superstition and folk medicine. Guided tours of the castle are available, which run every day from Tuesday to Sunday.

↑ Flowering plants brightening the whitewashed courtyard walls

JANEZ VAJKARD VALVASOR'S WORK

A traveller, historian and collector, Valvasor is primarily remembered for the four-volume work, *The Glory of the Duchy of Carniola* (Die Ehre des Herzogtums Crain), published in Nuremberg in 1689. It was the first fully researched description of central and western Slovenia, containing comments on history and human geography. The 3,500-page illustrated work remains valuable for researchers. Valvasor spent 15 years preparing the book and was ruined by the cost of its publication, which forced him to sell the castle in 1692. Printing was complex and expensive in the 17th century. Valvasor was a leader in the production of beautiful books and many people came to Bogenšperk Castle especially to study his technique. Accurately drawn townscapes were an important element of Valvasor's book on Carniola, which aimed to be a visually appealing complete guide to the nation's riches as well as a scholarly text. Valvasor ultimately sold his library to the Bishop of Zagreb, and died in poverty in Krško in 1693.

Clothes worn by Slovenians in the 17th century are displayed in the castle museum.

The former Library is the largest room in the castle.

There are 17th-century paper-making and printing machines on display in the Copper-engraving Workshop.

The study has period furnishings intended to recreate Valvasor's working life.

Bogenšperk Castle, its walls laid out in a neat square shape ↑

← Šmarna Gora rising beyond Ljubljana, reached via a number of trails *(inset)*

❹

Lake Zbilje
Zbiljsko jezero

🅐C4 🚶20 km (13 miles) NW of Ljubljana

A reservoir fed by the Sava river, man-made Lake Zbilje came into being with the construction of a dam at Medvode in 1953. It soon became a popular location for summertime swimming and boating, with the village of Zbilje at the lake's northern end offering a number of recreational facilities.

Stretching south of the village is a grassy lakeside area featuring cafés, a children's play park and boat-rental facilities, making it an excellent spot for a day trip. Although busiest in summer, the lake is a popular place for walks throughout the year, with abundant swans, ducks and other waterfowl adding to the charm. It's also possible to cross the lake by bridge, which leads across to the nearby village of Valburga.

EXPERIENCE MORE

❸

Šmarna Gora

🅐C4 🚶6 km (4 miles) N of Ljubljana 🚌 From Ljubljana 🌐smarnagora.com

Rising above Ljubljana's northern suburbs, the smooth-topped Šmarna Gora is a popular destination for Ljubljana dwellers seeking to stretch their legs. The hill is accessed via 15 well-maintained routes and has two peaks: the 676-m- (2,218-ft-) high Grmada lies to the west and the 669-m- (2,195-ft-) high Šmarna Gora lies to the east. Most people head straight for the latter, where the fortified Church of the Holy Mother crowns the summit, and expansive views of the city open up to the south. Also at the summit is the miraculous Bell of St Anthony. According to legend, Ottoman raiders were ordered to capture Šmarna Gora before noon. The bell tolled half an hour early, confusing the attackers and sending them into retreat. It is said that the wishes of those who ring the bell come true. The slightly taller Grmada also has some history attached: signal bonfires were lit atop it during period of the Turkish invasions.

The hill is particularly busy on fine Sundays, when it seems as if the entire city is swarming up and down its slopes. Numerous paths lead up the hill, although the most popular is the ascent that begins in the suburb of Tacen. A steeper approach heads up the eastern side of the hill from the village of Šmartno. Both suburbs are accessible by bus from central Ljubljana.

> **Rising above Ljubljana's northern suburbs, the smooth-topped Šmarna Gora is a popular destination for Ljubljana dwellers seeking to stretch their legs.**

⑤
Polhov Gradec Castle
Polhograjska graščina

🅰C4 🚗22 km (14 miles) W of Ljubljana; Polhov Gradec 61 🚌From Ljubljana ⏰10am–5pm Tue–Fri & Sun 🌐grad-polhovgradec.si

Nestling among wooded hills, the village of Polhov Gradec grew around its castle, a medieval stronghold that was rebuilt as an aristocratic residence during the Baroque period. During the late 16th century, the castle was owned by Jurij Kisl. A statesman, intellectual and soldier, Kisl distinguished himself in campaigns against the Ottoman Turks. His grandfather, Vid Kisl, founded the Fužine Castle in Ljubljana, now the Museum of Architecture and Design *(p110)*.

Polhov Gradec Castle now houses the Slovene Museum of Post and Telecommunications, which has colourful, entertaining displays. There are Morse code machines, telephones through the ages and postal uniforms. You can also admire the castle's richly stuccoed chapel or take a stroll in the 19th-century ornamental park.

---

⑥
Vrhnika

🅰C4 🚗32 km (20 miles) SW of Ljubljana 🚌From Ljubljana 🛈Tržaška cesta 1; www.visitvrhnika.si

Spread between low hills and within easy reach of Ljubljana, Vrhnika is a pleasant market town that was originally the Roman town Nauportum in the 1st century AD. Nothing from that period has survived. However, there is an ensemble of historic buildings near the central Cankarjev trg, starting with the octagonal St Leonard's Church, which faces the broad mansard roof of the former Court House.

IVAN CANKAR (1876–1918)

Few writers have shaped the modern Slovenian psyche in the way that Ivan Cankar has. The writer's vast output of poetry, novels and plays occupies a dominant position in the national culture, although his works rarely offered a flattering portrayal of Slovenian society. Cankar always supported the downtrodden, conveying a sense of sympathy for the aspirations of the poor. His most famous short story is *Hlapec Jernej* (Jernej the Bailiff), in which an ageing servant is deprived of his rights – a metaphor for Slovenia under Austrian domination. Cankar was a supporter of the Yugoslav ideal, but insisted on the uniqueness of Slovenian language and culture.

The most visited spot in town is the **Ivan Cankar Memorial House**, just west of the centre in the Na klancu district. It was here that the famous Slovenian writer Ivan Cankar was born in 1876. The house itself is not original, having been built on the site of the earlier Cankar family cottage, which burned down in 1880. Today, the interior houses a small collection of photographs, manuscripts and furniture.

Ivan Cankar Memorial House
🌐 🏠Na klancu 1 ☎(01) 755 1054 ⏰Apr–Oct: 9am–1pm Tue–Fri, 2–6pm Sat & Sun

↑ The pretty red roofs and rolling green hills that make up the town of Vrhnika

 7

Bistra Castle
Grad Bistra

⚠ C5 🚗 36 km (22 miles) SW of Ljubljana

Set against a hillside some 3 km (1 mile) east of Vrhnika, Bistra Castle began life as a Carthusian monastery founded by Ulrich III of Spannheim in 1260. Later an aristocratic residence, Bistra was an important centre for saw-milling throughout its history, and several reconstructed water-powered workshops lie alongside the stream that runs through the heart of the estate. The castle now provides a rather grand home to the fabulous **Slovene Technical Museum** (Tehniški muzej Slovenije).

Did You Know?

The first two Slovenian books ever printed are housed in the Slovene Technical Museum.

This is the country's largest museum, and the most worthwhile part is an outstanding collection of vintage automobiles, including more than 20 that once belonged to the Yugoslav president Josip Broz Tito. Look out for the armour-plated Packard Twelve that was presented to Tito by Stalin. Elsewhere, there are exhaustive displays of agricultural, forestry and fishing equipment, alongside early examples of steam power and electricity generation. Carrying on with the technological theme is a room devoted to Nikola Tesla (1856–1943), the prolific Serbian-born inventor who spent most of his career in the USA, developing alternating current, electric light systems and radio waves in the process. Classes and workshops are held at the museum on Saturdays, with many suitable for children.

Slovene Technical Museum

♿ 🕐 🏠 Bistra 6 🕐 Mar-May & Sep-Nov: 8am-5pm Tue-Fri, 9am-7pm Sat & Sun; Jun-Aug: 9am-7pm Tue-Sun 🌐 tms.si

 8

Iški Gorge
Iški Vintgar

⚠ C5 🚗 25 km (16 miles) S of Ljubljana

Flowing into the Ljubljana Marshes from the south, the Iška river cuts through the dolomite rock of the Bloke Plateau to form the Iški Gorge, a V-shaped valley with steep, densely wooded sides.

The most interesting stretches of the gorge lie just beyond the Gostišče Iški Vintgar, a guesthouse accessible via the paved road from the marshes. From the guesthouse, a footpath leads along the bank of the river, passing a sequence of cataracts and pools. The going gets more difficult as the gorge narrows, and visitors should be prepared to get their feet wet to be able to enjoy the waterfalls and rock formations of the gorge's upper stretches.

For those who want to explore the hilly terrain above the gorge, a path ascends west from the Gostišče Iški Vintgar towards the Orlek ridge, before descending

Trekking across a rock-strewn river that runs through the Iški Gorge

into an isolated dell. Here, a few wooden huts remain of the Krvavice Partisan Hospital, which operated on this site during World War II. More ambitious hikers can carry on uphill to the 1,107-m-(3,632-ft-) high summit of Krim hill, which offers wonderful views back across the marshes towards Ljubljana.

Ljubljana Marshes
Ljubljansko barje

🅰C4 🚗10 km (6 miles) S of Ljubljana 🅦ljubljan skobarje.si

Stretching beyond Ljubljana's southern suburbs, the grassy plain known as the Ljubljana Marshes began life as a shallow lake formed at the end of the last Ice Age. It was an important centre of Neolithic culture in the 4th millennium BC, when locals lived in woodpile dwellings above the lake's surface and used log-carved canoes to commute. With time the lake dried out, leaving a soggy area of peat bog. From the 18th century onwards, the digging of drainage ditches rendered the area suitable for agriculture, and in 1830 the marsh was sold off as plots, largely to soldiers for whom the land purchase offered exemption from further military service. The bogs were over-harvested for peat and only survive in isolated pockets nowadays. However, they remain an important breeding ground for birds, with herons, curlews and corncrakes among the

> WORLD'S OLDEST WHEEL
>
> In 2002, a remarkable discovery was made on the Ljubljana Marshes, when a wooden wheel - complete with wooden axle and wooden spear point - was unearthed. Subsequent radiocarbon dating determined the wheel - which was thought to be part of a two-wheeled cart, or pushcart - to be between 5,100 and 5,350 years old, making it the oldest such specimen in existence anywhere in the world. The wheel, which is made from oak and ash, now takes pride of place at the Ljubljana City Museum *(p80)*.

regular nesters. The best way to explore the marshes is by bike, thanks to a network of trails that run alongside the drainage channels.

The area's one prominent architectural attraction is the Church of St Michael (Cerkev sv Mihaela) in the village of Črna vas. Built between 1925 and 1939 by architect Jože Plečnik *(p101)*, the structure utilizes local wood as well as a mixture of grey limestone and red brick – a technique also employed in the National and University

Library *(p80)* in Ljubljana, and there are other elements of similarity between the two buildings. The ivy-covered bell tower, perforated with arches of various sizes, is one of Plečnik's most arresting creations. The church also features a nave raised above ground level to guard it against seasonal flooding, and is entered via an unusual arched stairway. Inside, simple wooden pews and timber ceiling beams contrast with the warm sheen of a striking high altar constructed with burnished copper sheets.

→

The ivy-clad exterior of the Church of St Michael, in the Ljubljana Marshes

→

An array of gorgeous tulips blooming in the Arboretum Volčji Potok

Arboretum Volčji Potok

🅰C4 📍22 km (14 miles) NE of Ljubljana; Volčji potok 3 🕐From 8am daily; closing times vary, check website 🌐arboretum-vp.si

Just north of the Domžale exit on the Ljubljana–Maribor motorway lies the Arboretum Volčji Potok, once Ljubljana University's botanical study centre and now the most popular horticultural attraction in the country. The site is huge, extending across 85 ha (210 acres) and has views of the Kamnik Alps.

Formerly a landscaped park belonging to the Souvan estate, the arboretum features 3,500 species of trees and shrubs, neat ornamental gardens and numerous floral displays. Seasonal attractions include a wide range of blossoms in May, over 1,000 varieties of roses, which bloom from June onwards, and an explosion of autumn colours in October. Also in autumn, an enjoyable pumpkin festival celebrates one of the country's best-loved vegetables.

Facilities for children include an attraction-packed play park, a maze and a tractor-pulled train dressed up to look like a vintage steam locomotive. There is also a pleasant summer café in which to relax.

Next door to the arboretum is an 18-hole golf course, one of only nine courses in Slovenia. It is located in a pine forest and surrounded by gorgeous scenery.

2 million

tulip bulbs bloom at Arboretum Volčji Potok each April, in a vibrant spring display.

Turjak Castle
Grad Turjak

🅰C5 📍25 km (16 miles) SE of Ljubljana 📞(01) 788 1006 🕐May–Oct: noon–7pm Sat & Sun

An important stronghold in the Middle Ages – with the first castle existing on this site as early as the 11th century – Turjak Castle got its present form in the 16th century, when the castle's characteristic barrel-shaped bastions and arcaded inner courtyard were built. The masters of the castle were the Auerspergs, who turned it into a key stronghold in Austria's defences against Ottoman incursions. The famous Andreas Auersperg led the Carniolan forces during the 1593 battle of Sisak, when a combined Croatian-Slovenian force crushed an advancing Ottoman army. Andreas is credited with the capture of a bridge crucial to the struggle, causing the enemy to flee.

Several rooms in the castle can be visited. These include the Renaissance Knights Hall and the Protestant castle chapel, which is decorated with 15th-century Gothic frescoes. The castle is unusual in having two chapels, with another Catholic one located on the west side of the building. Temporary exhibitions of arts and crafts are held in one of the towers. Below the castle are the ruins of alms-houses built by the owners for their ageing servants.

Daily cycle tours are offered to the castle from Ljubljana's Botanical Garden (p110). These are of medium difficulty and take roughly four hours.

Patriarch Peregrine I of Aquileia, who was keen to provide the Cistercian order with a base from which to spread their teachings. Stična Monastery was one of the richest in Slovenia and became an important centre of education and manuscript production. Heavily fortified in the 15th and 16th centuries to withstand Ottoman raids, Stična has retained its sturdy outer appearance to this day. Following Emperor Joseph II's decision to dissolve the big monasteries in 1781 Stična was abandoned. It was refounded in 1898 by Cistercian monks from Bavaria.

The 12th-century monastery church retains several original Romanesque features, but repeated rebuildings during the Baroque era bequeathed a bulbous belfry and an altar-filled interior. The monastery's administrative buildings now house the Slovene Museum of Christianity, which is crammed with reliquaries, candelabras and religious paintings. Highlights include 15th-century fresco fragments painted by Master Janez of Ljubljana and a dazzling chalice by Jože Plečnik (p101).

   12

Stična Monastery
Samostan Stična

🅐 D4 🏠 35 km (22 miles) SE of Ljubljana 🕑 8am–noon & 2-5pm Tue-Sat, 2-5pm Sun 🌐 mks-sticna.si

Set among meadow-carpeted hills just north of the main road from Ljubljana to Novo Mesto is Stična Monastery. It was founded in 1136 by

> **Heavily fortified in the 15th and 16th centuries to withstand Ottoman raids, Stična has retained its sturdy outer appearance to this day.**

↑ The 12th-century Stična Monastery, with its thick, whitewashed walls

STAY

Guesthouse Bistra
Beautifully located at the edge of the Ljubljana Marshes, this pretty guesthouse offers bicycle rentals to explore the area.

🅐 C4 🏠 Bistra 2, 1353 Borovnica

 €€€

Iskaretreat
This cosy, secluded chalet near the Iški Gorge is complete with a garden terrace that provides unbeatable mountain views.

🅐 C5 🏠 Iška 52, 1292 Ig 🌐 iskaretreat.com

 €€€

EAT

Trnulja
Delicious Slovenian cuisine is prepared from local produce on this eco-friendly farmstead in the Ljubljana Marshes. Accommodation is also available.

🅐 C4 🏠 Črna vas 267, Ljubljana 🌐 trnulja.com

 €€€

Krčmar gostinstvo, d.o.o. Stična
This relaxed spot, a three-minute walk southeast of the Stična Monastery, is great for families and serves up tasty, homely dishes.

🅐 D4 🏠 Stična 27, 1295 Ivančna Gorica 📞 (01) 787 7700

 €€€

EXPERIENCE
SLOVENIA

Hiking in the spectacular Julian Alps, Triglav National Park

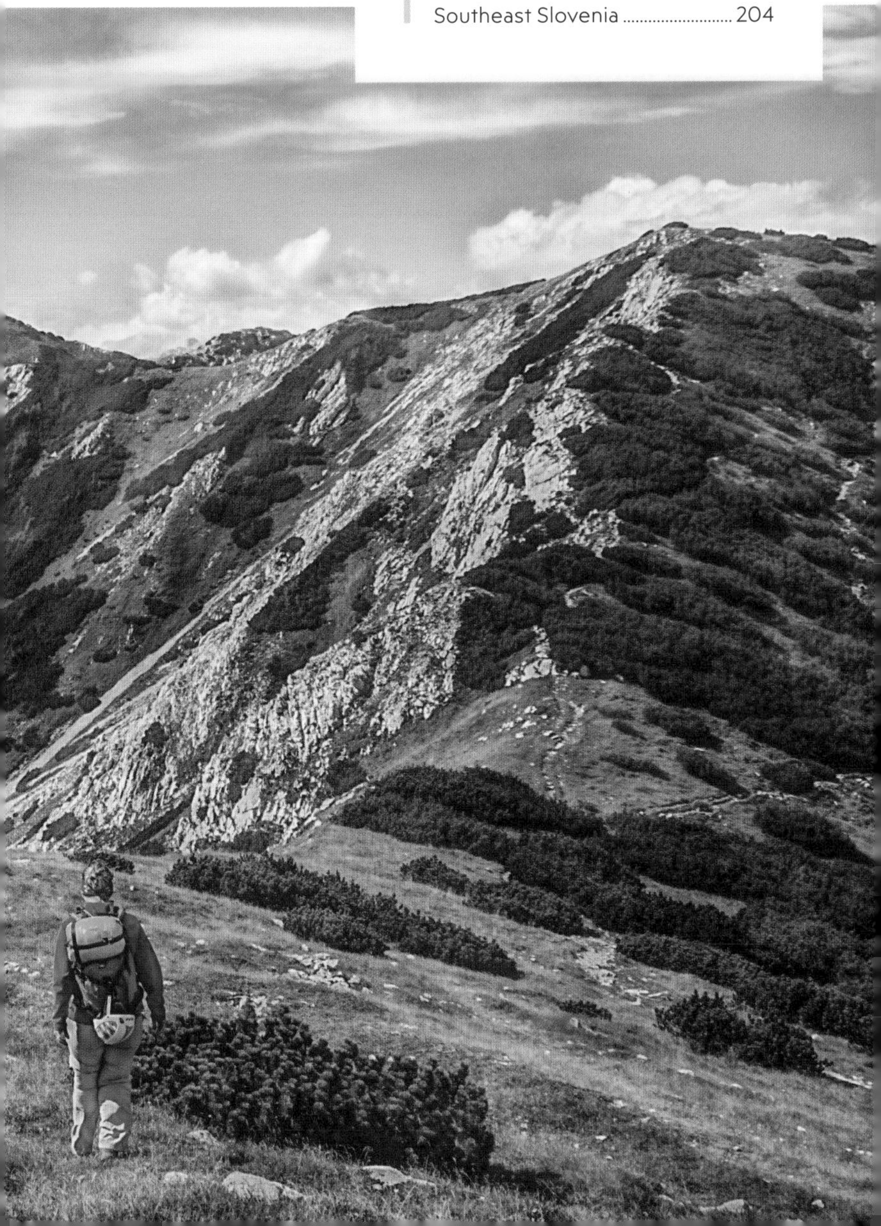

THE ALPS

This acclaimed and much-visited region of Slovenia is well known for the outdoor activities it offers, but the area is also rich in history. Excavations around Most na Soči reveal that an ample Bronze and Iron Age culture flourished in the upper Soča Valley. The Romans settled in the valley in the 1st century AD and established a military base at what is now Kranj. That site was developed in the 7th century by early Slavic tribes, who also established an island settlement at Lake Bled.

The 12th century brought a period of cultural vitality to this protectorate of Frankish aristocracies. Churches were built throughout the region and towns such as Radovljica, Kamnik and Kranj developed. The latter two emerged as important trade and religious centres in the Middle Ages and both served as capitals of Carniola until the Habsburgs won control of the area in the late 13th century. Until the 20th century, farming was the region's mainstay, and apiculture reached its zenith through Carnolian honeybee breeding in the 17th century.

Tourism began in the late 19th century, when Lake Bled morphed from a health retreat into a fashionable resort frequented by Viennese high society. The greatest upheaval in the region's history came during World War I, when the Soča Valley saw horrific fighting between Italian and Austro-Hungarian forces. Following the war, farming returned to the area and was joined by tourism in the 1990s.

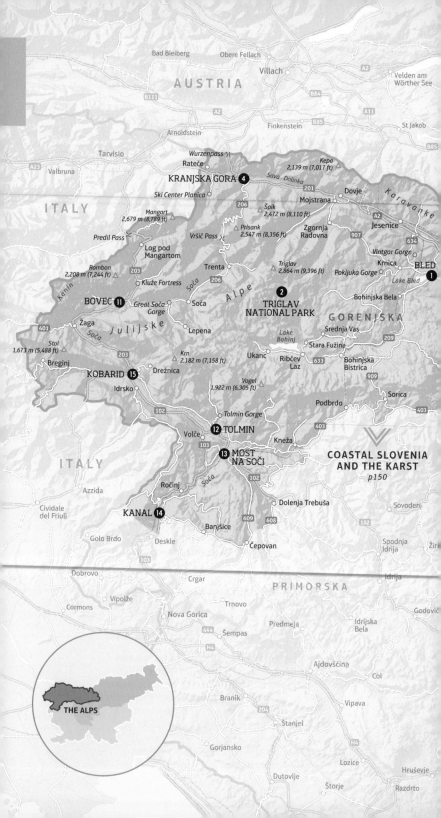

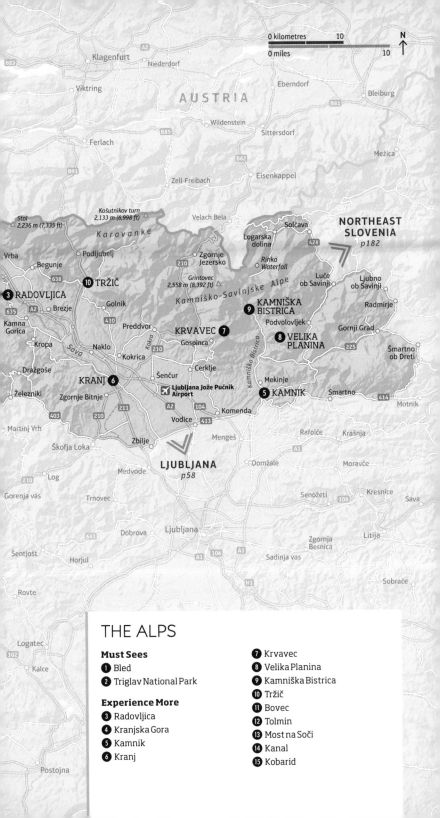

AUSTRIA

0 kilometres 10
0 miles 10

N

Klagenfurt
Niederdorf
Eberndorf
Bleiburg
Viktring
Wildenstein
Sittersdorf
Mežica
Ferlach
Zell-Freibach
Eisenkappel
Stol
2,236 m (7,335 ft)
Košutnikov turn
2,133 m (6,998 ft)
Velach Bela
Solčava
Vrba
Podljubelj
Zgornje
Jezersko
Logarska
dolina
NORTHEAST
SLOVENIA
p182
Begunje
10 TRŽIČ
Rinka
Waterfall
Luče
ob Savinji
Ljubno
ob Savinji
3 RADOVLJICA
Brezje
Golnik
Grintovec
2,558 m (8,392 ft)
Kamniško-Savinjske Alpe
Radmirje
Kamna
Gorica
Preddvor
**9 KAMNIŠKA
BISTRICA**
Gornji Grad
Kropa
Naklo
Kokra
Gospinca
KRVAVEC 7
Podvolovljek
**8 VELIKA
PLANINA**
Šmartno
ob Dreti
Dražgoše
Sava
Kokrica
Cerklje
Mekinje
Smartno
Železniki
KRANJ 6
Šenčur
Ljubljana Jože Pučnik
Airport
5 KAMNIK
Motnik
Zgornje Bitnje
Vodice
Komenda
Martinj Vrh
Zbilje
Mengeš
Rafolče
Krašnja
Škofja Loka
Medvode
**LJUBLJANA
p58**
Domžale
Moravče
Log
Trnovec
Senožeti
Kresnice
Sava
Gorenja vas
Dobrova
Ljubljana
Zgornja
Besnica
Litija
Šentjošt
Horjul
Sadinja vas
Sobrače
Rovte
Logatec
Kalce
Postojna

THE ALPS

Must Sees
1 Bled
2 Triglav National Park

Experience More
3 Radovljica
4 Kranjska Gora
5 Kamnik
6 Kranj

7 Krvavec
8 Velika Planina
9 Kamniška Bistrica
10 Tržič
11 Bovec
12 Tolmin
13 Most na Soči
14 Kanal
15 Kobarid

BLED

 B3 53 km (34 miles) NW of Ljubljana Lesce-Bled
🚌 Bled Jezero 🚏 ℹ️ Cesta svobode 10; www.bled.si

With its placid lake, fairy-tale island church, clifftop castle and girdle of grey mountains, Bled has become a visual trademark for the Slovenian tourist industry. Its key attractions today consist of boat trips to the island church and excursions into the alpine surroundings. Bled also makes a good base for exploring the nearby Triglav National Park (p132) and Lake Bohinj (p134). In winter, buses connect Bled with the skiing and snowboarding centre at Mount Vogel.

① Lake Bled

Just over 2 km (1 mile) long, 2 km (1 mile) wide and 30 m (98 ft) deep, Lake Bled (Blejsko jezero) fills a hollow gouged out by retreating glaciers towards the end of the last Ice Age. With wooded hills surrounding the lake and alpine peaks in the distance, it is nothing less than truly entrancing. The best way to enjoy the landscape is to walk along the asphalt path which leads right around the lake, a circuit that takes about two hours to complete. The most stunning views are from the western end, with the church spire on Bled Island (Blejski otok) set against the stupendous backdrop of the pretty snowcapped Karavanke Alps.

On the lake's southern shore stands Vila Bled, erstwhile summer house of Yugoslav president Josip Broz Tito (1890–1980), which has now been converted into an upmarket hotel.

② Bled Castle

🏠 Grajska cesta 25 🕐 Apr-Oct: 8am–8pm daily (Jul & Aug: to 9pm); Nov-Mar: 8am–6pm daily 🌐 blejski-grad.si

Dramatically located on a sheer cliff overlooking the lake's eastern end, Bled Castle (Blejski grad) began as the 11th-century stronghold of the Bishops of Brixen, who ruled over the area until 1803. Rebuilt by various owners over the years, the castle now houses an absorbing museum and a good restaurant. The former features a superb hoard of archaeological finds,

---

💬 **INSIDER TIP**
Row Your Boat

Much more enjoyable (and cheaper) than taking a traditional *pletna* at Lake Bled is to row yourself across to the island; hire a boat from the Castle Boat House or from opposite the Pension Pletna.

Cruising along the river on a canopied *pletna*, against a breathtaking backdrop

such as a bronze sword from around 1300 BC, bone harpoons and stone mortars. There's also coverage of the rapid development of tourism in the region. The beautifully frescoed Gothic chapel, wine cellar and herb gallery are worth a visit too.

Outside, the castle terrace commands an outstanding view, with the shimmering lake directly below and the Karavanke mountain range looming in the distance.

Bled Island

🕒 9am–4pm daily (Apr & Oct: to 6pm; May–Sep: to 7pm); 🌐 blejskiotok.si

Perched atop the hummock-shaped Bled Island, the Church of the Assumption (Cerkev Marijinega vnebovzetja) occupies a site that has been sacred for centuries. The island initially served pagan Slavs as a shrine, inspiring a famous episode in France Prešeren's epic poem *Baptism on the Savica (Krst pri Savici)*, in which the Slovenian prince, Črtomir, falls in love with Bogomila, the daughter of the island shrine's guardian.

After the region's conversion to Christianity, the island became a focus of Catholic pilgrimage. It has been associated with the cult of the Virgin Mary since the early Middle Ages, when a wooden chapel stood on the site of the current church. Pilgrimages boomed during the Baroque era, when the church was expanded and redecorated. Today, the island remains a popular place for pilgrimages on the Marian feast days, notably the Ascension and the Birth of the Virgin. These are traditionally all-night affairs

with participants arriving late in the evening and celebrating mass at 4am. The island can be reached via canopied boats (*pletna*), or you can row yourself. Visitors disembark at the bottom of a 99-step staircase that leads to the front door of the church. Inside are the fragmentary remains of some 15th-century frescoes illustrating the lives of the Virgin Mary and Jesus Christ.

Hanging from a small tower above the nave is the 15th-century Wishing Bell, presented to the church by a pilgrim whose prayers had been answered. It is believed that all those who ring the bell to honour the Blessed Virgin will also have their wishes granted.

EUROPE'S RENOWNED HEALTH RESORT

Bled owes its success as a resort to Swiss physician Arnold Rikli (1823–1906). An advocate of the benefits of sunshine, fresh air and clean water, Rikli founded the Institute of Natural Healing by Lake Bled in 1855. The first visitors sought cures for rheumatism, migraines, insomnia, and obesity. But as word of the spectacular scenery spread, they were joined by tourists and nobles. The resort has served as the summer residence for both Yugoslav King Aleksander I and President Tito.

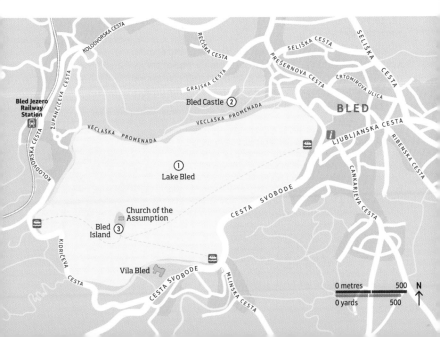

2 ⊛

TRIGLAV
NATIONAL PARK

🗺 B3 🚗 26 km (16 miles) W of Bled 🚌 From Bled 🛈 Bohinj: Ribčev
Laz 48; Mojstrana: Triglavska cesta 49; Trenta: Na Logu;
www.tnp.si

Encompassing verdant valleys, deep-blue lakes and soaring
peaks, Triglav National Park is, unsurprisingly, one of the
most visited places in the country. An outstanding network
of picturesque trails connect the varied areas of the park,
making it the perfect alpine paradise to explore.

Established in 1961, Slovenia's only national park is centred
on the country's highest mountain, the 2,864-m- (9,396-ft-)
high Triglav. Starkly beautiful outcrops of bare limestone
characterize the higher altitudes of the park, while its lower
reaches encompass forests of spruce and beech, which are
home to a fantastic range of flora and fauna. An annual wildflower festival is held in Bohinj in May and June, which highlights the incredible rich flora of the national park, showcased
alongside guided walks, workshops and delicious local cuisine.
    Other draws to the park include the Valley of the Triglav
Lakes, a sequence of seven glacial lakes surrounded by spruce
trees and boulders that is one of the area's most captivating
sights; and the Soča Trail, a 20-km (12-mile) route that follows
the Soča river as it carves its way through the Trenta Valley.

Did You Know?

Triglav is also a symbol of
Slovenia; the mountain's
silhouette appears
on the country's
national flag.

←

The park's gorgeous Lake Bohinj, encircled by mountains

1 The medieval Church of St John the Baptist stands at the edge of peaceful Lake Bohinj.

2 Beautiful alpine forget-me-not can be found at high altitudes throughout the park.

3 A climber traverses the rugged landscape of one of Triglav's intimidating peaks.

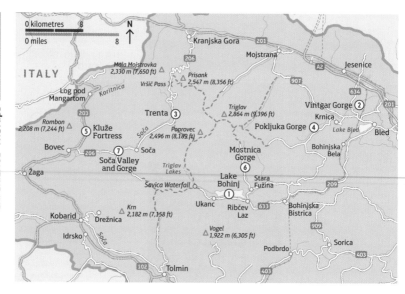

EXPLORING TRIGLAV NATIONAL PARK

STAY

Pri Plajeru
Stunningly located in the Soča Valley, this lovely, family-run farmstead offers chalet-style accommodation, organic produce and delicious meals.

🏠 Trenta 16a, 5232 Soča 🌐 eko-plajer.com

€€€

Chalet Hike & Bike
A cosy and very comfortable chalet across two floors (with a steep staircase), run by the owners of the excellent local tour operator, Hike & Bike. It sleeps six people and pets are welcome.

🏠 Stara Fužina 117, 4265 Bohinjsko jezero 🌐 hikeandbike.si

€€€

① Lake Bohinj

🏠 29 km (18 miles) SW of Bled 🚆 From Lesce-Bled 🚌 From Bled & Ljubljana 🛈 Ribčev Laz 48; www.bohinj.si

Tucked into the southeastern corner of Triglav National Park, Lake Bohinj (Bohinjsko jezero) is a beautiful expanse of water with high mountains on almost all sides and surrounded by some of Slovenia's best-preserved rustic villages. Fed by clear mountain streams, it is ideal for swimming and kayaking and an excellent base from which to explore the region's hiking trails. In winter, Vogel, to the south of the lake, is a popular spot for skiing and snowboarding, while the lake, if it freezes, provides a great opportunity for ice skating.

The small village of Ukanc, at the lake's western end, has pebbly beaches and is surrounded by Komna Plateau and Pršivec peak. A popular walking trail west from here leads to Slap Savica, a pair of waterfalls surrounded by high cliffs. Their waters feed the Sava river, which flows south-east to meet the Danube at Belgrade in Serbia.

On the slops of the Vogel mountain, the Vogel resort is a paradise for skiers in winter and hikers in summer. A cable car ascends from the shores of Lake Bohinj to a plateau that offers breathtaking views of the snow-clad Triglav massif to the north.

↑ A lone swimmer in a corner of Lake Bohinj in the Julian Alps

THE JULIANA TRAIL

The 270-km (168-mile) Juliana - or Julian Alps - Trail is a long-distance trail, designed to reduce overcrowding on Triglav and encourage hikers to explore the surrounding area. Running near the border with Italy, this self-guided, circular route leads hikers past green forests, rushing rivers and soaring peaks. The terrain is mostly flat, so it's great for novices and families.

With charming alpine farmhouses, Stara Fužina is one of the best-preserved traditional villages in western Slovenia. The 13th-century St Paul's Church on the outskirts of the village is also worth a visit. The meadows around Stara Fužina are dotted with canopied hay-drying racks or *kozolec*, a common feature of Slovenian farms.

The main settlement at the eastern end of Lake Bohinj is Ribčev Laz, which is famous for its dainty parish Church of St John (Cerkev sv Janeza). The church has some impressive late-Gothic frescoes.

Vintgar Gorge

📍 4 km (2 miles) NW of Bled 🚌 May–Sep: tourist shuttle from Bled 🕐 Late Apr–Oct: 8am–7pm daily 🌐 vintgar.si

Located just north of Bled *(p130)*, Vintgar Gorge is a 2-km (1-mile) ravine carved by the rushing waters of the Radovna river. It was discovered by chance in February 1891 during a period of unusually low water level in the river. The local mayor and a cartographer friend were amazed at the beauty of this usually impassable ravine and established a committee to construct wooden walkways to cater to the increasing number of visitors to Bled. The gorge became a major tourist attraction as soon as it opened in August 1893.

Visiting the gorge remains an exhilarating experience as the trail winds along sheer cliffs, passing gurgling rapids and whirlpools, crisscrossing the river on bridges. The walkway culminates at the 16-m (52-ft) Šum waterfall, which marks the northern end of the gorge. The cascade is at its most impressive during spring, when its thundering torrent throws up clouds of spray and even steam on very cold days. From here, Bled is within easy walking distance via a pretty footpath.

---

③
Trenta

📍 64 km (40 miles) W of Bled 🚌 Jun–Sep: from Kranjska Gora & Bovec 🛈 Trenta 31; www.soca-trenta.si

On the banks of the Soča river is Trenta – home to shepherds and lumberjacks. Its villagers led the first hikers into the Julian Alps in the late 1800s. Just uphill from the northern entrance to the village, Slovenia's only alpine botanical garden, the **Alpinum Juliana** (Alpski botanični vrt Juliana), spills down the hillside. The 600-plus alpine and karst species found here represent the diversity of the nation's alpine flora. There are plants from the Julian and Friuli Alps, the Karst region and pre-alpine meadows as well as from the Kamnik-Savinja Alps. The best time to visit the garden is in May and early June, when the flowers are in bloom.

Downhill, in the heart of the village, **Trenta Lodge** (Dom Trenta) contains an excellent information centre for Triglav National Park, as well as a local museum on geology and fauna.

Alpinum Juliana
⊘ 📍 Trenta 📞 (05) 388 9306 🕐 May–Sep: 8:30am–6:30pm daily

Trenta Lodge
⊘ 📍 Na Logu vi Trenti 🕐 Jan–Apr: 10am–2pm Mon–Fri; May–Oct: 10am–6pm daily (Jul & Aug: to 7pm) 🌐 soca-trenta.si

↑ Hikers following a lakeside wooden walkway through the Vintgar Gorge, which is bright with burnished autumn colours

④ Pokljuka Gorge

🚗 7 km (4 miles) W of Bled
🚌 From Bled

Not as popular as the Vintgar Gorge (p135), the 2-km (1-mile) Pokljuka Gorge, which spears into the national park west of Bled, is a destination for more isolated walking in pristine scenery. Although the gorge has some walkways, most of the route is along a permanently dry, rough riverbed, so walking boots are advisable.

Other sights in the gorge include the Pokljuka Cave (Pokljuška luknja), with a fallen roof that lets light into the cave; and tiny circular fields formed in the limestone depressions, known locally as *vrtci*, meaning little gardens. The prettiest formation is just beyond the ravine's narrowest part.

It is easiest to access the gorge from Krnica village, situated below the picturesque centre of the ravine, where the walls rise 40 m (130 ft) high. By bus, the ravine can be accessed along a short woodland path from Krnica. A car park is signposted above the village at the entrance of the ravine. Maps of the area are sold at the Bled information centre.

⑤ Kluže Fortress

🚗 84 km (52 miles) W of Bled 📞 (05) 388 6758
🕐 May & Oct: 10am-5pm Sat & Sun; Jun & Sep: 10am-5pm daily (to 8pm Sat); Jul & Aug: 9am-8pm daily

Impressively located between the Koritnica Gorge and Mount Rombon, Kluže Fortress is the last of a number of strongholds that once guarded the valley. It is believed that the Romans originally had a fort here, which was supplanted by a wooden fortress. Today's fortified bastion was built to serve as a command post during the Soča Front campaign. The fortress withstood Italian shelling, protected by its sheltered location and 2-m- (7-ft-) high reinforced walls.

Inside the fortress are displays on its history. The courtyard serves as the venue for mock battles organized by the Slovene Cultural and Historical Foundation in July and August. The gorge of the Koritnica river forms a 70-m- (230-ft-) deep natural moat around the fortress; the bridge across it offers great views of the Alps.

A path off the main road leads to Fort Hermann, the twin fortress that was nearly obliterated during the Soča Front campaign.

TOP 5 BEST HIKES IN THE PARK

Soška Pot
This 25-km (16-mile) trail meanders through the stunningly beautiful scenery of the Soča Valley.

Triglav Lakes
Hike to the magnificent Seven Lakes Valley, one of the most scenic spots in the entire national park.

Mostnica Gorge
This dramatic river gorge reaches up from Lake Bohinj, and is an ideal route for keen hikers.

Savica Waterfall
Follow a trail to the 78-m- (256-ft-) high Savica waterfall, source of the Sava Bohinjka.

Mala Mojstrovka
This 2,330-m (7,650-ft) peak is a popular destination from the Vršič Pass (p148), via its gentle southern slopes.

Kluže Fortress stands wedged above the Koritnica Gorge

↑ An impressive rock formation in the Mostnica Gorge

⑥
Mostnica Gorge

🏠 28 km (17 miles) SW of Bled ☎ (04) 574 7590
🚌 Jul–Aug: from Bled

The Mostnica river stretches north from Stara Fužina along the Voje Valley, where it has carved out a narrow 2-km (1-mile) gorge which features an array of interesting rock formations. A well-marked path follows the emerald-green river upstream to the 21-m- (69-ft-) high Mostnica waterfall. Along the way, the route passes four bridges including the Devil's Bridge (Hudičev most), which makes for one of the best viewpoints down into the gorge. Further up the valley the path crosses two footbridges. Iron ore was mined in the Voje Valley from the Bronze Age, and the bridges were built to allow it to be transported down the valley, giving the river its name in the process (Mostnica from *most*, meaning bridge). Note that the path along the river can be slippery after rain.

⑦
Soča Valley and Gorge

🏠 52 km (32 miles) SW of Bled 🌐 soca-valley.com

The Soča river is considered one of the most beautiful rivers in Europe, renowned for its distinctive emerald colour. Its most pristine spot is the gorgeous Great Soča Gorge, a narrow valley stretching for 750 m (2,460 ft). In summer, adventurous swimmers brave its icy, crystal-clear waters.

During World War I, the slopes above the river were the site of the largest mountain battle in history. In January 1915, in a bid to weaken

↑ Kayaking the gorgeously green waters of the Soča river

> **WALK OF PEACE**
>
> The Pot Miru, or Walk of Peace, is a 230-km (143-mile) hiking trail from Log pod Mangartom in Slovenia to Trieste in Italy, which links a series of World War I heritage sites along what was the front line between Italian and Austro-Hungarian troops, known as the Isonzo (or Soča) Front. Fighting here in 1915–1917 saw an appalling number of casualties, with some half a million deaths on both sides.

Austro-Hungary with a war on two fronts, the Allies lured Italy into the war with the promise of territorial gains. Italy sent 50 per cent of its forces over the border into the Soča Valley in Austro-Hungarian Slovenia. There are still many historical locations in the area dedicated to the memory of the brutal fighting here.

Beyond its history and natural beauty, the valley today is known for its excellent outdoor activities, with centres for whitewater rafting, hiking, canyoning and skiing.

EXPERIENCE MORE

❸

Radovljica

🅰B3 🚗5 km (3 miles) SE of Bled 🚋From Ljubljana and Kranj 🚌From Bled and Kranj 🅸Linhartov trg 9; www.radolca.si

The pretty core of Radovljica is one of the Gorenjska region's best-preserved old towns, defensively perched 75 m (246 ft) above the Sava river valley. Cocooned from traffic, Linhartov trg, the main square, is boxed in by painted Renaissance and Gothic burgher mansions that testify to medieval prosperity. The mansion at No 23 has a fresco of St Florian dousing a fire in the 18th-century town, while No 24, the Malijeva House (Malijeva hiša), retains a

---

BEEHIVE PANELS

No folk tradition is more Slovenian than that of painting beehive panels. During the 18th century, hives were created as shelf-like units allowing bee-keepers to harvest individual honeycombs without damaging the entire hive. The practice of painting on to their front panels emerged in the mid-1700s and reached its zenith in the 19th century. Reli-gious and floral motifs are popular panel themes, but the jokes and satirical images appeal the most: a hunter carried on a stretcher by his quarry, for example. The use of traditional painted panels dwindled in the 1900s, with the intro-duction of synthetic paints and the new larger hives seen today.

---

penalty bench used to chain criminals. The museum and gallery **Šivec House** (Šivečeva hiša) is late Gothic with Renaissance living quarters.

The square's architectural highlight is the large Thurn Mansion. Built as a ducal castle, then renovated into a palace and given a decorative Baroque façade, it houses the fascinating **Museum of Apiculture** (Čebelarski muzej). Here you'll find displays of quirky carved beehives, while a marvellous collection of painted beehive panels helps bring to life this Slovenian folk tradition. There's also a glass-sided observation beehive (the bees enter the façade of the building through a small glass tunnel), and there are displays covering the work of the pioneering apiarist Anton Janša, widely considered the father of modern beekeeping. A muni-cipal museum on the first floor documents the life of Slovenian dramatist Anton Tomaž Linhart (1756–95).

Off the square is the late-Gothic Church of St Peter (Cerkev sv Petra). It has a Baroque high altar with statuary by the architect

---

of St Nicholas's Cathedral in Ljubljana, Andrea Pozzo. The choir stalls have a carved boss depicting Pozzo himself.

Also of interest is the town's annual three-day Chocolate Festival (Festival čokolade), which is held in April.

Located just south of Radovljica, Kropa is a black-smiths' village that had 50 forge waterwheels in its 18th-century heyday. The **Iron Forging Museum** (Kovaški muzej) displays traditional wares, and a smithy opposite sells decorative ironwork. The nearby village of Brezje annually hosts about 300,000 pilgrims at the nation's most revered shrine: a miracle-working Madonna and Child painting in the Basilica of the Virgin (Marija Pomagaj).

Slovenia's most celebrated poet, France Prešeren (*p72*), was born in the village of Vrba, around 6 km (4 miles) north of Radovljica. Prešeren's Birth House (Prešernova rojstna hiša) has been converted into a small museum.

Šivec House

⊛ 🅰Linhartov trg 22 🕐Times vary, check website 🚫Mon 🌐mro.si

Museum of Apiculture

🅰Linhartov trg 1 🕐Times vary, check website 🌐mro.si

↑ Linhartov trg, the pretty main square of Radovljica that is lined by medieval mansions

Rugged peaks looming above the small town of Kranjska Gora

Iron Forging Museum

⊛ 🏠 Kropa 10 🕐 Times vary, check website 🌐 mro.si

Kranjska Gora

🗺 A3 🏠 39 km (24 miles) NW of Bled 🚌 From Bled, Bovec & Ljubljana 🛈 Kolodvorska ulica 1c; www.kranjska-gora.si

Beautifully located in the Sava Dolinka Valley beneath jagged alpine peaks, Kranjska Gora is the northern gateway to the Soča Valley (p137). This former dairy village was a key supply base for the Soča Front (p137) during World War I.

Since the 1930s it has been Slovenia's premier winter sports playground. In mid-March, the village hosts a number of ski events, including the Vitranc Cup in slalom, the giant slalom for the ski World Cup, and the World Ski-Flying Championship at Planica, the world's highest ski-jumping hill. In summer, Kranjska Gora is a popular base for hiking in Triglav National Park (p132). Starting at Mojstrana, 13 km (8 miles) east of Kranjska Gora, the

Triglavska Bistrica walking trail runs up the ruggedly beautiful Vrata Valley before reaching the forbidding north face of Mount Triglav.

Set proudly on the town's main square, the Church of the Assumption (Cerkev Device Marije Vnebovzete) dates from Kranjska Gora's earliest days in the 14th century. A Roman-esque bell tower survives from the original building, but the church has been rebuilt in Gothic style and features fine roof vaulting.

Beyond the church is **Liznjek House** (Liznjekova domačija), which was built in 1781 and provides a glimpse into the past of this traditional alpine village. This shingle-roofed residence has a brick ground floor and a smoke-stained "black kitchen". Traditional furnishings in the living quarters, such as painted trousseau chests and a grandfather clock, date back to the 1800s, as does the religious iconography in a tiny bedroom. The former stables have displays on local author Josip Vandot (1884–1944), a popular children's writer who penned tales about an inquisitive shepherd boy called Kekec.

Liznjek House

🏠 Borovška cesta 63 📞 (04) 588 1999 🕐 May-Oct: 10am-6pm Tue-Sat, 10am-5pm Sun; Nov-Apr: 9:30am-4pm Tue-Sat, 10am-4pm Sun

---

STAY

Skipass Hotel

This modern boutique hotel has ten stylish chalet-style rooms with balconies.

🗺 A3 🏠 Borovška cesta 95, Kranjska gora 🌐 skipasshotel.si

€€€

Hotel Linhart

An atmospheric hotel set in a beautifully restored 17th-century townhouse, located on Radovljica's main square.

🗺 B3 🏠 Linhartov trg 17, Radovljica 🌐 linharthotel.com

€€€

5

Kamnik

🅰 C4 🚗 52 km (32 miles) SE of Bled 🚂 From Ljubljana 🚌 From Ljubljana & Kranj ℹ Glavni trg 2; www.visitkamnik.com

This pleasingly old-fashioned town was a regional capital in the Middle Ages, and today retains some medieval attactions. The Franciscan Monastery (Frančiškanski samostan) off Glavni trg, the town's main square, has a library that houses a rare copy of the Bible (1584) by the Slovenian translator Jurij Dalmatin (1547–89); visits can be arranged through the tourist office. The attached Baroque Church of St James (Cerkev sv Jakoba) houses the Chapel of the Holy Sepulchre (Kapela Božjega groba), which was created in 1952 by Jože Plečnik and is full of striking motifs of the Resurrection.

↑ Zaprice Castle Museum, perched on a hillside above the town of Kamnik

Perched atop the rocky hillock at the end of Glavni trg is the so-called **Little Castle** (Mali grad). All that remains of this fortification, first documented in 1202, is a two-storey chapel. Its portal bears a Romanesque carving of angels and a crucifix, but the architecture within is Gothic and adorned with restored Baroque frescoes. Another reason to visit the chapel is the panorama it affords over Kamnik, up to the Kamniško-Savinjske Alps.

Šutna, the town's main street and Kamnik's former medieval thoroughfare, ends beneath the **Zaprice Castle Museum** (Medobčinski muzej Kamnik), where archaeological finds are housed within a restored Baroque castle. Exhibits include memorabilia of the 19th-century bourgeoisie and bentwood furniture from a local factory. Outside the museum is a lapidarium with specimens of traditional granaries from the Tuhinj Valley.

The Arboretum Volčji Potok, just 4 km (2 miles) south of Kamnik, and en route to Radomlje, is Slovenia's finest botanical park (p122). Its 88 ha (218 acres) are beautifully and creatively landscaped in a number of gardening styles.

Little Castle

⊗ 🏛 Glavni trg
🕐 Mid-Jun-mid-Sep: 9am-noon, 2-7pm daily

Zaprice Castle Museum

⊗ 🏛 Muzejska pot 3
🕐 Apr-Oct: 10am-6pm Tue-Sat; Nov-Mar: 8am-4pm Tue-Fri, 10am-4pm Sat
🌐 muzej-kamnik-on.net

→ Strolling down one of the wide, stone streets in Kranj's Old Town

---

EAT

Kunstelj

Historic, family-run inn serving delicious Slovenian dishes on its terrace overlooking the Sava Valley.

🅰 B3 🏛 Gorenjska cesta 9, Radovljica 🌐 kunstelj.si

€€€

Pension Milka

This charming family-run pension set beside glassy Lake Jasna has a fantastic restaurant. The menu focuses on fresh local delicacies.

🅰 A3 🏛 Vršiška 45, Kranjska Gora 🌐 pensionmilka.com

€€€

⑥
Kranj

C4 | 27 km (17 miles) SE of Bled | From Ljubljana | From Ljubljana, Bled, Kamnik & Škofja Loka | Glavni trg 2; www.visit kranj.com

Kranj is the country's fourth-largest settlement and an industrial centre. It features an appealing Old Town spread along a promontory, which was the site of early Celtic and Roman settlements.

Kranj is known for its links with France Prešeren (*p72*), the most celebrated of Slovenia's poets. The modest residence in which he spent the last three years of his life, **Prešeren House** (Prešernova hiša), contains his personal effects, including manuscripts, diaries and letters, as well as some original furnishings.

The heart of the Old Town is Glavni trg. Located on this square is the former city hall, which houses the **Gorenjska Museum** (Gorenjski muzej), with displays on regional

archaeology and charming exhibits of folk culture. The museum has a ceremonial Renaissance hall as well as sculptures by the Modernist sculptor Lojze Dolinar (1893–1970), a student of the Croatian sculptor Ivan Meštrovič (1883–1962). Also on the square is the grandest hall church in Slovenia, the Church of St Cantianus and Disciples (Cerkev sv Kancijana in tovarišev). The *Star of Beautiful Angels*, a fresco depicting angels, dating from the 15th century, adorns the ceiling of the nave. The church was built over the country's

largest Slavic graveyard. Visits to the ossuary can be arranged through the Gorjenska Museum.

Off the square is the Church of the Holy Rosary (Roženvenska cerkev) and next to it, a ceremonial stair-case by Jože Plečnik (*p101*).

Prešeren House
⟳ | Prešernova ulica 7
☎ (051) 615 388 | 10am–6pm Tue–Sun

Gorenjska Museum
⟳ | Tomšičeva 42
| 10am–6pm Tue–Sun
🅦 gorenjski-muzej.si

CARNIOLAN SAUSAGE

The Carniolan sausage (*Kranjska klobasa*) is a traditional smoked pork sausage from the historical region of Upper Carniola, around the town of Kranj. The filling - which consists of 75-80 per cent pork, along with 20 per cent bacon, sodium nitrate, garlic and pepper - is packed into pork casings, which are formed in pairs that are joined with a wooden skewer. Made by only 15 certified producers, *Kranjska klobasa* is traditionally served with sauerkraut, or with sour turnips, and freshly grated horseradish, and was granted protected geographical status by the EU in 2015.

↑ A pisted ski slope at Krvavec, rising above the clouds

7 🍴 ☕

Krvavec

🅰 C3 🚡 59 km (37 miles) SE of Bled 🔢 Grad 76; www.rtc-krvavec.si

Located just a 15-minute drive from Ljubljana's airport, this is the closest ski resort to an international airport in the world. Its proximity to Ljubljana itself as well as to Kranj *(p141)* ensures that this ski destination – located on the 1,853-m- (6,079-ft-) high Krvavec mountain – is one of the busiest in Slovenia. Access to the mountain summit, which is marked by a tall radio antenna, is by cable car from a small ski resort at Gospinca at an altitude of 1,480 m (4,856 ft). It can be reached via a narrow twisting road, or, during snowfall, by a cable car north of Cerklje. From Gospinca, marked trails ascend to the summit; the blue, 3-km (2-mile) Path of History (Poti zgodovine) takes visitors past a modern chapel and the excavated site of a 10th-century settlement.

The mountain also makes a popular destination in summer, when there are excellent opportunities for fair-weather activities such as walking and mountain biking.

8 🍴 ☕

Velika Planina

🅰 C3 🚡 76 km (47 miles) E of Bled 🚌 From Kamnik 🔢 Glavni trg 2, Kamnik; www.velikaplanina.si

The world's fourth-longest unsupported cable car, which starts midway up the Kamniško Bistrica Valley, provides access to the 1,666-m- (5,466-ft-) high Velika Planina. This mountain plateau is the best destination from which to get a sense of the Kamniško-Savinjske Alps *(p146)*. Like Krvavec, Velika Planina is a popular destination for skiing in winter and walking in summer. During summer the local herdsmen migrate to their picturesque settlements to graze cattle on the plateau's lush alpine meadows. Most of the unique, shingle-roofed wooden huts here were rebuilt after they were destroyed during World War II – the Germans suspected that this area was a base for resistance fighters. **Preskar's Hut** (Preskarjev stan), which survived the

onslaught, has been preserved as a museum. It is located about an hour's walk south of the upper cable car terminal, near the Church of Our Lady of the Snows (Kapela Marije Snežne).

Preskar's Hut

♿ 🏠 Kamniška Bistrica 2 🕐 Jul & Aug: 10am–4pm Sat & Sun

____

9 🍴

Kamniška Bistrica

🅰 C3 🚡 65 km (40 miles) E of Bled 🚌 From Kamnik 🔢 Glavni trg 2, Kamnik; (01) 831 8250

Around 4 km (2 miles) north of the lower cable car station to Velika Planina, the Kamniška Bistrica river valley terminates in a stupendous amphitheatre of Alps that are over 2,000 m (6,561 ft) high. Serious hikers can ascend from the car park at the terminal through pine woods and climb up to the saddles that lie between the jagged summits. A short walk takes you to the Orglice

↑ An idyllic crop of shingle-roofed mountain huts on Velika Planina

waterfall (Slap Orglice), which falls 30 m (98 ft) from a cleft. A similar walk leads to a hunting lodge – known as Plečnik's Mansion (Plečnikov dvorec) – that was built in 1932 for the Yugoslav King Aleksander I by Jože Plečnik (p101).

Tržič

🅰C3 🅰23 km (14 miles) E of Bled 🚌From Kranj & Radovljica 🏠Trg svobode 18; www.trzic.si

Lying just below the foothills on the Austrian border, the riverside town of Tržič was once synonymous with the artisan handicrafts of wheel- and shoe-making. Both withered in the face of industrial mass production, leaving the town a sleepy one-street place – only carriage-sized portals on the high street, Trg svobode, hint at the booming 18th and 19th centuries.

The excellent **Tržič Museum** (Tržiški muzej), located in a former tannery at the upper end of the town, illustrates shoe-making as well as the leatherwork trade that fed it. In the same building is the wonderful Slovenian Ski Museum, with all manner of exhibits dedicated to the national sport.

Around 3 km (2 miles) north lies the Dovžan Gorge (Dovžanova soteska). This slim ravine is a protected natural monument due to the abundance of Palaeozoic fossils found here, which were laid down when the area was covered by a warm shallow sea.

Tržič Museum
⌖ 🏠Muzejska ulica 11 🕐10am–6pm Tue–Sun 🌐trziski-muzej.si

> **Lying just below the foothills on the Austrian border, the riverside town of Tržič was once synonymous with the artisan handicrafts of wheel- and shoe-making.**

Bovec

🅰A3 🅰84 km (52 miles) W of Bled 🚌From Tolmin & Ljubljana; from Kranjska Gora (Jun–Sep) 🏠Golobarskih žrtev 8; www.soca-valley.com

Once a dairy centre, Bovec has transformed into a premier adrenaline sports destination in Slovenia, thanks to its spectacular setting between high alpine peaks and the china-blue Soča river.

Between April and October, several agencies organize whitewater rafting, kayaking and canyoning trips. There are signposted trails for mountain biking and a dedicated bike park; a brochure available in the tourist office outlines the routes. In winter the focus is on Kanin, which at 2,300 m (7,546 ft) is the highest skiing destination in Slovenia. It can be reached by a cable car that also provides access to high-altitude walking paths in summer, as well as a stunning view that stretches to the Adriatic Sea.

12 Tolmin

A4 ⧆ 75 km (47 miles) SW of Bled 🚌 From Bovec, Nova Gorica & Ljubljana 🛈 Petra Skalarja 4; www. soca-valley.com

This area's administrative centre, Tolmin warrants a visit for its absorbing archaeological collection in the **Tolmin Museum**. Displayed on the first floor are grave finds, jewellery and pottery that attest to the presence of sophisticated prehistoric cultures. Some items exhibited here were imported, such as an exquisite Attic cup that has become the trademark of the museum.

Located nearby are the Tolmin Gorge (Tolminska korita) and Dante's Cave (Zadlaška jama), both of which are worth seeing.

Tolmin Museum

♿ 🏛 Mestni trg 4 ⧆ 9am–4pm Tue–Fri, 1–5pm Sat & Sun 🌐 tol-muzej.si

Taking in the dramatic natural beauty of the Tolmin Gorge ↓

13 Most na Soči

A4 ⧆ 70 km (44 miles) SW of Bled 🚃 From Bohinjska Bistrica & Nova Gorica 🚌 From Tolmin & Idrija

One of the most advanced prehistoric settlements in Slovenia developed on this peninsula, which was created by the confluence of the Soča and Idrija rivers. Over 7,000 grave sites from the Bronze and Iron Age have been excavated here, ranking it among Europe's most important settlements. The Romans were here too, and an archaeological trail visits the remains of a Roman villa among its 21 sites. Other sites on this cultural treasure hunt include a re-created Bronze Age Hallstatt dwelling in the local school (accessed through the Tolmin Museum) and the Church of St Lucy (Cerkev sv Lucije).

Most na Soči is also home to a wide turquoise lake. It is artificial, created by a nearby hydroplant, but is lovely to look at nonetheless.

14 Kanal

A4 ⧆ 95 km (59 miles) SW of Bled 🚃 From Nova Gorica 🚌 From Most na Soči 🛈 Pionirska 2; www.tic-kanal.si

There is an iconic single-span bridge that crosses into this small town, from which competitors in the High Diving World Cup (held here in mid-August every year) plunge 17 m (56 ft) into the

Soča river below. On the opposite side of the bridge, an archway beside the church is a post-World War I rebuild of the 16th-century original.

Through this is the Kontrada courtyard, the oldest part of the town, which began as a castle in 1140 and developed into a square village protected by walls and two gatehouse towers. The tower on the north side survives and houses the **Galerija Rika Debenjaka**, which showcases the work of Kanal-born 20th-century artist Riko Debenjak. During the summer, an array of cultural activities are held in the square.

Galerija Rika Debenjaka

⊘ 🏠 Pionirska ulica bb 📞 (05) 163 6930 🕐 10am–noon Tue, 5–7pm Fri

---

 15

Kobarid

🅰A4 🏠 91 km (57 miles) SW of Bled 🚌 From Bovec, Nova Gorica & Ljubljana 🚉 Trg svobode 16; www.soca-valley.com

Italian influence can be seen throughout this charming town in Kobarid's shuttered houses, dusty pastel-painted façades and fine restaurants. Italy occupied Kobarid between the world wars and during the battle for the Soča Front (documented by American author Ernest Hemingway in his novel *Farewell to Arms*) until the first blitzkrieg in Europe finally broke the stalemate between Italy and Austro-Hungary.

Just off the main square, the excellent **Kobarid Museum** (Kobariški muzej), offers a compelling and sobering insight into the war. Other reminders of this bleak period can be seen along the **Kobarid Historical Walk** (Kobariška zgodovinska pot), whose 5-km (3-mile) circuit starts from Trg svobode.

Kobarid Museum

⊘ 🏠 Gregorčičeva 10 🕐 Apr–Jun & Sep: 9am–6pm daily; Jul & Aug: 9am–8pm daily; Oct–Mar: 10am–5pm daily 🌐 kobariski-muzej.si

Kobarid Historical Walk

⊘ ⊗ 🏠 Gregorčičeva 8 🕐 By appt only 🌐 potmiru.si

EAT

Hiša Franko

This is one of the finest restaurants in Slovenia, its kitchen headed by award-winning chef Ana Roš. Savour the impressive tasting menus showcasing delicious local produce.

🅰A4 🏠 Staro selo 1, Kobarid 🌐 hisafranko.com

 €€€

Martinov hram

Enjoy local specialities like fresh trout served outside on the lovely covered terrace at this Bovec guesthouse.

🅰A3 🏠 Trg golobarskih žrtev, Bovec 🌐 martinov-hram.si

 €€€

STAY

Hotel Dvorec

Rooms at this alpine hotel are sleek, simple and spacious. The restaurant is a good place to try the tasty local *frika* (fried potato and cheese hash).

🅰A4 🏠 Mestni trg 3, Tolmin 🌐 hoteldvorec.com

 €€€

Sanje ob Soči

A boutique hotel with a choice of stylish, uncluttered apartments and bedrooms. The breakfasts are delicious.

🅰A3 🏠 Mala Vas 105a, Bovec 🌐 sanjeobsoci.com

 €€€

A DRIVING TOUR
THE KAMNIŠKO-SAVINJSKE ALPS

Length 40 km (25 miles) **Stopping-off points** There are good cafés in the towns, and a tourist office in Luče ob Savinji **Terrain** The roads are narrow and winding

As the road twists uphill east of Kamnik, the farming villages and agricultural landscapes of the Dreta Valley give way to alpine settlements in the valley on the northern side of the Kamniško-Savinjske Alps. Off its upper reaches are two of the most beautiful alpine valleys in Slovenia – Robanov kot and Logarska dolina – each enclosed by a jagged wall of peaks. Opportunities for adventures abound in this region, so leave the car and journey into caves or hike through lush valleys.

*Accessed only via footpaths is the alpine valley of **Robanov kot**, with steep wooded slopes framing the 2,350-m- (7,710-ft-) high Ojstrica mountain. It is popular with walkers who seek unspoiled nature.*

*Lush meadows, speckled by wildflowers and clear rivers, backdropped by a wall of the Alps at its head, make the U-shaped valley of **Logarska dolina** one of the most picturesque.*

Podolševa

Savinja

Solčava

Kučnik

Logarska dolina

Strelovec △
1,763 m (5,784 ft)

Robanov kot

Savinja

*A footpath from the car park at the head of the valley leads to the 80-m- (262-ft-) high **Rinka waterfall**.*

Rinka Waterfall

FINISH

Ojstrica △
2,350 m (7,710 ft)

Krofička △
2,083 m (6,834 ft)

Križevnik △
1,910 m (6,266

Velika Zelenica △
2,214 m (6,834 ft)

Planjava △
2,392 m (7,848 ft)

Dleskovec △
1,967 m (6,453 ft)

Did You Know?

Logarska dolina means Loggers' Valley, referring to the timber industry that once thrived here.

↑ Water trickling down from the Rinka Waterfall in the Logarska dolina

Locator Map

Navigating a raft in the Savinja river, Ljubno ob Savinji ↑

Ancient limestone features and ice formations, preserved year long because of very low temperatures, can be viewed by carbide lamps inside the **Snow Cave***. Access to the cave, which is located in Raduha mountain, is via a forest road.*

A small town in the upper Savinja Valley, **Luče ob Savinji** *is where most of the local administrative infrastructure, including a bank, supermarkets, and cafés, is located.*

Ljubno ob Savinji*, located at the confluence of the Ljubnica and Savinja rivers, is home to a museum that documents the tradition of flosarji (rafters) in the town.*

Radmirje *is a pretty agricultural village known for its traditional kozolci haystacks and the Church of St Francis Xavier. Its treasury contains mantles gifted by Polish and French royalty.*

The main attractions in the small town of **Gornji Grad** *are the Cathedral of Sts Hermagor and Fortunat, and the summer residence of the Ljubljana bishops. The latter houses an ethnographic museum.*

Presečnikov vrh
△ 1,573 m (5,161 ft)

△ Sedlo
1,274 m (4,180 ft)

Snow Cave

Ljubenske Rastke

Primož pri Ljubnem

Raduha

Struge

428

Savinja

Bukovnik

Luče ob Savinji

428

924

Ljubno ob Savinji

Juvanje

Lučnica

Arničev vrh △
1,116 m (3,661 ft)

Radmirje

Okonina

225

Florjan pri Gornjem Gradu

Meliše

△ Lepenatka
1,425 m (4,675 ft)

Podhom

Gornji Grad
▷ **START**

Bočna

Dreta

Zgornji Dol

225

0 kilometres   4

0 miles   4

N ↑

A CYCLING TOUR
VRŠIČ PASS

Length 24 km (14 miles) return **Stopping-off point** Lake Jasna **Terrain** Asphalt road, with cobblestones on corners. This is a demanding route with a long, steep climb involving around 820 m (2690 ft) of ascent **Nearest town** Kranjska Gora, reached by bus from Ljubljana or Jesenice

The cycle ride from Kranjska Gora to the Vršič Pass – Slovenia's highest paved road at 1,611 m (5,285 ft) – offers epic views of the Julian Alps. It's quite a climb, over a relentless series of 24 switchbacks, but the route follows a well-maintained asphalt road, and the scenery is simply breathtaking as you pedal into one of the most beautiful areas of Triglav National Park. Be sure to leave time to explore some of the sites along the way.

Start at **Kranjska Gora** (p139), a ski resort town at the confluence of the Sava Dolinka and Pišnica rivers.

Take a break at **Lake Jasna** and, if you're feeling peckish, pedal over to Pension Milka, one of the best restaurants in the area.

Shortly after passing Lake Jasna, follow the road through the magnificent **Triglav National Park** (p132).

There's a prominent **rock window** on Mt Prisank, which can be seen from one of the hairpin bends.

Erjavčeva koča is one of several mountain huts near the pass where you can stop to rest your legs.

From the **Vršič Pass** you can admire the stunning views south over the Trenta Valley; several hiking trails strike out from the pass here.

The road here is known as the **Russian Road**. It was built in WW1 by Russian prisoners of war.

Pause at the **Russian Chapel**, which was built in 1916 as a memorial to Russian prisoners working on the road, who were killed earlier the same year in an avalanche.

START/FINISH · Kranjska Gora · Pension Milka · Jasna · Lake Jasna · Škrbinjek 1,341 m (4,399 ft) · Kurji vrh 1,762 m (5,781 ft) · Rušica 2,075 m (6,808 ft) · Mavrinc 1,272 m (4,173 ft) · Stržič 1,876 m (6,155 ft) · Vavovje 1,810 m (5,938 ft) · Prednje Robičje 1,941 m (6,368 ft) · Mt Prisank viewpoint · Russian Chapel · Nad Šitom Glava 2,080 m (6,824 ft) · Erjavčeva koča · Velika Mojstrovka 2,333 m (7,654 ft) · Vršič Pass · Bavha 1,706 m (5,597 ft) · Osojna Glava 1,678 m (5,505 ft) · Prisank 2,547 m (8,356 ft) · Mala Pišnica · Pišnica

Did You Know?

On the northern side of Mt Prisank is Ajdovska Deklica (Pagan Girl), a natural carving in the shape of a face.

Snowy peaks towering over the rugged terrain of the Vršič Pass ↑

COASTAL SLOVENIA AND THE KARST

Western Slovenia has long been the meeting point of Slav and Italian cultures. The region's inclusion in Slovenia was largely the result of the partisan struggles of World War II and memories of the Communist-led liberation movement are still cherished. War memorials are an important feature of regional towns and many streets and squares are still named after partisan heroes. Many Italian speakers left the coastal towns when they were awarded to Slovenia after World War II, but Italian is the official language and street signs are bilingual. Slovenia's short Adriatic coastline is packed with variety. Historic ports such as Koper and Piran, which were ruled by Venice for five centuries, still bear that city's architectural imprint.

The region's arid sunny climate have long produced some of Slovenia's best-known wines, including the famous crisp white wines from the Goriška Brda and Vipava regions, and the sharp red teran from the coast. The spectacular mix of cultural influences is evident in the food as well, with menus fusing seafood from the Adriatic with truffles, mushrooms and home-cured ham, *pršut*, from the inland towns and villages.

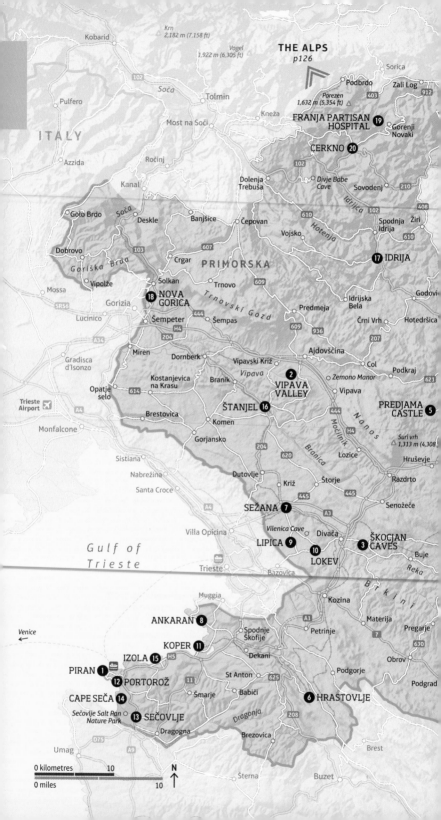

COASTAL SLOVENIA AND THE KARST

Must Sees
1. Piran
2. Vipava Valley
3. Škocjan Caves
4. Postojna Caves
5. Predjama Castle

Experience More
6. Hrastovlje
7. Sežana
8. Ankaran
9. Lipica
10. Lokev
11. Koper
12. Portorož
13. Sečovlje
14. Cape Seča
15. Izola
16. Štanjel
17. Idrija
18. Nova Gorica
19. Franja Partisan Hospital
20. Cerkno
21. Postojna
22. Pivka Cave
23. Križna Cave
24. Pivka Park of Military History
25. Planina Cave
26. Rakov Škocjan Regional Park
27. Lake Cerknica
28. Snežnik Castle
29. Snežnik Plateau
30. Ilirska Bistrica
31. Reka River Valley

The coastal town of Piran, overlooked by the campanile of St George's Cathedral

③
Piran Art Gallery

🏠 Tartinijev trg 3 ⏰ Jun-Aug: 9am–2pm and 8–10pm Tue–Sun; Sep–May: 10am–5pm Tue–Sun 🌐 obalne-galerije.si

Located just off the square, the Piran Art Gallery (Obalne galerije Piran) is one of the best places to see modern art in southwestern Slovenia. On Cankarjevo nabrežje, a short distance south of Tartinijev trg, is another branch of the gallery – the Herman Pečarič Gallery – housed in a beautiful late 19th-century building. The gallery's schedule of contemporary exhibitions is augmented by a display of paintings and graphics bequeathed to the town by local artist Herman Pečarič (1908–81), best known for his Istrian land- and seascapes.

④
Prvomajski trg

Northwest of Tartinijev trg is a maze of alleys and a trio of minor squares, of which the largest, Prvomajski trg, has an elaborate Baroque fountain. Built in 1776, the fountain is

①
PIRAN

🅰 A6 🏠 120 km (75 miles) SW of Ljubljana 🚌 From Koper and Portorož 🛈 Tartinijev trg 2; www.portoroz.si

A delightful warren of pastel-coloured houses squeezed on to a small peninsula, Piran represents coastal Slovenia at its most charming. The town only became part of Slovenia in 1954, and is home to a cluster of fishing boats and some excellent seafood restaurants.

①
Tartinijev trg

Piran is centred around the oval-shaped Tartinijev trg, which occupies the former inner harbour. The harbour was filled in in the 19th century and the resulting space was named after local-born violinist and composer, Giuseppe Tartini (1692–1770). The square's focal point is a 19th-century statue of the composer.

Other buildings of note in the square include the Neo-Renaissance Town Hall (Občinska palača), built in 1879, and the wine-red 14th-century Venetian House (Benečanka hiša). Nearby, the Neo-Classical St Peter's Church (Cerkev sv Petra)

contains a 14th-century crucifix that shows Jesus nailed to a fork-shaped cross thought to symbolize the Tree of Life.

②
Tartini House

🏠 Kajuhova 12 📞 (05) 663 3570 ⏰ Jun–Aug: 9am–noon, 6–9pm Tue–Sun; Sep–May: 11am–2pm Fri, 11am–4pm Sat & Sun

In a small plaza north of Tartinijev trg, Tartini House (Tartinijeva hiša) has a modest collection of the composer's heirlooms, including one of his violins, Tartini's death mask, old musical scores and artworks inspired by Tartini's music.

STAY

Art Hotel Tartini
Sleekly furnished, with enchanting views over Piran's main square, this boutique hotel has a rooftop garden and a cocktail bar.

🏠 Tartinijev trg 15 🌐 arthoteltartini.com

€ € €

fronted by an imposing pair of statues symbolizing Law and Justice. A stone cherub holding an amphora stands on one corner of the balustrade; on rainy days, water gushes out of the amphora.

---

 ⑤

Sergej Mašera Maritime Museum

📍 Cankarjevo nabrežje 3
📞 (05) 671 0040 🕙 9am–5pm Tue–Sun 🌐 pomorski muzej.si

On the southeastern side of the harbour, this museum (Pomorski muzej Sergej Mašera) is named after the Yugoslav naval commander who drowned in April 1941 when he destroyed his ship off the Croatian coast to prevent it from falling into enemy hands. Exhibits include various underwater archaeological finds and 18th-century model ships.

 GREAT VIEW
Town Wall

A steep walk uphill from the cathedral is a stretch of the town wall, built in 1470. You can scale the gate tower and walk along the parapet, which offers a sumptuous panorama of the town and surrounding coast.

 ⑥

St George's Cathedral

📍 Adamičeva ulica 📞 (05) 673 3440 🕙 10am–5pm Wed–Mon

St George's Cathedral (Stolna cerkev sv Jurija) is a single-nave structure begun in 1641. The church can be accessed via a passageway from the small Parish Museum (Župnijski muzej) in the baptistry. The church's freestanding campanile is a faithful copy of that in St Mark's Cathedral in Venice.

⑦

Shell Museum

📍 Tartinijev trg 15
🕙 Times vary, check website 🌐 svet-skoljk.si

Piran's Shell Museum (Čarboni Svet Školjk) is a spectacular exhibition of over 3,000 shells from across the world, formed from the private shell collection of local biologist Jan Simič.

---

⑧

Museum of Underwater Activities

📍 Župančičeva 24 🕙 Jun–Sep: daily; Oct–May: Fri–Sun 🌐 muzejpodvodnih dejavnosti.si

This small but absorbing museum (Muzej podvodnih dejavnosti) relates the history of diving in the Adriatic Sea. There is a section devoted to underwater warfare, too.

VIPAVA VALLEY

🗺 B5 🕐 58 km (36 miles) N of Koper 🚌 From Nova Gorica and Ljubljana
ℹ Glavni trg 1; www.vipavskadolina.si

Stretching in a line between Nova Gorica and Podnanos, the Vipava Valley is a slash of vivid green below rocky hills and karst plateaux that has long been known as an excellent wine-producing area.

One of the oldest wine-growing regions in Slovenia, the Vipava Valley has been producing outstanding wines since the Roman times thanks to it's mild, sub-Mediterranean climate. Though it produces both red and white varieties, the valley is especially renowned for its white grapes, including the common varieties of Chardonnay and Sauvignon as well as the indigenous Zelen and Pinela. As such, small, family-owned wineries dot the landscape, and are one of the main reasons to visit the valley.

Beyond it's wine-producing capabilities, the Vipava Valley is also a haven for outdoor enthusiasts, with hiking and cycling trails found around every bend of the rolling landscape. The two main towns in the valley, Vipava (p158) and Ajdovščina (p158), are great starting points for exploration. Whether touring on foot, bike or behind the wheel, you'll be rewarded with pristine rural scenery, vineyards bordering the roadside, terracotta roofed medieval villages, and fine restaurants serving seasonal, local produce to dip into.

CYCLING TOUR

One of the best ways to explore the Vipava Valley is by bike. For an easy, circular route with no shortage of vineyards, head south-west from Vipava to the village of Goče, then through the Branica Valley. Cross the Vipava river and turn east, through Ajdovščina and past Zemono Manor, to arrive back in Vipava.

Pale sunlight filtering down on to the lush fields of the Vipava Valley

① Vipava Valley is well known for its exceptional wine production.

② Mountain biking is a popular way to explore the valley.

③ There are pretty old stone streets in Vipava town.

EXPLORING VIPAVA VALLEY

Vipava

🏛 58 km (36 miles) N of Koper 🚌 From Nova Gorica & Ljubljana 🛈 Glavni trg 1; www.vipavskadolina.si

Pressed against the sheer grey flanks of the Nanos ridge, the small town of Vipava stands at the centre of the Vipava Valley wine producing area. Dominating the main square is the ochre 17th-century mansion built by the Lanthieri Counts, who ruled over Vipava until World War I. A building on the town's main square houses the tourist information centre and the **Vinoteka Vipava**, where white wines made from the indigenous Zelen and Pinela grapes are available for sampling and purchase.

Beyond the square, Vipava's street plan of narrow twisting alleyways protects houses from the *burja*, the bone-chilling northeasterly wind that blasts down from the mountain ridges above. Alleyways behind the main square lead to an attractive waterside area near the source of the Vipava river, which emerges from the limestone slopes of Nanos

mountain. From here, trails lead up towards the jagged ruins of Vipava's 13th-century castle. For those keen to embark on longer hikes, several marked paths lead up towards Nanos's main ridge, beyond which lies a rolling plateau of evergreen forest and pastures. Perched on a small hill 2 km (1 mile) west of Vipava is the 7th-century Zemono Manor, a famously beautiful arcaded building, which now houses the Pri Lojzetu restaurant.

Vinoteka Vipava

🏛 Glavni trg 1 📞 (05) 368 7041 🕒 Mid-May–mid-Sep: 9am–7pm Mon–Fri, 9am–1pm & 3–7pm Sat & Sun; mid-Sep–mid-May: 9am–5pm Mon–Fri, 9am–1pm Sat

---

The scenic hillside town of Vipavski Križ, overlooked by a hulking mountain ↑

Ajdovščina

🏛 65 km (40 miles) N of Koper 🚌 From Ljubljana and Nova Gorica 🛈 Prešernova ulica 9; www.vipavskadolina.si

The second main town of the Vipava Valley, semi-industrial Ajdovščina began life as a Roman fortified camp, the ruins of which can still be seen around town. It became an important centre of milling and metalworking in the Middle Ages, with workshops that were powered by the gushing waters of the Hubelj river. More recently, Ajdovščina has become noted as the home of the Pipistrel aviation company, whose innovative gliders can frequently be seen at the airfield west of town.

Relics from Ajdovščina's ancient origins are most visible on the eastern side of the centre, where a surviving medieval gateway and adjoining section of Roman wall preside over a grassy park facing the river. Inside the gate lies a tightly woven web of narrow streets, where the **Veno Pilon Gallery** (Pilonova galerija) honours the locally born painter, Veno Pilon (1896–1970), with displays of paintings and mementos from his lifetime. The collection starts with Pilon's subtly dramatic watercolours of the Russian town of Lipeck, where he was interned as a prisoner of war during World War I. Most striking of Pilon's later works are the Expressionist portraits, in which the sitters

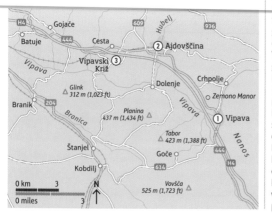

Must See

Today, Križ is a scenic but sleepy settlement, with long stretches of defensive wall intact, and the stark remains of the fortress looming above the eastern end.

are portrayed with overlarge hands, asymmetrical faces, or elongated torsos.

A 30-minute walk on a well-signed and easy-going nature trail on the northern side of town leads to the source of the Hubelj river, which emerges from the rocky hillside in the form of a gushing waterfall.

The town is almost entirely encircled by tranquil, empty mountains, making it a great location for hiking and mountain biking all year round.

Veno Pilon Gallery
Ⓐ Prešernova 3
Ⓒ 9am–6pm Tue–Fri, 3–6pm Sat & Sun Ⓦ venopilon.com

 ③
Vipavski Križ
Ⓐ 67 km (42 miles) N of Koper

Occupying a low ridge in the middle of the Vipava Valley, Vipavski Križ was an insignificant village until the late 15th century, when the Counts of Gorizia needed a forward line of defence to protect themselves against Ottoman attacks. Križ was turned into a fortress, with the ensuing influx of soldiers, builders and churchmen transforming it into a major regional centre.

Today, Križ is a scenic but sleepy settlement, with long stretches of defensive wall intact, and the stark remains of the fortress looming above the eastern end. The town's original design has been maintained, with clusters of close-packed terracotta roofs edging up the hillside. Dominating the town is the 17th-century Capuchin Monastery Church (Cerkev Kapucinskega Samostana), famous for a Baroque painting of the Holy Trinity which hangs upon the high altar. The monastery's **Library** holds a prized collection of manuscripts and prayer books. The most renowned item is the script of the *Škofja Loka Passion Play (Škofjeloški pasijon)*, the oldest Slovene play.

Library
Ⓒ 9am–noon, 1–5:30pm Tue–Sat

EAT

Gostilna Podfarovž
Seat yourself on the terrace perched above one of the Vipava river's six springs, and tuck into beautifully prepared dishes.

Ⓐ Ulica Ivana Šceka 2, Vipava Ⓦ podfarovz.si

€€€

STAY

Majerija
A subterranean guest-house, where each room is named after a herb from the garden.

Ⓐ Slap 18, Vipava
Ⓦ majerija.si

€€€

Did You Know?

Škocjan is one of only four cave systems in the world listed as a Natural – rather than a Cultural – UNESCO Site.

Light streaming in through the ↑ vast mouth of the Škocjan Caves, and *(inset)* The Bowls formations

ŠKOCJAN CAVES
ŠKOCJANSKE JAME

B5 38 km (24 miles) NE of Koper From Koper and Ljubljana; nearest station is Divača, 3 km (2 miles) N of caves For tours only; times vary, check website park-skocjanskejame.si

Located in rolling countryside just outside the town of Divača, the Škocjan Caves are one of Slovenia's most spectacular karst features, and one of the largest cave complexes in the world.

Velika Dolina (literally, Great Valley) is where the Reka river disappears underground, carving out the chambers of the Škocjan Caves before re-emerging near the Adriatic Sea. This UNESCO World Heritage Site's labyrinthine complex of caverns and passageways is reckoned to be the world's largest network of subterranean chambers, and, to this day, remains only partially explored. About 3 km (2 miles) of passageways are open to the public, accessible by a 90-minute guided tour. As well as a spectacular array of stalagmites and stalactites, visitors can marvel at underground waterways and rock bridges, as well as an unusual sequence of formations known as The Bowls.

The surrounding landscape, which features limestone gorges, pastureland, traditional stone-built villages and deciduous forest, is a protected nature area. The restored barns of Škocjan Village contain a number of museum collections, with a model of the cave system and Bronze Age archaeological finds among the exhibits.

TOP 4 CAVE HIGHLIGHTS

The Bowls
These unique cup-like formations, arranged in tiers and formed by the sediment left by dripping water, is one of the more unusual sights here.

Cerkvenik Bridge
The walk across this man-made bridge, hovering 45 m (148 ft) above the twisting underground Reka river, is utterly breathtaking.

The Organ
This is one of the most alluring rock formations, so-called due to a ribbed curtain of limestone that resembles the pipes of a church organ.

Paradise Cave
Among Škocjan's set-piece caverns, the Paradise Cave is famous for the fluted pillars of rock that connect the floor to the ceiling.

↑ Lush greenery cloaking the rugged sides of Velika Dolina (Great Valley)

④ 🗡 🎿 🍴 🖥 🛍

POSTOJNA CAVES
POSTOJNSKA JAMA

🅰 B5 📍 53 km (33 miles) S of Ljubljana 🚆 From Ljubljana
🕐 For tours only; times vary, check website 🌐 postojnska-jama.eu

Slovenia's most popular natural attraction, Postojna Caves constitute the longest subterranean system in the country, with over 20 km (12 miles) of chambers and tunnels. Inside, magnificent formations of stalactites and stalagmites seem to stretch endlessly in all directions.

The caves were formed by the seeping waters of the Pivka river and its tributaries, which carved out several levels of underground galleries over a period of roughly three million years. The caves were first opened to visitors in 1819, with Austrian emperor Francis I as the guest of honour. The site currently receives just under half a million visitors a year, making it one of Europe's most popular natural attractions.

Lasting 90 minutes, guided tours begin with a train ride into the heart of the caves, followed by a walk through a series of halls with intricate rock formations. The 3.5-km- (2-mile-) long underground railway offers an exhilarating introduction to the caves, speeding visitors through illuminated chambers. With the train swerving between dangling stalactites, it is almost like a fairground ride. Back near the cave entrance is the Concert Hall, a vast space where performances are sometimes held.

> **The 3.5-km- (2-mile-) long underground railway offers an exhilarating introduction to the caves.**

Did You Know?

At Christmas time, local actors and musicians stage a "living nativity" within the caves.

↑ Visitors gathering inside one of the huge caverns within the complex

OLM

The Olm (*Proteus anguinus*) – or "human fish" – is an aquatic cave salamander found in the underground karst world of Slovenia. This mysterious creature can survive without food for 10 years. The Olm's appearance – long tail, snake-like body and short legs – led to the belief that they were baby dragons. Completely blind, the Olm is extremely sensitive to light, and the use of the bright lights in flash photography can damage its skin and even lead to the animal's death.

↑ A pathway winding past massive, dramatic rock formations inside the Postojna Caves

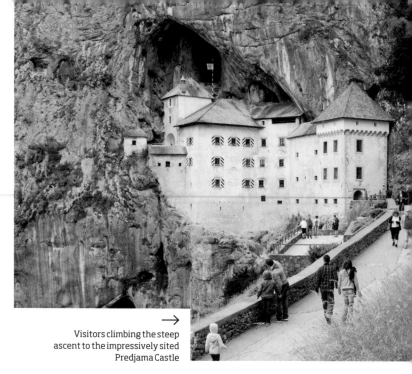

→

Visitors climbing the steep
ascent to the impressively sited
Predjama Castle

PREDJAMA CASTLE
PREDJAMSKI GRAD

Ⓐ B5 **⌂ 13 km (8 miles) NW of Postojna** **◔ Daily; times vary, check website**
Ⓦ postojnska-jama.eu

**There are few fortresses more dramatically situated than Predjama
Castle, which sits halfway up a hillside carved into a huge cave. Wander
the period interiors, and then tour the impressive karst caves below.**

The site was fortified in the 13th century,
although most of what can be seen today is
the result of 16th-century rebuilding. Most
famous of the castle's many owners was the
15th-century knight Erasmus Lueger. In July,
a tournament is held here to celebrate the
medieval period with jousts and parades.

ERASMUS LUEGER

Born in Trieste, Erasmus Lueger became
the owner of Predjama Castle in 1478.
He fell foul of the authorities after killing
one of the emperor's kinsmen, and a year-
long siege of the castle was mounted as
a result. The defenders brought in food
through a secret tunnel, but Erasmus
was ultimately killed by a cannonball.

Accessible via wooden bridges that could be
hastily removed, Predjama was considered
impregnable. A reconstructed drawbridge
leads to the part that is located within the cave.

The 16th-century furnishings and costumes
displayed in the restored dining room provide
an insight into the aristocratic lifestyles of the
time when castles became residential chateaux.
There are also a series of tableaux featuring
wax dummies throughout the castle; one room
shows a prisoner being tortured prior to inter-
rogation in the inquisitor's room next door.

Also of interest is the castle's tender and
moving pietà. Located in the Chapel of St Anne,
a serene white space decorated with wooden
pews and a simple cross, the pietà dates from
1420 and is one of the high points of late-
Gothic art in Slovenia. Karst caves below the
castle can be visited by guided tour.

↑ Wax dummies and period furnishings inside the castle

GREAT VIEW
Upper Vantage Point

The views offered from this seemingly impregnable castle are as impressive as you might expect. Staircases ascend to the highest of Predjama Castle's five levels, from where the viewing terrace affords an extensive panorama of the beautiful valley spread out below.

EXPERIENCE MORE

6

Hrastovlje

B6 20 km (13 miles) SE of Koper From Koper Titov trg, Koper; (05) 664 6403

The rustic village of Hrastovlje is home to one of Slovenia's most outstanding medieval treasures: the 12th-century **Church of the Holy Trinity** (Cerkev sv Trojice), a simple Romanesque structure sheltered behind a defensive wall.

The church's interior is covered with dazzling frescoes from 1490 by local artist John of Kastav. The most famous frieze is the *Dance of Death*, in which a jolly-looking company of skeletons lead the old and young, rich and poor alike towards the grave.

Many of the other scenes feature biblical stories but with the main characters clad in 15th-century attire, providing a fascinating insight into the lifestyles of the period. Particularly imaginative are the scenes depicting the Book of Genesis and the Journey of the Magi. Ceiling panels carry delightful illustrations of local country life at different stages of the annual agricultural cycle and through the seasons.

Church of the Holy Trinity
Hrastovlje 19a 9am-noon, 1-5pm daily

7

Sežana

B5 45 km (28 miles) NE of Koper Partizanska 2; www.sezana.si

An unassuming market town serving the hill villages of the western Karst, Sežana is an important hub for travellers to nearby attractions such as the Lipica Stud Farm *(p166)* and the Vilenica Cave *(p168)*. It also holds a variety of minor attractions in its own right, the most popular of which is the restful **Botanical Gardens**.

The gardens were laid out by the Scaramanga family, a Trieste-based trading dynasty who were enthusiastic horticulturalists. An elegant 19th-century palm house sits amid geometrically arranged flowerbeds, while beyond it lies an extensive arboretum containing evergreens that help to keep the gardens colourful all year round.

Botanical Gardens
Partizanska cesta 2
Times vary, check website
vrtsezana.si

↑ Beautifully painted ceiling panels within the Church of the Holy Trinity in Hrastovlje

The settlement of Ankaran, which hugs the slopes of the Mirje peninsula ↑

8

Ankaran

A6 28 km (17 miles) NE of Piran From Koper
Regentova 2; www.visitankaran.si

The quiet town of Ankaran grew around a former Benedictine monastery, which was abandoned in 1641 after a plague. It became a hotel in the 1920s and a huddle of holiday villas were subsequently built. Today, Ankaran makes a good base for coastal walks, with paths leading west towards the rugged cape of Debeli. Alternatively, the well-signposted Bebler Mountain Path (Beblerjeva planinska pot) climbs inland from the town's centre to the ridgetop village of Hrvatini.

9

Lipica

B5 48 km (30 miles) NE of Koper From Sežana
lipica.org

Located by the Italian border near Sežana, the village of Lipica takes its name from the linden trees that are widespread in this area (the Slovenian word *lipa* means linden). The village is synonymous with the Lipizzaner horses bred here since 1580. Established by the Habsburg Archduke Charles II of Styria, the **Lipica Stud Farm** crossed Andalucian horses with local steeds – horses from this area were already noted for their endurance and strength – resulting in the graceful white Lipizzaner horses. Lipica (part of the Habsburg Empire at the time) was chosen since its climate and the surrounding rocky landscape compared favourably with those of Spain. The breed immediately found favour with the prestigious Spanish Riding School in Vienna, which was established in the 1700s, and has been considered aristocratic in the equine world ever since. All of today's Lipizzaners are descended from four breeding lines, which can be traced back to the 18th century.

During the nearly 450 years of its existence, the stud farm has witnessed a frequently turbulent history. In 1797 the herd was evacuated to Hungary to escape the approach of Napoleon's army, and it was moved to Hungary a second time in 1809. During World War I, the herd was evacuated to Laxenburg near Vienna and Kaldrup in what is now Czechia, with only those at Laxenburg returning to

Lipica following the war. During World War II, the herd (and studbooks) were taken by the German army to Hostau, with the herd only being recaptured and returned through a bold military mission led by General Patton in 1945.

Today, Lipica has riding stables, a hotel, a nine-hole golf course, a Carriage Museum and the Museum Lipikum (Muzej lipicanca). There are over 350 horses at Lipica, many of which can be seen grazing in the extensive paddocks that adjoin the stud farm. Tours of the stables allow visitors to see the creatures at close quarters, while presentations by the

Did You Know?

The heart-shaped leaves of Slovenia's linden trees are a national symbol.

LIPIZZANER HORSES

The Lipizzaner horses at Lipica are all bred from Spanish, Arabian, Italian and local stock from the Karst region. The foals are born dark-coloured, and develop their distinctive off-white coats only after the age of five. The best time to see the Lipizzaners is in the morning, when they are released from the stables at 9am and come galloping down a broad avenue to the paddocks. While Lipica is the original Lipizzaner farm, the Austrians established a new stud in Piber after the break-up of the Habsburg Empire in 1918.

Classical Riding School show the highly trained horses performing complex routines. Horse-drawn carriage tours of the farm and pastures are available from April to October. Enthusiasts can book one-week courses ranging from horse riding for beginners to advanced dressage training.

Occupying a room in one of the older stable complexes is the **Avgust Černigoj Gallery** (Galerija Avgusta Černigoja), honouring Černigoj (1898–1985), the Modernist artist who spent the last years of his life at Lipica. The collection ranges from Constructivist paintings from the artist's youth to the collages he worked on in his later years. The gallery is designed according to the avant-garde aesthetics of Černigoj's early years, with grey metal staircases, bright red pillars and a circular viewing platform on the second floor.

Lipica Stud Farm

⊛🐎🍴🏨 ◘Apr-Sep: 10am–5pm daily; Oct–Mar: 10am–3pm Tue–Sun

Avgust Černigoj Gallery

⊛ ◘Apr-Sep: 10am–5pm daily; Oct–Mar: 10am–3pm Tue–Sun

← A group of Lipizzaner horses cantering around a paddock at Lipica Stud Farm

Lokev

🅰B5 🕐38 km (24 miles) NE of Koper 🚌From Sežana

Lokev is a typical Karst village of modest stone houses. It is famous for the local home-cured ham (*pršut*) that is sold in the shop at the huge drying shed (*pršutarna*). At the village centre is a castellated round tower built by the Venetians in 1485. It now houses the **Tabor Military Museum** (Vojaški muzej Tabor), a private collection containing mementos from both world wars. Exhibits include the uniform of General Svetozar Borojevič, commander of the Austro-Hungarian forces on the Soča Front (*p137*), and weapons used by the partisan brigades that liberated western Slovenia from Fascist occupiers in 1945.

Located amid forest and scrub just north of the village, **Vilenica Cave** (Jama Vilenica) was one of the first of the Karst caverns to become a tourist attraction, receiving visitors as early as the 17th century. However, it lost prominence when the nearby Postojna and Škocjan Caves were discovered. Visits to Vilenica were revived in 1963, and about 450 m (1,480 ft) of stalactite-encrusted passageways can be seen as part of a guided tour. The Dance Hall, the biggest of Vilenica's chambers, serves as the venue for readings during the Vilenica International Literature Festival, which brings together Slovenian and Central European poets.

Tabor Military Museum

⊛ 🅰Lokev 66a 📞(05) 767 0107 🕐9am–noon, 2–6pm Wed–Sun

Vilenica Cave

⊛⊛ 🕐Apr–Oct: 3 and 5pm Sun 🌐vilenica.com

🕚

Koper

🅰A6 🕐20 km (13 miles) NE of Piran 🚉🚌From Ljubljana 🛈Titov trg; www.visit koper.si

Now Slovenia's main port, Koper began as a small Roman settlement known as Insula Caprea (Goat Island). It became a trading centre under the Venetian Empire, and has an attractive Old Town rich in Venetian-influenced architecture. The city was home to a largely Italian-speaking population until it became part of Slovenia in 1954. The Italian heritage is everpresent; street signs are bilingual and many of the locals speak Italian. Modern Koper is girdled with industrial zones, but the city retains its historic character in its core of medieval streets.

> **Many of central Koper's narrow alleyways meet at Tito Square (Titov trg), home to some spectacular old buildings.**

Many of central Koper's narrow alleyways meet at Tito Square (Titov trg), home to some spectacular old buildings. The most eye-catching is the Praetorian Palace (Pretorska palača), a striking example of Venetian-Gothic style. Opposite the palace is the 15th-century Loggia, which has Venetian-Gothic windows and a 16th-century statue of the Virgin and Child. A side door leads to the Galerija Loža, a gallery for contemporary artists.

On the eastern side of Titov trg is the Cathedral of the Assumption (stolnica Marijinega vnebovzetja), a pleasing amalgam of Baroque and Romanesque elements. On the right side of the transept is a painting entitled *Virgin and Child Accompanied by Saints*, attributed to the Venetian painter Carpaccio, who is thought to have once lived in Koper. Hidden behind the main altar is the medieval sarcophagus of local protector St Nazarius, with an effigy of the saint on the lid. One side of the slab has a delicately carved relief of Nazarius holding a model of Koper. Slightly away from the cathedral is the Venetian-style **City Bell Tower**, a medieval defensive tower that was turned into a belfry in the 15th century. Steep steps lead up to a bird's-eye view of the city centre.

One of the Old Town's most characterful buildings is the Fontico. A 15th-century grain warehouse, it is now occupied by municipal offices and has a busy exterior studded with the crests of local merchant families. Next door is the plain ochre Church of St Jacob (Cerkev sv Jakoba), a simple 14th-century Gothic structure.

↑ The atmospheric interior of the Vilenica Cave, located just outside Lokev

↑ Praetorian Palace and *(inset)* the Fontana da Ponte, both of which stand on Tito Square in Koper

The delightfully elaborate Fontana da Ponte is located in a pretty Old Town square. The fountain dates from 1666, and has an octagonal base spanned by an arch in the form of a balustraded bridge. On the southern end of the square is the Muda Gate, a 16th-century archway with reliefs of the city's official symbol – a fiery-tongued sun with a smiling face.

Occupying the Belgramoni-Tacco Palace, the **Regional Museum** (Pokrajinski muzej) hosts a rich collection of fossils, archaeological finds and medieval stonework. Paintings on display include a panorama of Koper in the 1600s and a copy of the *Dance of Death* fresco from the Holy Trinity Church, Hrastovlje *(p165)*. Exhibitions of historical interest are held in the Muzejska galerija, two doors further down.

The western entrance to Koper's Old Town is marked by the Taverna, a buttressed stone structure. Originally a salt-storage warehouse, the building gets its name from the number of inns that were once clustered around it. It is now a venue for popular summer concerts.

Surrounded by an atmospheric maze of alleys, the **Ethnographic Collection** (Etnološka zbirka) fills a beautifully restored Venetian-Gothic house. The displays include utensils, costumes, and dry-stone construction techniques of the Karst.

City Bell Tower
⊛ ⌂Titov trg ⌚9am-4:30pm daily (mid-Jun-Sep: to 7:30pm)

Regional Museum
⊛ ⌂Kidričeva 19 ⌚8am-4pm Tue-Fri, 10am-4pm Sat & Sun ⓦpokrajinskimuzej koper.si

Ethnographic Collection
⊛ ⌂Gramšijev trg 4 ☎(05) 663 3586 ⌚8am-4pm Tue-Fri, 10am-4pm Sat & Sun

EAT

Gostilna za Gradom
This quirky seafood restaurant outside the centre of Koper is well worth the trip. Expect impeccable service and playful dishes like bread rolls shaped as sea urchins or hedgehogs.

⌂A6 ⌂Kraljeva 10, Koper ☎(05) 628 5505

Muha
Tuck into delicious regional dishes washed down with a glass of local Teran or Refošk wine in the Karst's oldest inn, which dates from 1679. The gnocchi, in particular, are mouthwatering.

⌂B5 ⌂Lokev 138a, Lokev ☎(05) 767 0055 ⌚Thu & Fri

Portorož

🅰A6 🚗2 km (1 mile) SE of Piran 🚆🚌From Koper, Ljubljana and Piran ℹObala 16; www.portoroz.si

Draped along a curve of Piran Bay, Portorož is Slovenia's biggest and most stylish beach resort. Despite the presence of a grand Habsburg-era hotel – the Kempinski Palace, built in 1911 – most of Portorož dates from the post-World War II period; a number of modern hotels, cafés and casinos border the palm-lined main boulevard. There is a large crescent of beach made up of imported sand – there are no naturally sandy beaches on this part of the Adriatic. Boutiques selling major fashion labels and jewellery cater to an increasingly upmarket clientele, and the resort also offers a buzzing, varied nightlife.

As well as being very busy during the summer, Portorož is a popular spa resort throughout the year, thanks to a warm microclimate and the therapeutic qualities of the local seawater.

The **Portorož Auditorium** (Avditorij) is well worth a visit, offering a year-round programme of music, drama and film. In summer, the venue stages concerts in its outdoor amphitheatre.

Portorož Auditorium

🏠Senčna pot 10
🌐avditorij.si

SALT PANS OF SEČOVLJE

Sečovlje has been known for salt production since the Middle Ages, although it was only in the 19th century that it became the region's main industry. Dykes were constructed across the bay, creating shallow pans in which seawater would evaporate, leaving pure salt crystals. The salt was then raked into piles and loaded on to barrows, before being exported all over the Mediterranean. The pans were neglected during the Communist period and the quality of the salt declined. Today, Sečovlje salt crystals, Piranske soline, make popular gastronomic souvenirs.

Sečovlje

🅰A6 🚗9 km (6 miles) SE of Piran 🚌From Portorož

A small village just short of the Croatian border, Sečovlje is famous for the salt pans that stretch across the neighbouring Gulf of Piran. This arrestingly beautiful man-made grid of shallow pools is important both as a wildlife sanctuary and an industrial heritage site. Although salt extraction still takes place in a section of the pans, since 2001 they have been protected under the **Sečovlje Salt Pan Nature Park** (Krajinski park Sečoveljske soline).

The main entrance to the park is at the northern end of the pans and is easy to reach on foot or by bike from Portorož. A dyke-top path leads towards the visitors'

centre, which has a display on conservation issues. A second entrance is at the southern end of the salt pans by the Croatian border – the access road is in a no-man's land between the Slovene and Croatian frontier posts. This leads to the **Sečovlje Salt Museum** (Sečoveljske muzej), located in a block where seasonal workers used to live.

A unique area of man-made wetland, the pans are home to flora typical of salty marshland environments, and serve as an important stop-off for migrating birds. Nesting species include the yellow-legged gull, the common tern and the Kentish plover; white egrets often hunt in the area.

Sečovlje Salt Pan Nature Park

🏠Parecag 290, Sečovlje
🕐Times vary, check website 🌐kpss.si

Sečovlje Salt Museum

 🌀 📅 🅰 Sečovlje 📞 (05) 671 0040

---

⑭

Cape Seča
Rt Seča

🅰 A6 📅 5 km (2 miles) SE of Piran 🚌 From Portorož

Dominating the horizon south of Portorož is Cape Seča, a hilly peninsula with holiday cottages, vineyards and olive groves. The olive-covered western flanks of the cape provide stunning views of the Sečovlje salt pans filling the bay that forms the border between Slovenia and Croatia.

A path leads around the cape from the southern side of Portorož's yachting marina on to an open stretch of seafront beneath grey-brown cliffs. Just beyond the cape's western-pointing tip is the Cactus Garden (Vrt kaktusov), a privately owned collection open to the public during the summer months. Another route from Portorož goes over the ridge of the cape, passing **Forma Viva**, an open-air sculpture park. The park features over 130 modern and abstract works.

Forma Viva
🅰 Seča 152 🕐 24 hrs daily 🌐 obalne-galerije.si

← Clear turquoise waters lapping against the shores of Portorož resort

↑ An appealing lavender souvenir shop within the Old Town of Izola

⑮

Izola

🅰 A6 📅 11 km (7 miles) NE of Piran 🚌 From Koper 🛈 Sončno nabrežje 4; www. visitizola.com

A lively fishing port, Izola is a typical Mediterranean town of narrow alleys, shuttered windows and potted palms, all squeezed onto a thumb-shaped peninsula. It is one of the most pleasant spots in Slovenia for a seaside stroll, with its horseshoe-shaped harbour bordered by seafront gardens fragrant with rosemary, lavender and sage. Stretched around the peninsula's northern end is a sequence of concrete bathing platforms, each offering lovely views across the bay towards Koper *(p168)* and Trieste.

Dominating the high ground at the heart of the peninsula is the Church of St Maurus (Cerkev sv Mavra), which has a striped façade and a freestanding belfry. Below the church is the former palace of the Besenghi degli Ughi family, sporting fancy wrought-iron window grilles and a stone balustrade adorned with carvings of human faces. It is now a music school.

Hidden in the alleys of the Old Town is the **Parenzana Museum** (Muzej Parenzana), celebrating the narrow-gauge railway line that once ran through Izola from Trieste in Italy to Poreč in Croatia. Closed in 1937, the Parenzana is remembered through old photographs and a model of a short stretch of the line displayed in the museum. The museum's collection of model locomotives recalls the days when the Izola-based toy manufacturer Mehanotehnika, active from 1954 to 2008, produced train sets that were popular with children across the former Yugoslavia. Today the railway line serves as a foot- and cycle-path.

Parenzana Museum
 🅰 Alme Vivoda 3 🕐 9am–3pm Mon–Fri 🌐 parenzana.net

🔍 HIDDEN GEM
Parenzana

The Parenzana is a 123-km (76-mile) transborder cycle route that meanders through northeast Italy, Slovenia and Croatia *(www.parenzana.net)*. Much of the trail is free from other traffic, so it makes a relaxing way to explore this region.

16
Štanjel

B5 **59 km (37 miles) NE of Koper** **From Nova Gorica and Sežana** **From Nova Gorica and Sežana** **stanjel.eu**

The best-preserved of the ridgetop settlements to the southwest of the Vipava Valley (*p156*) is Štanjel, once an important way station on the trade route between Vipava and the coast. Sacked by Ottoman raiders in 1470, the town was refortified in the 16th century by the Kobenzl family.

The main approach to the town leads through the west gate, adorned with the deer and eagle motifs of Štanjel's coat of arms. Presiding over a a knot of unpaved alleys lined with cottages is the cone-shaped belfry of St Daniel's Church (Cerkev sv Danijela), a late-Gothic structure with Baroque altars.

On Štanjel's hill is the 16th-century castle (kaštel), much of which is in ruins. Occupying one of the castle buildings is the **Lojze Spacal Gallery** (Galerija Lojzeta Spacala), housing a collection of works by the Trieste-born artist Lojze Spacal (1907–2000), famed for his depictions of the Karst and the coast. Staff at the gallery also show visitors around the nearby Karst House (Kraška hiša), a traditional hill-village home.

Just beyond the Karst House, the town's eastern boundary is marked by the Kobdilj Tower (Kobdiljski

↑ A round tower and weathered sculpture making up the ruins of Stanjel's castle

stolp), a gateway topped with castellations. Running in an arc below the tower is Ferrari's Garden (Ferrarijev vrt), a landscaped park that has a lake with a Venetian-style bridge.

Lojze Spacal Gallery
⊗ **Grad Štanjel**
(05) 769 0197 **Daily**

17
Idrija

B4 **102 km (63 miles) N of Koper** **From Ljubljana** **Mestni trg 2; www.visit-idrija.si**

Accessed via winding roads, Idrija's location at the base of a valley is spectacular. Mining began here in 1490, and Idrija soon became the second-largest mercury-mining centre in Europe, providing 13 per cent of the global output.

After mining came to a halt in 2008, the town became a major centre of industrial tourism. This mining heritage is apparent everywhere in Idrija, particularly in the **Town Museum** (Mestni muzej), housed in the Gewerkenegg

Castle on a hilltop above the centre. One section is devoted to the manufacture of Idrija lace, a home industry begun by miners' wives to supplement modest family incomes, and still going strong today.

A first-hand experience of mining conditions is provided at **Anthony's Shaft** (Antonijev rov), a network of tunnels to the south of the castle. A tour starts at the Šelštev House, leading visitors down the shaft itself, where past mining techniques are demonstrated.

Several other industrial monuments are strewn around the centre of the town: the pit-head pavilion at Francis's Shaft (Jašek Frančiške) a display of mining machinery, while the nearby Miner's House (Rudarska hiša) reveals the cramped living conditions of 19th-century families. On the western outskirts of town is a large stone building containing the Kamšt, a vast waterwheel built in 1790 to pump floodwater from the mineshafts below.

Immediately beyond the Kamšt is the Zgornja Idrijca Landscape Park, where a path runs alongside the Rake – a man-made water course that fed the waterwheel. Keen walkers can follow forest trails towards the Klavže, 18th-century dams that controlled the flow of water on local mountain torrents, making it possible to float locally cut timber downstream.

Town Museum

 ⬙Prelovčeva 3
⬙9am–6pm daily
Ⓦmuzej-idrija-cerkno.si

Anthony's Shaft

⬙Kosovelova 3
⬙Times vary, check website
Ⓦcudhg-idrija.si

18

Nova Gorica

⬙A4 ⬙85 km (53 miles) N of Koper ⬙From Ljubljana
⬙Delpinova 18b; www.novagorica-turizem.com

The main administrative centre of western Slovenia, Nova Gorica owes its origins to post-World War II peace treaties, which awarded the city of Gorizia to Italy but left the villages immediately to the east in Slovenian hands. The Slovenians built a new town on their side of the border, intended to serve as an economic and social centre for the local rural population. Largely

Did You Know?
—
Idrija is renowned for its *žlikrofi*: ravioli-like pockets of pasta stuffed with potato, bacon and onion.

constructed in the 1950s, the town centre has a grid-plan appearance. However, there is a wealth of historical sights throughout the suburbs.

Dominating a hill south of the centre, the **Franciscan Monastery of Kostanjevica** (Frančiškanski samostan na Kostanjevici) started out as a Carmelite foundation in the early 17th century. It was refounded by the Franciscans in 1811 and holds the burial vault of France's last Bourbon king, Charles X (1757–1836).

Just east of central Nova Gorica, Kromberk Castle is a Renaissance chateau surrounded by ornamental gardens. It provides a grand home for the **Nova Gorica Museum** (Goriški muzej), whose art collection spans everything from Gothic altar panels to graphic prints. The museum's engaging ethnographic and archaeological collections are housed in the **Villa Bartolomei** in Solkan, a leafy suburb made up of summer villas.

Spanning the Soča river on Solkan's northern boundary is the 1906 Solkan railway bridge (Solkanski most), its 85-m- (280-ft-) high central arch the biggest of any stone-built bridge in the world. To the east of the bridge is Sveta Gora hill, its summit crowned by the **Sveta Gora Monastery** (Frančiškanski samostan Sveta Gora) and its Pilgrimage Church of the Assumption. The church holds a 16th-century picture of the Virgin that is believed to answer the prayers of the faithful.

Franciscan Monastery of Kostanjevica

⬙Škrabčeva ulica 1
⬙9am–noon & 3–5pm Mon–Sat, 3–5pm Sun
Ⓦsamostan-kostanjevica.si

Nova Gorica Museum

⬙Grajska 1
⬙Times vary, check website Ⓦgoriskimuzej.si

Villa Bartolomei

⬙Pod Vinogradi 2 ⬙May–Oct: 3–8pm Sat & Sun; Nov–Apr: 1–5pm Sat & Sun
Ⓦgoriskimuzej.si

Sveta Gora Monastery

⬙Sveta Gora 2
Ⓦsvetagora.si

↓ Nova Gorica's Franciscan Monastery of Kostanjevica

EAT

Proteus

Named after the infamous "human fish" *(p163)*, this restaurant serves up mouth-watering dishes.

B5 Titov trg 1, Postojna postojnska-jama.si

€€€

Storja pod Stopnicami

A lovely, trattoria-like spot with checked tablecloths and delicious home-cooked meals.

B5 Ulica 1 Maja 1, Postojna storja.si

€€€

STAY

Pri Ancki

A cosy guesthouse with a few colourful, simply furnished rooms. Breakfast is served round a communal table.

C5 Casermanova ulica 9, Cerknica (031) 644279

€€€

 19

Franja Partisan Hospital

Partizanska bolnica Branja

B4 25 km (16 miles) N of Idrija Apr–Sep: 9am–6pm daily; Oct: 9am–4pm daily; Nov–Mar: by appt only muzej-idrija-cerkno.si

In the densely wooded and picturesque Pasica Gorge lies the Franja Partisan Hospital, a timber-built field hospital used by Slovenian resistance fighters during World War II. Active from December 1943 to 1945, the hospital's 13 wooden huts once housed wards that were fully equipped with x-ray machines, operating theatres and an electricity generator. Over 1,000 partisans and Allied soldiers were treated here during the war, with medical supplies dropped by Allied aircraft throughout Slovenia. Staff and patients were blind-folded on their way to and from the hospital to ensure maximum secrecy. Converted into a memorial after the war, the site was named after partisan doctor Franja Bojc Bidovec (1913–85), the hospital administrator from January 1944 until the war's end.

The site was almost totally destroyed by major floods in September 2007, but thanks to a faithful reconstruction, the splendid monument still welcomes visitors.

20

Cerkno

B4 20 km (13 miles) NW of Idrija From Idrija Močnikova 2; www.visitcerkno.si

Stretched out beneath the 1,632-m- (5,354-ft-) high ridge of Mount Porezen, the village of Cerkno is a popular base for summer hiking and winter skiing. The main attraction in the village itself is **Cerkno Museum**, which contains an arresting collection of wood-carved carnival masks worn by the local pre-Lenten revellers, the *laufarji*.

The Cerkno tourist office can organize visits to the Divje Babe Cave, a major archaeological site that is rich in Neanderthal remains, between April and September. In 1996, archaeologists discovered what is claimed to be the world's oldest musical instrument, a 60,000-year-old flute carved from bear bone. Today, the bone is exhibited in the National Museum of Slovenia, Ljubljana *(p98)*, although the question of whether it is really a flute or simply a bone with holes in it is the subject of long-running academic debate.

↑ A simple wooden building within the Franja Partisan Hospital

← Pivka river sinkhole, which lies beside the popular Postojna Caves

Cerkno Museum

 Bevkova 12 🕑 9am–3pm Tue–Fri, 10am–1pm & 2–6pm Sat & Sun 🌐 muzej-idrija-cerkno.si

---

㉑
Postojna

🅰 B5 🚗 53 km (33 miles) S of Ljubljana 🚆🚌 From Ljubljana ℹ Tržaška cesta 59; www.visit-postojna.si

The history of the town of Postojna, situated midway between Ljubljana and the Adriatic coast, is inextricably linked with that of the famous Postojna Caves (p162). The arrival of the railway in 1857 made the caves accessible to visitors from all over Central Europe. This spurred the development of Postojna itself, which was transformed from a provincial market town into a major administrative centre. The town fell under Italian rule after World War I, and it became a heavily garrisoned military base on the frontier with the erstwhile Kingdom of Yugoslavia. Barrack buildings can still be seen on the outskirts of town. The **Karst Museum**, which occupies the former garrison headquarters, has on display exhibits relating to the natural history, archaeology and ethnography of the entire Karst region. The museum's star exhibit is the Predjama Cache, a modest but exceptional hoard of ten, 16th-century objects – goblets, candlesticks, a chalice – that were found wrapped in a rotting piece of linen in the castle cellar in 1991.

Karst Museum

 Kolodvorska 3 🕑 Times vary, check website 🌐 karstmuseum.com

㉒
Pivka Cave
Pivka jama

🅰 B5 🚗 3 km (2 miles) N of Postojna 🕑 For tours; Jul–Aug: 9am & 5pm, Sep–Jun: by appt

Just north of the entrance to the Postojna Caves is the lesser-known Pivka Cave. A steep descent via a stairway and a walk along the path beside a submerged stretch of the Pivka river takes visitors to the caverns. A man-made passageway leads through to the neighbouring Black Cave (Črna jama), so named due to the smooth, black calcite rock that gives lustre to some of the caverns.

THE CERKNO LAUFARJI

Cerkno's most unusual carnival custom involves the *laufarji* (runners), local young men who cavort through the village in stylized costumes welcoming the spring. They appear on the first Sunday of the year and increase in number as the weeks go by. Their main task is to accompany the *Pust* - a symbol of winter that has to be confronted, tried and symbolically executed on Shrove Tuesday before spring can commence. The *Pust* is policed by a masked group called the *terjasti*, who also entertain the public by dancing and leaping.

23

Križna Cave
Križna jama

C5 **30 km (19 miles) SE of Postojna** **Apr–Sep** **krizna-jama.si**

Famous for its subterranean lakes, Križna Cave offers one of Slovenia's unique speleological experiences. Fed by underground water sources from both the Bloke and Cerknica plateaus, the 8-km- (5-mile-) long cave contains a string of 22 lakes, separated from each other by smooth rock barriers formed by mineral deposits.

Guided tours last about an hour and begin with a trip through Bears' Corridor – so-called because of the huge number of skeletons of the prehistoric cave bear found here – before culminating with a boat trip on the first of the cave's lakes, a shallow body of water with sloping stone banks that resemble inviting beaches at first sight. For those who wish to explore more, there are longer four-hour tours, which use small dinghies to venture further into the underground lake and river system. This journey terminates at the Calvary Hall,

Did You Know?

One of the most impressive bear finds displayed in the Križna Cave is a 56-cm- (22-inch-) long skull.

where a submerged forest of stalagmites glitters beneath the crystal-clear water. This longer tour is limited to four people per day, so it is best to reserve well in advance.

Križna Cave is not fully fitted with electric lighting so visitors are supplied with portable lamps on entering the cave, making the tours through the darkness all the more atmospheric.

The temperature inside the cave remains a constant 8° C (47° F) through the year and it is advisable to wear or carry some warm clothing.

The Križna Cave is also an important habitat for bats, with seven different species nesting here during winter.

24

Pivka Park of Military History
Park vojaške zgodovine

B5 **16 km (10 miles) S of Postojna** **Times vary, check website** **parkvojaskezgodovine.si**

Occupying the former Italian and subsequently Yugoslav barracks at the southern end of Pivka village is this major collection of military artifacts. Much of the exhibition is made up of artillery pieces and tanks used by Italian and German occupiers during World War II. There is also military hardware used by the Yugoslav People's Army in the ten-day conflict of June/July 1991.

A circular walking route named the Trail of Military History (Krožna pot vojaške zgodovine) runs up and down the neighbouring hills, passing fortifications dating from the interwar era, when the area was a highly militarized zone on what was then the Italian–Yugoslav border. The whole trail takes about four hours

to negotiate, although you can choose a shorter 45-minute stretch that runs to Primož hill, site of an interwar Italian artillery fort.

Planina Cave
Planinska jama

■ B5 ■ 12 km (8 miles) NE of Postojna ☎ (041) 338 696 ☐ For tours: Jul-Aug: 5pm daily, Apr-Jun & Sep: 3pm & 5pm Sun, Oct-Mar: by appt only

The Planina Cave is one of Slovenia's most spectacular water caves. It has passage-ways carved by the subterra-nean Pivka river, which flows here from Postojna Cave, and the Rak, which flows from the Rakov Škocjan Gorge. The rivers meet inside Planina to form the Unica river, which emerges from the cave's northern end. It is an import-ant habitat for the amphibious *Proteus anguinus (p163)*, which can be seen swimming in the rivers. Tours of the cave take visitors through the huge arched tunnel carved by the Unica before ascending to the Great Hall. Deeper four-hour explorations of the cave, including dinghy trips on subterranean lakes, must be booked well in advance.

Kayaking on popular ↑ Lake Cerknica, which is fringed by reeds

Rakov Škocjan Regional Park

■ C5 ■ 7 km (5 miles) E of Postojna ■ notranjski-park.si

Rakov Škocjan is a rugged limestone canyon formed by the collapse of an under-ground tunnel carved by the rushing waters of the Rak

←
Taking a dinghy through one of the subterranean lakes in the Križna Cave

river. Parts of the tunnel still survive in the form of two rock bridges, with the delicate 40-m- (140-ft)- high arch of the Small Natural Bridge (Mali naravni most) marking the eastern end of the gorge. The lower, but much longer, Great Natural Bridge (Veliki naravni most) lies 3 km (1 mile) further down. A well-marked trail runs between the two bridges. At the far end of the Great Natural Bridge, the Rak disappears into Tkalca Cave before joining the Pivka river in the Planina Cave.

Lake Cerknica
Cerkniško jezero

■ C5 ■ 22 km (14 miles) E of Postojna ■ notranjski-park.si

Just south of the town of Cerknica is the "disappearing" Lake Cerknica, a broad karstic depression that fills with water during wet spells, especially during the spring thaw, but gradually dries as

the water seeps away into its porous limestone underlay. The lake is in a constant state of growing and shrinking, and may disappear entirely during dry summers, when it becomes a reedy marsh. At its fullest extent the lake covers an area of 26 sq km (10 sq miles).

Lake Cerknica is a popular venue for boating and fishing in spring. It is surrounded by a network of quiet country roads, which make for ideal cycling terrain. The lake's popularity with ducks, corn-crakes and wading birds has made it a major attraction for birdwatchers.

 GREAT VIEW
Lake Gazing

Of the many spectacular viewpoints around Lake Cernica, the pano-ramic vista from nearby Mount Slivnica (1,114m/ 3,655 km) is the most breathtaking. The assent itself is also a pleasant hike.

 Snežnik Castle and its perfect reflection in the glassy surface of its lake

the highest precipitation in the whole of Slovenia, which mostly falls in winter as snow – hence the name Snežnik, which translates roughly to mean snowy.

Snow remains for much of the year on the upper slopes of the 1,796-m- (5,892-ft-) high Veliki Snežnik, the cone-shaped mountain at the centre of the plateau. Despite a bare, rocky summit, Veliki Snežnik is not a difficult climb for seasoned hikers.

Veliki Snežnik is a long day's walk from both Snežnik Castle and the other main starting point, Ilirska Bistrica. Alternately, you can drive to Sviščaki, a small settlement just east of Ilirska Bistrica, which has a mountain hut, and pick up the shorter trail to the mountain from there.

The other major holiday centre on the plateau is Mašun, which is situated midway between Snežnik Castle and Veliki Snežnik. It has B&B accommodation in the local farmhouses and a floodlit ski slope during winter.

28

Snežnik Castle
Grad Snežnik

C5 **38 km (24 miles) SE of Postojna** **(01) 705 7814** **Apr–Sep: 10am–6pm daily; Oct–Mar: 10am–4pm Tue–Sun**

A Renaissance chateau rising behind picturesquely turreted walls, Snežnik Castle was owned by some of Slovenia's leading landowning families throughout the centuries.

Guided tours of the site (which are obligatory and take place every hour) lead visitors through a series of historic interiors, each filled with a rich array of period furniture. Outside, the castle's verdant landscaped park is the perfect place for a relaxing stroll.

Did You Know?

Dormice still inhabit this region in large numbers, so you're sure to spot some if exploring the woods.

The castle's former dairy now houses the **Snežnik Dormouse Museum**, which informs visitors on traditional dormouse-hunting techniques, as well as different ways to cook the animal once it is caught. There is also a display of hats fashioned from dormouse fur.

Snežnik Castle is one of the main trailheads for mountain biking, horse riding and walking on the Snežnik Plateau.

Snežnik Dormouse Museum

Grad Snežnik **(01) 705 7516** **Mid-May-Oct: 10am–noon & 3–7pm Wed–Fri, 10am–1pm & 2–7pm Sat & Sun**

29

Snežnik Plateau
Snežniška planota

C6 **40 km (25 miles) SE of Postojna** **Loz; (08) 160 2853**

The Snežnik Plateau is a typically rugged limestone landscape characterized by rocky outcrops, frequent abysses and dense forests. The plateau enjoys some of

30

Ilirska Bistrica

B6 **33 km (21 miles) S of Postojna** **From Ljubljana** **Gregorčičeva 2; www.zelenikras.si**

A quiet and uneventful town located on the road and rail route linking Ljubljana with the Croatian port of Rijeka, Ilirska Bistrica is best known as a starting point for walkers who wish to explore the nearby Snežnik Plateau.

At the centre of the town is St Peter's Church, which has a Gothic presbytery, a collection of 17th-century Baroque altars, and paintings by 20th-century artist, Tone Kralj. Around the church lies an engaging little huddle of 19th-century buildings.

The information centre in the town can help organize private accommodation here.

31

Reka River Valley

⚑ B/C6 ⚑ 37 km (23 miles) S of Postojna

Rising on the south side of Snežnik Plateau, the Reka river – which is one of the largest rivers in Slovenia – flows northwest before disappearing into the Škocjan Caves (p160), only to emerge 33 km (21 miles) later on the Italian side. To the west of Ilirska Bistrica, the river is particularly scenic.

The swift flowing waters were once used to power sawmills, such as in the **Novak Farmstead** (Novakova domačija) below Smrje village.

THE ŠKOROMATI OF HRUSICA

Located on the Brkini Plateau to the west of Ilirska Bistrica, Hrušica village is famous for preserving pre-Lenten carnival customs with pagan undertones. Revellers, known as the *škoromati*, run through the streets on the Saturday before Shrove Tuesday, clad in sheepskin jerkins and wooden masks *(right)*. They are led by the sinister *škopiti*, a black-clad figure wielding huge tongs. His job is to catch unmarried girls and smear them with ash, ensuring their fertility. On Ash Wednesday, an effigy known as the *Pust* is burned outside the village, to guarantee good fortune and healthy crops for the coming year.

The restored 19th-century mill has a waterwheel and a traditional farmhouse kitchen.

Just north of Smrje, the riverside village of Prem is a fine example of the stone-built settlements that once characterized the area. The well-preserved 13th-century **Prem Castle** (Grad Prem) offers fine views. It houses artifacts found at Bronze Age hill forts on the Brkini Plateau south of the river.

Novak Farmstead
⚑ Topolc 75C ◷ By appt
ⓦ novakov-mlin.eu

Prem Castle
◈ ⚑ Prem ◷ Apr–Jun & Sep–Oct: 10am–2pm Mon & Wed–Fri, 11am–5pm Tue, 10am–6pm Sat & Sun; Jul–Aug: 10am–7pm daily
ⓦ gradprem.si

> **The Snežnik Plateau is a typically rugged limestone landscape characterized by rocky outcrops, frequent abysses and dense forests.**

↑ Autumnal colours and an ethereal mist within a forest just outside Ilirska Bistrica

A DRIVING TOUR
GORIŠKA BRDA REGION

Length 45 km (28 miles) **Stopping-off points** The area is full of wineries; the most popular is Vinoteka Brda in Dobrovo **Terrain** There are single-lane roads in the region

Stretching northwest of Nova Gorica is the Goriška Brda region, characterized by green slopes and hilltop villages. It is one of Slovenia's foremost wine regions, famous for the light white rebula as well as international varieties such as Merlot and Chardonnay. Wine can be tasted at innumerable local establishments, ranging from big wineries in the main villages to family farmsteads out on country roads, so bring a designated driver and unwind.

Did You Know?

The Goriška Brda region is home to more than 150 wine producers.

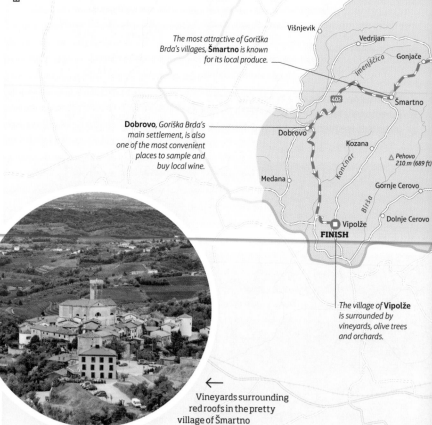

Strmec 501 m (1,643 ft)

*The most attractive of Goriška Brda's villages, **Šmartno** is known for its local produce.*

Višnjevik

Vedrijan

Gonjače

Imenjščica

402

Šmartno

Dobrovo, *Goriška Brda's main settlement, is also one of the most convenient places to sample and buy local wine.*

Kozana

△ *Pehovo 210 m (689 ft)*

Medana

Gornje Cerovo

Dolnje Cerovo

□ Vipolže
FINISH

*The village of **Vipolže** is surrounded by vineyards, olive trees and orchards.*

← Vineyards surrounding red roofs in the pretty village of Šmartno

↑ The remarkable Solkan Bridge snaking through lush forest

Locator Map

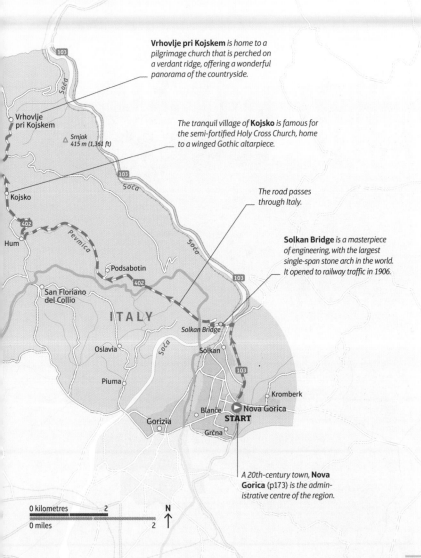

Vrhovlje pri Kojskem *is home to a pilgrimage church that is perched on a verdant ridge, offering a wonderful panorama of the countryside.*

The tranquil village of **Kojsko** *is famous for the semi-fortified Holy Cross Church, home to a winged Gothic altarpiece.*

The road passes through Italy.

Solkan Bridge *is a masterpiece of engineering, with the largest single-span stone arch in the world. It opened to railway traffic in 1906.*

Vrhovlje pri Kojskem

△ Srnjak 415 m (1,361 ft)

Kojsko

Hum

Podsabotin

San Floriano del Collio

ITALY

Oslavia

Piuma

Solkan Bridge

Solkan

Kromberk

Blanče

Nova Gorica **START**

Gorizia

Grčna

A 20th-century town, **Nova Gorica** *(p173) is the administrative centre of the region.*

0 kilometres   2
0 miles   2

N ↑

NORTHEAST SLOVENIA

The northeastern part of Slovenia incorporates the historical regions of Lower Styria and Prekmurje. Lower Styria formed the southern part of the medieval Duchy of Styria, which existed within the Holy Roman Empire initially under a succession of Bavarian and Frankish rulers. In the Middle Ages, the Lower Styrian lands were ruled by the Counts of Celje, one of the most powerful dynasties in the region at that time, whose extensive territory was not relinquished to the Habsburgs until the 15th century. In 1918 along with the rest of Slovenia, it became part of the Kingdom of Yugoslavia.

Prekmurje has close links to Hungarian culture, having been annexed by the Kingdom of Hungary in the Middle Ages. Maribor, the largest city in northeast Slovenia, developed as a market town in the Middle Ages, thriving on trade along the Drava. Following the Nazi invasion of the Kingdom of Yugoslavia in 1941, Maribor was heavily bombed by the Allies, with around half the city being destroyed. In the years since, however, it has recovered to become Slovenia's second city and a cultural powerhouse, taking the title of European Capital of Culture in 2012.

NORTHEAST SLOVENIA

Must Sees
1. Celje
2. Maribor
3. Ptuj

Experience More
4. Rogatec Open-Air Museum
5. Velenje
6. Kope
7. Slovenj Gradec
8. Roman Necropolis
9. Dravograd
10. Šentanel
11. Peca Underground Mine
12. Rogaška Slatina
13. Rogla
14. Laško
15. Žiče Monastery
16. Slovenske Konjice
17. Štatenberg Manor
18. Church of the Virgin Protectress
19. Ljutomer
20. Ormož
21. Radenci
22. Velika Polana
23. Lendava
24. Bogojina
25. Moravske Toplice
26. Murska Sobota

↑ The red-roofed town of Celje, as seen from the Old Castle

 ①

CELJE

⚐ E4 **⌖ 100 km (62 miles) N of Novo Mesto** **🚉 From Ljubljana, Maribor & Velenje** **🚌 From Ljubljana, Maribor & Murska Sobota** **ℹ Glavni trg 17; www.celje.si**

The nickame "City of Counts and Princes" seems largely inconsistent with the modest appearance of Slovenia's third-largest town. Though damage during World War II erased the town's medieval glory, Celje's riverside core still harbours appealing museums and a splendid castle.

① Glavni trg

Ringed by cafés and shaded by plane trees, this picturesque cobbled square is a favourite place for locals to relax. It developed as the administrative heart of the Old Town and is surrounded by the Baroque townhouses of wealthy citizens. The house at No 8 still retains its frescoes. A votive Marian pillar (1776) stands at the centre above statues of St Rok, protector against plague, St Florian, Catholic firefighter, and St Joseph, the patron saint of families and workers. The

pillar itself was installed two centuries ago and became the place where criminals were publicly shamed. Mounted into a townhouse behind the pillar is a tombstone from Celeia, the Roman centre over which Celje was founded.

② St Daniel's Church

⛪ Slomškov trg

Celje's principal church (Cerkev sv Danijela) stands on Slomškov trg, a square named to honour a 19th-century bishop, Anton Martin Slomšek,

who was born near Celje and beatified in 1999. This large Gothic church was built in the early 14th century to replace a smaller predecessor when Celje's wealth and power had begun to rise.

Within the church's dark, atmospheric interior are several frescoes, and there are fine tombstones of the Celje dukes in full armour in one aisle. The highlight of the church is the late-Gothic chapel – named Chapel of Our Lady of Sorrows after its medieval pietà – to the altar's left.

Located behind the church is the Water Tower, the most impressive bastion of medieval defences, so called for its riverside location.

③   Celje Regional Museum

⛪ Muzejski trg 1 **🕐 Mar-Oct: 10am-6pm Tue-Sun; Nov-Feb: 10am-6pm Tue-Sat** **🌐 pokmuz-ce.si**

Located in a Renaissance palace, the Celje Regional Museum (Pokrajinski muzej

> The Celje counts built the Old Castle's four-storey defensive Friedrich Tower, from which there are magnificent views over the city and the lush hills of the Lower Savnija Valley.

Celje) showcases the town's past, from prehistory to the early 20th century and its ducal rulers. A ghoulish case contains 18 of their skulls. The other star attraction is a painted ceiling (1600) that was uncovered during renovation of the ceremonial hall in 1926 and is so fragile that it is kept in dim light. Art historians dispute its attribution to the Dutch master, Almanach. Its trompe l'oeil is a spectacular work with guards and noblewomen gazing down from galleries that seem to fade into the distance, while images of the four seasons and battles frame the edges.

Elsewhere, rooms hold a selection of furnishings and oil paintings in styles ranging from Renaissance to Biedermeier, while other sections of the museum contain prehistoric archaeology.

Old Castle

🏠 Cesta na grad 78
🕐 Times vary, check website 🌐 grad-celje.com

The scale of one of Slovenia's largest castles, Stari grad, testifies to Celje's power under late-medieval counts. Originally a Romanesque stronghold on a sheer bluff southeast of the centre, the castle acquired its form during the late 14th century. The Celje counts built a palace and the four-storey defensive Friedrich Tower, from where there are magnificent views over the city and the lush hills of the Lower Savnija Valley. The castle is also now a hugely popular venue for concerts in the warmer summer months, as well as traditional medieval-themed events which hark back to the town's history.

Museum of Recent History

🏠 Prešernova 17 🕐 9am-5pm Tue–Fri, 9am–1pm Sat, 2–6pm Sun 🌐 muzej-nz-ce.si

This museum (Muzej novejše zgodovine), found in the Town Hall, offers an entertaining narrative of Celje from the late 19th century. Short films introduce local history and the "Street of Craftsmen" upstairs. There is also a splendid recreation of shops and ateliers with the mid-20th century with displays of tools and ephemera.

The museum also contains Herman's Den (Hermanov brlog), the only children's museum in Slovenia. This wonderful collection features more than 300 toys from all over the world.

EAT

Stari Pisker
The characterful "Old Pot" has a menu packed with meaty treats, including burgers, steaks and BBQ skewers.

🏠 Savinova ulica 1
🌐 stari-pisker.com

€€€

DRINK

Tamkoučiri
This artsy, alternative café-cum-bar offers decent coffee and a superb range of craft beers. In warmer weather, head out to the sweet little garden terrace.

🏠 Gosposka ulica 1a
📞 (04) 132 9261

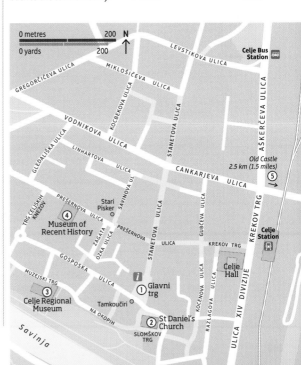

②

MARIBOR

🅰E3 🚗57 km (35 miles) NE of Celje 🚆🚌From Ljubljana, Celje & Dravograd 🚌From Ljubljana, Celje, Ptuj & Murska Sobota 🛈Partizanska 6; www.maribor-pohorje.si

Slovenia's second-largest city, Maribor occupies a strategic and picturesque location on the Drava river. Once an important trading centre, today the city has a mix of old and new architecture; the riverside quarter of Lent offers the most attractive Baroque buildings.

①

Maribor Castle and Regional Museum

🏛Grajska 2 🕐10am-6pm Tue-Sat, 10am-2pm Sun 🌐museum-mb.si

Dominating the northern end of Castle Square (Grajski trg), Maribor Castle (Mariborski grad) was built in 1478 to protect Maribor from Ottoman attacks. Once the Turkish threat receded, the castle became an aristocratic residence. Today, it is home to the Regional Museum (Pokrajinski muzej),

which displays folk costumes, military uniforms, furniture and Gothic and Baroque religious art. The 18th-century Rococo staircase here, adorned with statues, is remarkable.

②

Cathedral of St John the Baptist

🏛Slomškov trg 📞(02) 251 8432 🕐Dawn-dusk daily

Just southwest of the castle, Maribor's medieval cathedral (stolna cerkev sv Janeza

Krstnika) is predominantly Gothic in style, although a characterful Renaissance bell tower was added in 1601. The interior decorations date mostly from the Baroque period, although some exquisitely carved medieval stone stalls remain in the choir. A chapel to the left of the main altar is dedicated to Bishop Anton M Slomšek, who promoted the Slovenian language at a time when Maribor was ruled by a German-speaking elite.

③

Glavni trg

The town's long, rectangular main square took shape in the 13th century, when Maribor was emerging as a major commercial centre in the region. On its northern side is the Town Hall (Rotovž), with

Map

0 metres 200 N
0 yards 200

KREKOVA ULICA RAZLAGOVA ULICA
GRAJSKA ULICA
TRG GENERALA MAISTRA
GREGORČIČEVA ULICA
GLEDALIŠKA UL.
Maribor Castle and Regional Museum ①
Mal'ca
Railway station 550 m (600 yards)
TRG SVOBODE
SLOVENSKA ULICA
PARTIZANSKA CESTA
GRAJSKI TRG
Basilica of Our Mother of Mercy
Cathedral of St John the Baptist
SLOMŠKOV TRG ②
TRG BORISA KRAIGHERJA
GOSPOSKA ULICA
JURČIČEVA UL.
TRG LEONA ŠTUKLJA
OROŽNOVA ULICA
POŠTNA UL.
LEKARNIŠKA UL.
ROTOVŠKI TRG
Town Hall
OB JARKU
VETRINJSKA ULICA
SVETOZAREVSKA ULICA
ULICA VITA KRAIGHERJA
KOROŠKA CESTA
St Alosius's Church
③ Glavni trg
ULICA KNEZA KOCLJA
ŽIDOVSKA UL.
Old Vine Lent ④
Grill Ranca
Synagogue ⑤ The Jewish Quarter
VOJAŠNIŠKA UL.
USNJARSKA ULICA
Water Tower
Drava
Glavni most
⑥ Mariborsko Pohorje 5.5 km (3.5 miles)

Did You Know?

Maribor's Old Vine is the only plant in Slovenia with its own dedicated museum (and anthem).

↑ Attractive buildings in Maribor, lining the edge of the city's river

an onion-domed clock tower and an arcaded Renaissance courtyard at the back. In the square's centre is an ornate Baroque Plague Column (kužno znamenje), raised in 1743 to commemorate the 17th-century plague.

Lent

Downhill from the city centre is the charming riverside Lent quarter, which was once a busy port from where rafts put together from local timber began their journey along the Drava and Danube rivers.

Today, Lent is a bustling neighbourhood, its well-preserved Baroque houses home to modern art galleries, cafés and bars. Growing along the façade of one of the waterfront houses is the 400-year-old famous Old Vine (Stara trta), believed to be the oldest vine in the world. Marking Lent's western boundary is the Judges' Tower (Sodni stolp), a barrel-shaped medieval structure with a curious mansard roof. To the east is the rather peculiar 16th-century Water Tower (Vodni stolp), featuring a pentagonal ground plan and a tall, tapering roof.

The Jewish Quarter

Immediately inland from the Water Tower is the Jews' Tower (Židovski stolp), a quadrangular structure attached to a short stretch of the surviving city wall. The narrow lanes by the tower were once home to Maribor's Jewish community, who were an important presence in the city from the 13th century until their extermination by the Nazis during World War II. The beautifully restored 14th-century **Synagogue** (sinagoga) now houses an exhibition devoted to local Jewish heritage.

Synagogue

 🏠 Židovska 4 🕐 8am–4pm Mon–Fri, 9am–2pm Sun 🌐 sinagoga maribor.si

Mariborsko Pohorje

🏠 Pohorska ulica 60

Just south of the Old Town is the Zgornje Radvanje suburb, from where a cable car takes you up to the Mariborsko Pohorje massif. You can enjoy a number of outdoor activities here, with skiing and snowboarding from December to

March at the well-equipped resort of the same name, which offers 80 km (48 miles) of pistes. It is also a popular destination for walking, hiking, horse riding, cycling or simply relaxing. The well-marked 75-km (46-mile) Pohorje Biking Transversal and Bike Park Pohorje is a world cup race venue catering to mountain bikers.

EAT

Grill Ranca
Enjoy fast food, Balkan style, at this hugely popular riverside spot.

🏠 Dravska ulica 10
📞 (02) 252 5550

€€€

Mal'ca
This buzzy day-time restaurant offers five different dishes each day, two of which are always vegetarian.

🏠 Slovenska ulica 4
🕐 Sat & Sun
🌐 malcamimogrede.si

€€€

← The Church of St George rising above the close-packed buildings of Ptuj

the late-Gothic original. Statues depict the Roman emperor Trajan, who awarded Ptuj full colonial rights, and St Victorin, the town's first bishop in the early 4th century.

A statue on the votive column in the middle of Mestni trg depicts St Florian, protector against fire, as a Roman soldier. This statue is a replica of the original, which was erected in 1745 after four catastrophic fires hit the city in a span of 60 years. The column seems to be working – the inferno in 1744 was Ptuj's last.

PTUJ

F3 • 30 km (19 miles) SE of Maribor • ☐ ☐
ℹ Slovenski trg 5; www.ptuj.info

Scenically located on the banks of the Drava river, Ptuj is furnished with a wealth of monuments that testify to a history spanning two millennia. The town was founded in AD 69 and blossomed in the Middle Ages, but its influence was weakened by the Ottoman Turkish attacks. Today, Ptuj is dotted with red-tile roofs and Gothic buildings set along pretty alleyways.

① Church of St George

 Slovenski trg
📞 (02) 748 1970

Built in the 9th century over a Roman basilica, the Church of St George (Cerkev sv Jruija) is an atmospheric hybrid of late-Romanesque and Gothic styles whose walls are decorated with frescoes. The abundance of finely carved altars reveals the medieval town's wealth. The church's most acclaimed work of art, protected in a glass case in the vestibule, is a 14th-century sculpture of St George slaying the dragon.

The baptismal chapel contains a lovely 15th-century colour-saturated polyptych of the death of the Virgin Mary by Konrad Laib, a Salzburg master influenced by Italian high art.

② Mestni trg

The tidy main square, popular with locals for their morning coffee and evening drinks alike, has been the civic heart of Ptuj since medieval times. The grandest of the historic buildings on the square is the Germanic Neo-Gothic Town Hall, built in 1907 to replace

③ Minorite Monastery

 Minoritski trg
📞 (02) 748 0310

The Minorite order set up this monastery (Minoritski samostan) when they arrived in Ptuj in 1261. Having survived the purges of Joseph II in 1784 and persecution by the Nazis, the order still remains in the monastery, which possesses what is said to be the oldest Baroque façade in Slovenia. In the library is one of only three surviving New Testaments by the 16th-century Lutheran Primož Trubar, who published the first books in the Slovenian language. Visits to the library can be arranged through the tourist office.

 PICTURE PERFECT
Marvellous Monastery

Inside the Minorate Monastery is a beautiful summer refectory that offers a unique addition to any photo album. Get up close to the rich frescoes and stucco work for the best shots.

THE KURENT

Somewhere between a fertility ritual and a rite of spring, the Kurent is named for its Kurenti – scary figures who dress in sheepskins on Shrove Tuesday and gambol between houses, clanking cowbells to scare off evil and winter spirits. Spectators smash clay pots for luck and some women gift handkerchiefs to win favour with the male Kurenti.

The adjoining modern church is a replica of the one that was destroyed by Allied bombs in 1945 – only the Gothic presbytery remains of the original.

Ptuj Castle

⌂ Na gradu 1 📞 (07) 748 0360 ⏰ 10am–6pm daily (mid-Oct–Apr: to 5pm)

Salzburg archbishops built Ptuj Castle (Ptujski grad) in the 11th century. It was leased to the lords of Ptuj and made into a palace by the Leslie Dynasty in the 17th century. The lower floors house period furnishings and objets d'art, while the floors above display musical instruments, costumes of Ptuj's famous Kurent carnival and devotional art.

Orpheus Monument

⌂ Slovenski trg

This 5-m- (16-ft-) high Roman tombstone stands where it was unearthed sometime in the Middle Ages. Carved from white Pohorje marble for a 2nd-century mayor of Poetovio, and later used as a medieval pillory, this monument (Orfejev spomenik) is named after the worn relief of Orpheus, the legendary musician in Greek mythology. Carvings in the tympanum depict Selene, goddess of the moon. More modest tombstones from Poetovio are mounted around the base of the City Tower (Mestni stolp) behind, a campanile that doubled as a watchtower during Turkish raids. One wing of the polyptych shows St Hieronymus holding a model of the original church.

Dominican Monastery

⌂ Muzejski trg 1 ⏰ Apr–Sep: 10am–6pm Tue–Sun 🌐 dominikansamostan.si

Floral stucco and sgraffiti and a candy-pink colour scheme give the Dominican Monastery (Dominikanski samostan) the most joyful façade in Ptuj. The decoration was added to the original Gothic building that housed the order after it arrived in Ptuj around 1230. Inside, Gothic vaults provide an atmospheric setting. The shell of the old church itself is now a concert hall.

Mithra Shrine

⌂ 2 km (1 mile) W of Ptuj

A pavilion, signposted off Mariborska cesta, shelters the remains of the 3rd-century Mithra Shrine. Its finest relief depicts the Roman sun god Mithras as he sacrifices a bull to create the world. Prize finds are displayed in the Dominican Monastery.

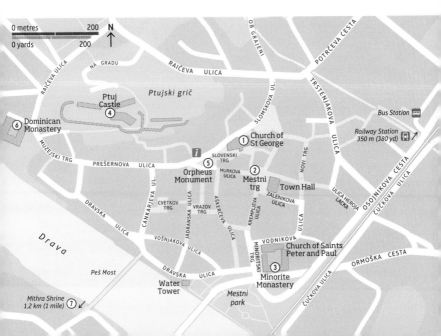

EXPERIENCE MORE

Rogatec Open-Air Museum

Muzej na prostem Rogatec

F3 ⏱ 8 km (5 miles) NE of Rogaška Slatina; Ptujska cesta 23 🚉🚌 From Rogaška Slatina ⏱ Apr–Nov: 10am–6pm Tue–Sun 🌐 rogatec.si

The market town of Rogatec is home to the largest open-air museum in Slovenia. Ten agricultural buildings gathered from Štajerska in northern Slovenia have been rebuilt to simulate a village, providing an insight into rural and religious folk culture between the 18th and early 20th centuries.

The centrepiece cottage – the boyhood home of Slovenian poet Jože Šmit (1922–2004) – has hollowed tree trunks for gutters. The windows of the room in the *hiška* (home) where the older daughters of the house slept have hinged iron grilles to deter amorous suitors. Traditionally, the hinges were left unoiled so that it would be difficult to open the windows.

The village also has a *toplar* (double hayrack) unique to Slovenian rustic architecture, and a 1930s grocer's store selling traditional souvenirs.

Demonstrations of domestic crafts such as baking, smithery and basket-weaving from corn husks are sometimes staged late on Friday or Saturday afternoons during the high season.

Velenje

D3 ⏱ 24 km (15 miles) NW of Celje 🚉🚌 From Celje and Ljubljana 🛈 Stari trg 3; www.velenje-tourism.si

Slovenia's fifth-largest town and one of the newest, Velenje is an architectural relic of Communist Yugoslavia. It grew rapidly in the 1950s as the country's coal mining expanded. The town architect thought that since miners spent days underground, the town should be filled with light and space: something achieved via tower blocks and squares. Though Velenje shed its formal name of Titovo Velenje (Tito's Velenje) in 1990, the city's main square Titov trg is still home to a statue of Yugoslav Communist revolutionary Josip Broz Tito.

A 13th-century stronghold that used to control trading routes, **Velenje Castle** (Velenjski grad) crowns a low hill to the south of town. The **Velenje Museum** (Muzej Velenje) hosts 10 different collections. Exhibits include sacral and folk works, African art and ritual objects, and modern Slovenian art.

Rural housing and *(inset)* stark interiors at the Rogatec Open-Air Museum ↓

Skiers descending a gently pisted slope in Kope's resort

The **Coal Mining Museum of Slovenia** (Muzej premogovništva Slovenije) offers tours to explore the shafts below.

Velenje Castle & Museum

⊛ 🏠 Ljubljanska cesta 54
🕐 10am–6pm Tue–Sun
🌐 muzej.velenje.si

Coal Mining Museum of Slovenia

⊛⊛⊛⊛ 🏠 Stari Jašek, Koroška cesta 🕐 9am–4:30pm Tue–Sat 🌐 muzej.rlv.si

---

Kope

🅰 E3 🏠 63 km (39 miles) N of Celje 🛈 Glavni trg 21, Slovenj Gradec; www.pohorje.org

A narrow road running east from Slovenj Gradec ascends slowly through villages to this small resort among the highest hills of the Pohorje massif. It is a popular destination for skiing as the snow cover can last from November to late spring, while in summer, hikers and families come for the clean, cool air and easy walking trails.

Hour-long walks from a car park at an altitude of 1,370 m (4,500 ft) ascend to the neighbouring peaks, Velika Kopa and Črni vrh. From the latter, at 1,540 m (5,060 ft), the path continues to hilltops Mali Črni vrh and Ribniški vrh to reach a pretty alpine lake covered with waterlilies.

Slovenj Gradec

🅰 D3 🏠 51 km (32 miles) NW of Celje 🚌 From Celje and Velenje 🛈 Glavni trg 24; www.slovenjgradec.si

Reputedly the coldest town in Slovenia – 40 years ago, schoolchildren would be sent home because the ink froze in their pens – this small town is better known as the birthplace of composer Hugo Wolf (1860–1903) and for its artistic heritage that dates to the 18th century, when a local workshop made sacred sculpture. A Modernist arts collective in the 1930s spawned the **Gallery of Fine Arts** (Galerija likovnih umetnosti), a pastel-tinted medieval building with modern sculpture. The gallery hosts works by local 20th-century artists such as Jože Tisnikar and international

names such as Ossip Zadkine, a Russian-born, Paris-educated Cubist. The building was originally the town hall and the exhibits of regional archaeology in the incorporated **Slovenj Gradec Museum** (Koroški pokrajinski muzej) are displayed in old cells. These include glass and jewellery from Colatio, a 3rd-century Roman settlement that preceded Slovenj Gradec.

The Church of St Elizabeth (Cerkev sv Elizabete) lies on Trg svobode, off Glavni trg. Its sombre, late-Romanesque exterior conceals a late-Gothic interior with Baroque furnishings. Austrian sculptor Johan Jacob Schoy (1686–1732) carved an altar so large it just squeezes into the presbytery while the altarpiece is by Franz Strauss, leading artist of the town's Baroque workshop.

The adjacent Church of the Holy Spirit (Cerkev sv Duha) contains fragments of Roman tombstone embedded in its walls and Gothic frescoes of Christ's martyrdom. The tourist office can provide access when mass is not in progress.

Gallery of Fine Arts

⊛⊛ 🏠 Glavni trg 24 🕐 9am–6pm Tue–Fri, 10am–1pm & 2–5pm Sat & Sun 🌐 glu-sg.si

Slovenj Gradec Museum

⊛⊛ 🏠 Glavni trg 24 🕐 9am–6pm Tue–Fri, 10am–1pm & 2–5pm Sat & Sun 🌐 kpm.si

---

JOŽE TISNIKAR (1928-98)

Few Slovenian painters are as instantly recognizable as Jože Tisnikar. After an impoverished childhood as one of eight children to an alcoholic father, he took a job working with cadavers in the pathology department of Slovenj Gradec hospital. The experience shaped his work. *Autopsy* (1955) established the style of the self-taught artist: haunted and bleak.

Crows under the Cross (1974) by Tisnikar, typical of his style

↑ Simple details on a tomb within the Roman Necropolis

The richest carving adorns the mausoleum of the Ennius family. The style of its reliefs dates it back to the mid-1st century AD. It is fronted by an image of Europa being carried out to sea by Zeus disguised as a bull, and canopied by a richly carved baldachin are images of the Ennius family. Both monuments were created when Celje was at its most wealthy. The oldest tomb, that of Gaius Vindonius Successus, and the simple 3rd-century tomb of Statucius Secundianus, reflect the rise then wane of a rich society. A section of the old Roman road lies to the east of the cemetery.

> With good views, friendly locals and a sleepy pace of life, Šentanel is a lovely destination at which to sample rural tourism.

the Romanesque Church of St Vitus (Cerkev sv Vida), built in 1170, when Dravograd first found mention in the records.

10

Šentanel

A D2 **⌂** 78 km (49 miles) NW of Celje

This sleepy farming hamlet clusters around the Church of St Daniel, from which it gets its name, on a south-facing hillside. With good views, friendly locals and a sleepy pace of life, Šentanel is a lovely destination at which to sample rural tourism, stop overnight in a traditional alpine farmhouse or try the local cider (*mošt*) in the village-centre inns. Opposite the church are two farmsteads with a few small rooms. The village is also a popular base for some of Slovenia's finest mountain-biking trails.

8

Roman Necropolis
Rimska nekropola

A D4 **⌂** Ob rimski nekropoli 2, Šempeter, 12 km (8 miles) W of Celje **🚌** From Celje **⌚** Apr: 10am–3pm daily; May–Sep: 10am–4pm daily (Jun–Aug: to 5pm); Oct: 10am–4pm Sat & Sun **🌐** td-sempeter.si

In 1952, villagers digging in an orchard in the town of Šempeter discovered a female statue, thereby unearthing a well-preserved Roman cemetery on the former Ljubljana to Celje road. The cemetery survived the reigns of the Roman emperor Trajan and the Severi Dynasty (AD 96–235), but was abandoned around AD 270 when the Savinja river flooded. The silt preserved the 100-plus mausolea of Celeia (Celje) families, which have been reconstructed; the park is called Roman Necropolis.

The most impressive epitaph is the marble mausoleum of the Spectatii, a 8-m (26-ft) monument built for a Celje dignitary and his family. An image of Medusa at the apex was intended to protect their remains from grave-robbers, while on the base are reliefs of Roman civilization.

9

Dravograd

A D2 **⌂** 60 km (37 miles) NW of Celje **🚌** From Maribor **🚌** From Maribor, Celje, Velenje and Slovenj Gradec **ℹ** Trg 4 julija 50; www.dravograd.si

On the Austrian border, this small town wraps around the confluence of the Drava, Meža and Mislinja rivers. Its location made it strategic for rafters, who bound felled logs at its quay then transported them to Hungary, Romania and Serbia. Pleasure trips by raft (*flos*) are organized for groups.

Dravograd's name was tarnished in the last century, due to its association with a Gestapo prison in the basement of the town hall. In its five cells, punishment and torture was meted out to Slovenian resistance fighters and troublesome Russian prisoners who were forced to build a hydroelectric dam on the Drava river. The cells can be accessed, via the tourist office, during weekday office hours. Nearby in the town centre is

→ The imposing façade of the Grand Hotel Rogaška in Rogaška Slatina

Peca Underground Mine

Podzemlje Pece

D2 **46 km (29 miles)
NW of Celje; Glančnik 8,
Mežica** **From Dravograd
& Črna na Koroškem** **Park
kralja Matjaža, Center 100;
www.podzemljepece.com**

Although the Romans are
believed to have sourced lead
ore from Mount Peca, it was
not until 1665 that a mine was
dug at Mežica to extract lead
and zinc. Mining intensified in
the early 20th century and
when the mine ceased production in 1994, about 19 million tonnes (21 million tons)
of ore had been extracted.
Visitors can tour the mine by
train or by bicycle. A museum
tells of local mining life.

Rogaška Slatina

E4 **88 km (57 miles) NE
of Novo Mesto** **From Celje**
From Celje and Maribor
**Zdraviliški trg 1; www.
visit-rogaska-slatina.si**

No other Slovenian spa town
retains the air of its imperial
heyday like

Rogaška Slatina. Austro-
Hungarians acclaimed the
therapeutic power of the
town's thermal waters after
the Croatian viceroy Petar
Zrinski was cured here in
1665. The arrival of Archduke
Johann von Habsburg in 1810
hastened Rogaska Slatina's
development into a fashionable destination for Austro-
Hungarian royalty and
Viennese high society.

Its heart is the central park,
Zdraviliški trg, with manicured
lawns and flowerbeds. Here,
the Habsburg-era health spa,
Zdraviliški dom, now the Grand
Hotel Rogaška, is one of the
grandest Neo-Classical buildings in Slovenia and has a
ballroom in which composer
Franz Liszt once entertained
imperial spa-goers.

The original 19th-century
drinking temple lends its name
to Rogaška Slatina's Temple
mineral water, on sale throughout Slovenia. The focus of
many of today's visitors is the
modern drinking hall (pivnica)
at the far end of the square.
Several mineral springs,
including Donat – a potent
magnesium-rich water –
spout within this hall. The hall
also offers massages, Fango
mud treatments and
aromatherapy.

STAY

Rotovnik-Plesnik

A warm welcome awaits
at this friendly farm stay
that serves local dishes.

D3 **Legen 134 A,
Slovenj Gradec**
rotovnik-plesnik.si

Kmetija Marjanca

Take in stunning views
through floor-to-ceiling
windows at this farm.

E4 **Spodnji
Kostrivnica 5, Podplat,
3 km (2 miles) from
Rogaška Slatina**
tk-marjanca.net

Visitors can also spend time
in the **Rogaška Riviera**, a
complex of indoor and
outdoor thermal mineral-
water pools.

Rogaška Riviera
Celjska cesta 5 **Daily**
rogaska-resort.com

↑ Thermal pools beneath a vast glass roof at Laško's modern spa complex

 13

Rogla

🅰 E3 📍 36 km (22 miles) N of Celje 🚌 From Zreče
ℹ Cesta na Roglo 15, Zreče; 🖥 rogla.eu

The rounded highlands north of Slovenske Konjice are the central section of the Pohorje massif. Once home only to isolated dairy farmsteads and a cottage timber industry, the lightly forested upland is known today for its ski resort on the summit of Rogla, north of the town of Zreče. Once the snow thaws, hiking and mountain biking take over on a variety of trails through alpine meadows and pine forests.

↑ Skiing along a tree-fringed run in the ski resort of Rogla

 14

Laško

🅰 E4 📍 11 km (7 miles) S of Celje 🚉🚌 From Celje
ℹ Valvasorjev trg 1; www.lasko.info

The road to the south of Celje follows the Savinja river to this small town famous as the home of the lager, Laško pivo. It was first brewed in 1825 by the owner of a honey and mead shop that grew into one of the largest breweries in Yugoslavia. The town's brewery (pivovarna) lies to the south of the medieval town centre and houses a small museum with displays on brewing techniques. Tours include a beer tasting with the welcome accompaniment of savoury pastries.

Laško's second claim to fame is its mineral springs. The Romans, medieval missionaries and the Austro-Hungarian Emperor Franz Josef I (r 1848–1916) himself bathed in the 34° C (93° F) waters that bubble up just north of the Old Town. Today's spa resort is a modern complex named Thermana Park Laško, which features a host of indoor and outdoor pools.

The town also boasts the early Gothic Church of St Martin (Cerkev sv Martina), which has a Romanesque tower.

🔍 HIDDEN GEM
Escape Room Enigmarium Laško

Have a go at the world's first brewery-themed escape room, which was established in the same house where the town's first barrel of beer was brewed. It lasts up to an hour, and is great fun.

 15

Žiče Monastery
Žička kartuzija

🅰 E3 📍 Stare Slemene 24, Loče, 20 km (12 miles) NE of Celje 📞 (03) 759 3110
🕐 Apr-Oct: 10am-6pm Tue-Sun; Nov-Mar: 10am-4pm Thu-Sun

Celebrated for its peace and isolation in the Valley of St John, Žiče Monastery might well be the most evocative ruin in Slovenia. The Carthusian monastery was founded in 1160 – the story goes that St John appeared in a dream to the Styrian ruler Otakar III of Traungau (1124–64), who had recently returned from the Crusades, and instructed him to create a self-sufficient community. The monastery withstood Turkish raids behind high defence walls in the 15th century and prospered until its dissolution by Emperor Joseph II in 1782.

At the heart of the complex is the shell of the Romanesque Church of St John the Baptist (Cerkev sv Janeza Krstnika) and a Gothic chapel. Surrounding buildings have been restored and now house a museum with a lapidarium; the cellar of the acclaimed winemaker Zlati grič; and, in a defence tower, an apothecary that sells medicinal liquors and herbal cures prepared to ancient Carthusian recipies (open in summer only). The Gostišče Gastuž (1467) by the entrance is reputed to be Slovenia's oldest operating inn.

Slovenske Konjice

E3 **19 km (12 miles) NE of Celje** From Celje, Ljubljana and Maribor **Stari trg 29; www. slovenskekonjice.si**

Persevere through the modern suburbs and the Old Town certainly lives up to the charm suggested by Slovenske

Konjice's tagline: "City of Flowers and Wine". Historic townhouses, painted in shades of peach, cream and butterscotch with flowerbox-lined windows, stretch along the banks of a stream that is spanned by tiny bridges. A local tale explains that these early 18th-century houses survived where their medieval predecessors burned because their builders had incorporated sacred boulders from the Žiče Monastery in the walls. The village-like medieval core, Stari trg, is enchanting. At Stari trg 15, the Riemer Gallery (Galerija Riemer) displays a private collection of period furniture and art amassed by a wealthy local businessman. Tours can be organized through the tourist office.

Another attraction is the Church of St George (Cerkev sv Jurija), an unusual two-nave Gothic construction with a frescoed Baroque chapel. Beyond it is the Trebnik Manor (Dvorec Trebnik), an erstwhile 17th-century residence, which now serves as a gallery and shop where organic herbal beauty products and foods are sold.

Štatenberg Manor
Dvorec Štatenberg

E3 **Štatenberg 86, Makole, 18 km (11 miles) SW of Ptuj** **10am–10pm Wed–Sun** **dvorecstatenberg.si**

Set above the valley 9 km (6 miles) west of Ptujska Gora, this two-storey palace was commissioned by Count Ignaz Maria Attems in the early 18th century. Intended to replace a medieval castle in nearby Makole, it was designed by an Italian architect and served as a summer residence for the aristocratic Styrian family.

The four-wing palace was created in one go and has not been altered by subsequent owners. While decades of neglect have left the exterior semi-derelict, the courtyard is a delight of restrained Baroque style. There is a restaurant on the palace's ground floor. The rest of the interior, much of which is in poor condition, can only be seen on tours. The highlight is the ceremonial two-storey hall in the central wing, where the Attems held banquets and balls beneath a ceiling whose allegorical frescoes are framed by stucco work. The surrounding English-style parkland is pleasant to explore, and angling is possible.

A lush vineyard in Slovenske Konjice, known as the "City of Flowers and Wine"

18
Church of the Virgin Protectress
Cerkev Marije Zavetnice

 F3 🏛 **11 km (7 miles) SW of Ptuj** 📞 **(02) 794 4231** 🚌 **From Ptuj**

Dating from the beginning of the 15th century, the Church of the Virgin Protectress is located above Ptujska Gora village. Funded by Ptuj's Lord Bernard III, the church was fortified during Turkish incursions in the middle of the century. According to a local legend, the Virgin Mary draped her cloak over the hill as a black cloud to conceal the church from raiders – a miracle that elevated it to one of the most revered churches in Slovenia. The story is probably related to the extraordinary *Virgin as Protector* (1410) high altar, the highlight of a beautifully spacious three-nave Gothic interior. Its centrepiece depicts a host of angels lifting the Madonna's dusty green cloak to reveal a kneeling crowd sheltered beneath. Among the 82 aristocrats, clergy and commoners depicted are Bernard III with his wife Valburga, presumably the two figures on the Virgin's left staring back at viewers. The south aisle contains a superb high-Gothic baldachin that was created to canopy the tomb of Celje's Count Frederick II; the three-star crest of the Celje Dynasty – adopted in 1991 on the national flag – is just one feature within this exquisite carving. In the sanctuary, to the right of the main portal, is a finely executed Gothic fresco of St Dorothy and Jesus in the rose garden, with its donor depicted kneeling at the side.

19
Ljutomer

G3 🏛 **44 km (27 miles) NE of Ptuj** 🚌 **From Ormož and Murska Sobota** 🚌 ℹ️ **Glavni trg; www. visitjeruzalem.com**

This region to the south of the Mura river has long been associated with horse breeding; its administrative and cultural centre, Ljutomer, hosted the country's first horse-racing meet – the second in the Austro-Hungarian Empire – in 1875. Between April and September the racing society stages trotting races on two Sunday afternoons a month.

Ljutomer's heart is its spacious main square, Glavni trg, with a votive plague column of the Virgin Mary and saints Rok and Boštjan (1729). The **Ljutomer Museum** in the former town hall at the back of the square focuses on the Tabor Movement in Ljutomer (1868–71), when young Slovenian intellectuals initiated mass open-air forums (*tabors*) to rally support for a united Slovenia.

Ljutomer Museum

 🏛 **Glavni trg 2** 📞 **(02) 581 1295** 🕐 **8am–3pm Mon–Fri**

20
Ormož

G3 🏛 **23 km (14 miles) E of Ptuj** 🚌 **From Ptuj & Murska Sobota** 🚌 **From Ptuj** ℹ️ **Kolodvorska cesta 9; (02) 741 5356**

A location on a terrace abutting the Slovenian border has put Ormož on the front line throughout modern history. Between the 15th and 17th centuries, the town was attacked by Hungarians and Ottoman Turks, prompting the lords of Ormož to fortify the 13th-century castle. **Ormož Castle** retains the Romanesque tower, but the Baroque courtyard palace is the product of renovation during peacetime in the 18th century. Allegorical Classical paintings line the first floor and are the highlight of the castle's small museum, which

 ←

The incredibly ornate high altar within the Church of the Virgin Protectress

← Sunset over a tiny village near Ormož, the surrounding hillside lined with vineyards

also has displays on the town's history. The museum's exhibits include photographs from the Ten-Day War (27 June–6 July 1991) when Ormož was again back on the barricades of Slovenia as tanks of the Yugoslav Army invaded from Croatia (p56).

The countryside north of Ormož is idyllic to explore. Isolated houses are scattered atop hills whose sun-drenched slopes nurture the vineyards of one of the country's premier wine regions. Details of the wine cellars (vinska klet) are available at the tourist office.

About 11 km (7 miles) north of Ormož lies the somnolent wine village, Jeruzalem. The story goes that it was christened by German Crusaders who were reminded of the Holy City by the local hospitality. They are said to have brought

 GREAT VIEW
Jeruzalem Vineyards

Savour fabulous views of the pretty terraced vineyards that surround this hilltop village near Ljutomer – look out, too, for the klopotec, wind-powered rattles devised to scare off birds.

a pietà icon, a replica of which is on the altar of the Church of St Mary (Cerkev sv Marije).

Ormož Castle

 ⬆ Kolodvorska 9
📞 (02) 741 7290 ⏰ 8am–3pm Mon-Fri, 9am–2pm Sat

㉑

Radenci

🅰 F2 ⬆ 31 km (19 miles) N of Ptuj 🚌 From Ljutomer and Murska Sobota ⊠ sava-hotels-resorts.com

Until the arrival of a young Austrian medical student, Karl Henn, in 1833, local peasantry believed the 30–33° C (86–91° F) waters that bubbled up from the ground at Radenci were caused by the cooking of subterranean witches. Henn, by then a doctor, returned to the area in 1869 and began to export the naturally carbonated water to the imperial court in Vienna and the papal palace in Rome. The water remains popular throughout Slovenia.

The medicinal spa resort established by Henn in 1882, Zdravilišče Radenci, is located at the eastern fringe of a large wooded park. Its waters are believed to treat cardiovascular problems. Renovation has

added Terme Radenci, a spacious modern spa hotel with a wellness centre and large thermal swimming pool.

㉒

Velika Polana

🅰 G2 ⬆ 63 km (39 miles) NE of Ptuj

From late spring, this village in southeast Prekmurje hosts more breeding pairs of white storks than anywhere else in Slovenia. Around ten couples, who mate for life, migrate here, travelling 12,000 km (7,450 miles) from sub-Saharan Africa. For five months, until early August, the birds stalk frogs and small rodents in the wetlands near the Mura river and then return at dusk to their nests – large baskets of twigs perched on roofs, chimneys and even telegraph poles. These nests are repaired and expanded over successive migrations and can grow very heavy. Locals welcome the returning birds, which folklore maintains are a sign of good luck and a premonition of a new baby in the family.

Locally born writer Miško Kranjec (1908–83) eulogized this area and the storks' nests in his works.

The Church of the Holy Trinity, which sits on a hillside above Lendava

white storks. The village's main attraction is the Church of the Ascension (Cerkev Gospodovega vnebohoda), which was remodelled by Jože Plečnik (p101) in his idiosyncratic style; it is popularly known as Plečnik's Church (Plečnikova Cerkev). The church's spire is a cylindrical construction, crowned by a curious turret. The interior has been transformed from a single-nave Baroque construction into an impressive hall-like space that is broken only by a massive marble column in the centre. From this radiate four whitewashed arches, all the more impressive for their simplicity. The most curious element is the wooden high altar, which has locally made pottery dangling from it. The church's oak-beamed ceiling is covered with ceramic plates glazed in the colours of the Prekmurje countryside.

㉓ Lendava

G2 🚗72 km (45 miles) NE of Ptuj 🚌From Murska Sobota and Moravske Toplice 🛈Glavna ulica 38; www.lendava-lendva.si

Lendava is the easternmost town in Slovenia. Founded by Romans, it developed into a medieval market town under Hungarian feudal rulers. The L-shaped **Lendava Castle** (Lendavski grad) sits on a terrace above the town. It houses a municipal museum whose displays include Bronze Age archaeology and folk art from Hetés, a Hungarian region known for its textiles.

During the 19th century the town had a thriving Jewish population, and although the Jewish community was deported by Hungarian forces during World War II, the town's **Synagogue** has been restored and is now one of only two in Slovenia. Its galleried hall has a small display on local Jewish history and plays host to temporary art exhibitions.

Perched among vineyards above the town is the **Church of the Holy Trinity** (Cerkev sv Trojice). It has a mummified corpse on display, which legend

says is that of Captain Mihael Hadik, who died defending his hometown from Turkish forces in 1603 – a deed so noble that his corpse was preserved by its own sanctity. Although Hadik died in battle, his body was not found until 1733, in reality preserved by the extremely lime-rich soil in which it lay.

Lendava Castle

⊗ 📍Banffyjev trg 1 ☎(02) 578 9260 🕒8am–4pm Mon–Fri, 9am–2pm Sat

Synagogue

⊗ 📍Trg Györgya Zale 1 ☎(0) 577 6020 🕒10am–4pm Tue–Sun

Church of the Holy Trinity

⊗ 📍Lendavske gorice ☎(02) 578 8330 🕒11–11:30am, 3:30–4pm Tue–Sun 🔒During snowfall

㉔ Bogojina

G2 🚗56 km (35 miles) NE of Ptuj 🚌From Murska Sobota

Bogojina is a village of Hungarian-style L-shaped cottages, many of which are crowned by large nests of

㉕ Moravske Toplice

G2 🚗54 km (34 miles) NE of Ptuj 🚌From Murska Sobota 🛈Kranjčeva 3; www.moravske-toplice.com

Several hot-water springs were discovered on the Prekmurje plains during the search for oil in the 1960s. This is where the spa town of Moravske Toplice

Did You Know?

Artist Janez Aquila painted himself into his frescoes in Martjanci as a tonsured monk.

> **Bogojina is a village of Hungarian-style L-shaped cottages, many of which are crowned by large nests of white storks.**

was established. The mineral-rich waters here proved hugely popular with those seeking relief from rheumatism.

Every day in summer, hundreds of visitors come to the **Terme 3000** spa to take a dip in the thermal waters. The resort's complex of hotels and pools includes a medical facility, a wellness centre offering massages and saunas, and it is a popular holiday area.

The small village of Martjanci lies 2 km (1 mile) to the east of Moravske Toplice. Although its church appears to be an anonymous Gothic construction, its presbytery contains the finest medieval frescoes in the Prekmurje area. They were painted in 1392 by the artist Janez Aquila, and are intended to represent a heavenly Jerusalem. Apostles – St Peter with the key to the pearly gates, St James with his

staff and shell of pilgrimage and St George spearing a dragon – are depicted mingling with dying Crusaders while saints look on from the roof.

Terme 3000
🏠 Kranjčeva ulica 12 🕐 Daily
🌐 sava-hotels-resorts.com

26
Murska Sobota

🅰 G2 📍 47 km (29 miles) NE of Ptuj 🚋 From Ljubljana & Ptuj 🚌 From Radenci, Maribor & Celje
ℹ Slovenska ulica 41; www.visitmurskasobota.si

Until it was absorbed into the Kingdom of Serbs, Croats and Slovenes in 1919, Murska Sobota was a backwater of Hungary, and therefore has few historical monuments. Today, the town is the capital of the Prekmurje region. The **Museum of Pomurje** (Pomurski muzej) in Murska Sobota Castle (Murski grad)

is worth a visit. An erstwhile residence of the counts of Murska Sobota, this massively turreted Renaissance palace sits in an English-style parkland in the centre of the town. The restored Baroque festive hall is arguably the highlight among the museum's ethnology and archaeology exhibits. One section has black pottery jugs crafted by potters in the northeastern village of Filovci, and displays on customs of the region. One room details the liberation of Murska Sobota by Russia, after a second Hungarian occupation at the end of World War II. A Soviet-style victory monument in the town centre celebrates the Red Army's arrival in April 1945.

Museum of Pomurje
🎟 🏠 Trubarjev drevored 4 🕐 9am–5pm Tue–Fri, 9am–1pm Sat, 2–6pm Sun 🌐 pomurski-muzej.si

The Museum of Pomurje and *(inset)* its interiors in Murska Sobota ↓

A CYCLING TOUR
THE DRAVA

Length 30 km (18 miles) **Stopping-off point** Gostilna Modra frankinja is a pleasant restaurant to the north of Miklavž na Dravskem polju **Terrain** Mostly level, asphalt trails and quiet roads, with only 45 m (147 ft) of ascent, make this easy cycling **Nearest stations** Maribor and Ptuj

The epic Drava Cycle Route runs through a total of four countries in Europe: Italy, Austria, Slovenia and Croatia. The lenghty 145 km (90 miles) section that crosses Slovenia is split into six stages between Dravograd, on the border with Austria, and Ormož, on the border of Croatia. The stage between Maribor and Ptuj is one of the most beautiful sections. Conveniently reached by train, this rewarding route offers easy cycling along the right bank of the Drava and takes in a succession of natural and cultural sites.

START
Maribor
Lent
Malečnik
Brezje
Tezno
Miklavž na
Dravskem polju
Rogoza
Skoke

*Begin this tour in Slovenia's second-largest city, **Maribor** (p188), which sits on the banks of the River Drava, between the forests of Pohorje and the vineyards of Slovenske gorice.*

*Lent, the oldest part of Maribor, is home to the **Old Vine** – which, at over 400 years old, is believed to be the oldest grapevine in the world.*

*At **Miklavž na Dravskem polju**, stop by the Roman burial mound, which dates from around AD 100. These tombs contained urns holding the ashes of the deceased.*

↑ Cycling past the verdant vineyards which overlook the city of Maribor, the beginning of this scenic tour

0 kilometres   3
0 miles   3

N
↑

Fairy lights draped over a colourful street in the historic town of Ptuj ↑

Follow the gentle course of the **River Drava**, which passes through Slovenia on its way to join the River Danube, near Osijek in Croatia.

INSIDER TIP
Go off road

If you're feeling a bit more adventurous, return to Maribor along the more hilly left bank of the river, which features 263 m (863 ft) of ascent and only half the route on paved roads.

Rest your legs at this low-lying **floodplain** alongside the Drava; it's a Natura 2000 Site, where some 250 species of birds have been recorded.

Finish your cycle in **Ptuj** (p190), one of the oldest towns in Slovenia; there's a great viewpoint of Ptuj's castle if you cross the footbridge to Drava's left bank.

A short detour takes you to **Hajdina**, which was once a centre of Mithraism (a cult worshipping the Indo-Iranian deity Mithras). A shrine found here is the oldest known temple dedicated to Mithras in this part of the Roman world.

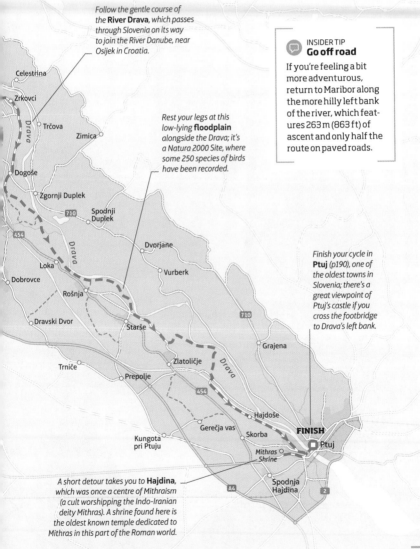

Celestrina
Zrkovci
Trčova
Zimica
Drava
Dogoše
Zgornji Duplek
Spodnji Duplek
710
454
Dvorjane
Loka
Drava
Vurberk
Dobrovce
Rošnja
Dravski Dvor
Starše
710
Grajena
Trniče
Zlatoličje
Drava
Prepolje
454
Hajdoše
Gerečja vas
FINISH
Kungota pri Ptuju
Skorba
Ptuj
Mithras Shrine
Spodnja Hajdina
A4
2

Autumn colours within one of southeast Slovenia's forests

SOUTHEAST SLOVENIA

The historical region of Lower Carniola, which corresponds with the southeast area of Slovenia, was part of the Windic March that was first mentioned in the 7th century. Later it became part of the Duchy of Carniola, a state within the Holy Roman Empire that was under Habsburg rule from the 14th century, and which was divided in the 17th century into Upper, Inner and Lower Carniola. The town of Novo Mesto, with its carefully preserved Old Town, was founded in the 14th century and was the main cultural centre of Lower Carniola. It is also an important archaeological site, with numerous Iron Age objects having been discovered there.

In 1918 Lower Carniola became part of the Kingdom of Yugoslavia, along with the rest of modern Slovenia. From around 1330, the Kočevje region was settled by Gottschee Germans, who brought with them their own culture and a distinctive Bavarian dialect. They lived peacefully in the area for some 600 years, until their forced resettlement by the Nazis during Hitler's occupation of Slovenia in the 1940s.

Throughout the 20th century, southeast Slovenia remained largely untouched by the rapid industrialization taking place elsewhere in the country. As a result, the region has retained its rural charm and today its unspoilt forests and sweeping valleys offer visitors a peaceful retreat.

Gornji Grad

Šempeter   Žalec

Ljubljana Jože
Pučnik Airport

Kamnik

Trojane

A1

Izlake   Trbovlje

104

A2

Domžale

Moravče   Litija   Podkraj

108

Zidani Most

Ljubljana   Radeče

POSAVJE

Budna Vas

LJUBLJANA
p58

Šmartno

A2

417   Gabrovka   738

Grosuplje   448   Ivančna
Gorica

416

Rakitna   448   A2   Mirna   Mokrono

216   Muljava   Luža   **GALLERY OF
NAIVE ARTISTS**
Trebnje   **13**

650

106   Velike
Lašče   Podgorica   **ŽUŽEMBERK 6**   Dobrava   651

648   649   Mala Bučna vas

106   Žlebič   Žvrče   **D O L E N J S K A**   **NOVO MESTO 7**

419

**CHURCH OF THE
ASSUMPTION 3**   Prevole   Smuka   216

4 RIBNICA   Stari Log   **2**   **11 DOLENJSKE
TOPLICE**

**COASTAL
SLOVENIA AND
THE KARST**
p150   Dolenja vas   106   **KOČEVSKI
ROG**   Mozelj

214   *Baza 20*

Koblarji   *Veliki Rog
1,099 m (3,605 ft)*   216

653   Podpreska   Grčarice   Črnošnjice   Semič

655   **1 KOČEVJE**   218

Čabar   Gotenica   Livold

Kočevska
Reka   106   Mozelj   217   **ČRNOMELJ 8**

32   Brezovica

Osilnica   Ribjek   Briga   **KOLPA
VALLEY**   Stari trg   218

657   **5**   919

C R O A T I A   3

Delnice

A1   Vrbovsko   42

**SOUTHEAST
SLOVENIA**

0 kilometres   10

0 miles   10   N

NORTHEAST
SLOVENIA
p182

SOUTHEAST
SLOVENIA

Experience

The pleasant town of Kočevje, its buildings reflected in a still lake

EXPERIENCE

Kočevje

🗺️ D6 📍 17 km (11 miles) SE of Ribnica 🚍 From Ljubljana and Novo Mesto 🌐 kocevsko.com

During World War II, the Kočevski Rog plateau was a wellspring of Partisan Resistance. Kočevje, on the Kočevski Rog, hosted the inaugural assembly of the Delegates of the Slovenian Nation. This assembly, held between 1 and 3 October 1943, effectively led to the birth of the modern Slovenian nation.

The parliament was held at Šeškov dom, which is now the **Regional Museum** (Pokrajinski muzej). The hall where the delegates convened bears a banner that reads *Narod si bo pisal sodbo sam* (The nation shall choose its fate alone). It also displays superb reportage-style sketches of the assembly as well as of the Partisan Resistance by the 20th-century Novo Mesto-born artist, Božidar Jakac. A section in the museum covers the lifestyles and the sudden flight of the Germanic Gottscheer population from Kočevski Rog in 1941.

Another memento of partisan activity is the heroic monument to the Communist struggle, erected postwar in the central square.

Regional Museum

⊛ 🏛️ Prešernova 11 📞 (051) 269 972 🕐 8am-3pm Mon-Fri, 10am-1pm Sat 🌐 pmk-kocevje.si

Kočevski Rog

🗺️ D5 📍 37 km (23 miles) SE of Ribnica 🌐 kocevsko.com

The limestone plateau east of Kočevje is cloaked in one of Europe's last virgin forests, its pine and beech woods home to brown bears, wolves and lynx. Habsburg rulers resettled German immigrants, known as Gottscheers, in this remote region from the 14th century. The immigrants made the area one of the most developed in the region by the early 20th century but fled fearing reprisals at the outbreak of World War II.

The Partisan Resistance set up camp here in 1943 and established Baza 20, located 7 km (4 miles) west of the town of Dolenjske Toplice *(p213)*. Concealed in limestone depressions, this nerve centre for the anti-Fascist struggle was never discovered despite several attempts by the Nazis, and is preserved as the only serving headquarters of European wartime resistance. At its peak, around 200 people lived and worked in the 26 huts, which contained a

> **The limestone plateau east of Kočevje is cloaked in one of Europe's last virgin forests, its pine and beech woods home to brown bears, wolves and lynx.**

Assumption, the most revered pilgrimage church of the Dolenjska region. The church's octagonal design, which is fronted by a curious arcade and capped with a lantern, introduced the Lombardy Mannerist style to Slovenia and was later copied throughout Dolenjska. The frescoed Holy Steps were added to the rear of the church in 1780 to accommodate the flood of pilgrims.

The church's plain interior only heightens the impact of the spectacular Baroque furnishings decorated in shades of ruby, emerald and gilt. The carved high altar by the 17th-century sculptor Jurij Scarnos is especially rich – a riot of gilded carvings on which Mary is lifted heavenwards by a flock of cherubs.

hospital, workshops, a printing press and barracks. All but two display boards, are empty, and yet the silent forest makes the visit a haunting experience.

The base is now tainted by the partisans' massacre of thousands of pro-German Slovene Home Guard in the forest at the end of the war. Their mass graves were a secret until the 1970s and the exact number of people executed remains unknown. Tours are available April through October.

❸
Church of the Assumption
Cerkev Marijinega Vnebovzetja

🗺 C5 🚗 6 km (4 miles) W of Ribnica; Nova Štifta 3 📞 (01) 836 9943

Perched on a hill and shaded by ancient linden trees in the tranquil farming village of Nova Štifta is the mid-17th-century Church of the

to trade in his territory in 1492. As a result, peddlers hawked locally made spoons, butter pats, wicker sieves, wooden buckets and even toothpicks throughout the Habsburg Empire.

A fascinating collection of woodcraft as well as displays on the peddlers' lifestyle are highlights of the Municipal Museum in **Ribnica Castle** (Grad Ribnica), a restored Renaissance stronghold situated on a river islet. The town is also an excellent spot to pick up some handcrafted souvenirs, and visitors can purchase such items at the tourist office.

Located in front of the castle is the Church of St Stephen (Cerkev sv Štefana). Its two bell towers, crowned with Classically inspired obelisks and pediments, were designed by the Modernist architect Jože Plečnik (p101).

Ribnica Castle
⊘ 🗺 Škrabčev trg 40 📞 (01) 836 9335 🕙 10am–1pm, 4–7pm Tue–Sun

❹
Ribnica

🗺 C5 🚗 43 km (27 miles) SE of Ljubljana 🚆 From Ljubljana 🛈 Cesta na Ugar 6; www.visitdolenjska.eu

The modest market town of Ribnica is the oldest settlement of western Dolenjska, and has long been renowned for its woodcraft. The town's cottage industry flourished when, in an attempt to restore prosperity after Turkish raids, the Austrian Emperor Frederick III (r 1452–93) gave Ribnica free licence

A basket-maker at work within one of Ribnica's markets

↑ Kolpa river winding through the scenic green valley of the same name

5
Kolpa Valley

🅰D6 🚗49 km (31 miles) S of Ribnica 🛈Osilnica 16; www.osilnica.si

Due to its natural beauty and the fact that it is one of the cleanest – and, in summer, warmest – rivers in Europe, this tranquil river valley is a favourite holiday destination among Slovenians. Walking and fishing are popular, as is

rafting on the gentle rapids on the section that snakes along the Croatian border. The hub of all the activity is Osilnica, 18 km (11 miles) west of the border crossing. It has the only bank and super-market in the area, as well as the Stane Jarm Gallery (Galerija Staneta Jarma), featuring works of local sculptor Stane Jarm (1931–2011). Gallery visits can be organized at the tourist office.

East of Osilnica, in Ribjek, the diminutive Church of St Egidius (Cerkev sv Egidija) is a pretty shingle-roofed structure dating from 1681, with naive frescoes and painted glass windows, a traditional Slovenian folk art. It is said that the guard depicted on the right of the high altar is a commandant who fought in one of the many Turkish incursions of the 16th century.

Another folk hero of the valley is Peter Klepec, a shep-herd boy who is said to have been given superhuman strength by local fairies. Legend relates that he uprooted the largest tree in the valley to defeat Turkish forces. This is depicted in a roadside sculpture by Stane

RAFTING ON THE KOLPA

The clear Kolpa river provides delightful opportunities for rafting between April and September. While rafting on small whitewater rapids is possible early in the season, tranquil trips on inflatable rafts or canoes take prece-dence in midsummer; the river is at its swiftest between Stari trg and Vinica. Hotel Kovač in Osilnica and Tine & Co on Stari trg organize rafting trips.

Jarm a short distance west of Ribjek; the figure wields a tree and glares eastwards.

6
Žužemberk

🅰D5 🚗24 km (15 miles) W of Novo Mesto 🚌From Ljubljana and Novo Mesto 🆆zuzemberk.si

The geographical and administrative hub of the broad Krka river valley, this market town was built around a defence tower in the Middle Ages. **Žužemberk Castle** (Grad Žužemberk) was built in the 16th century by the Auersperg princes and retained offices, a court and prison cells until it began to collapse in 1893. It was reduced to a shell in 1945, but restoration, ongoing since the 1960s, has returned some of the visual impact of its five circular bastions. The castle now serves as a venue for concerts between June and September.

Žužemberk Castle
🏛Grajski trg 1 📞(07) 388 5180 🕐Jul & Aug: 10am–6pm Sat & Sun

7

Novo Mesto

🅐D5 🚗58 km (36 miles) E of Ribnica 🚆From Ljubljana 🚌From Dolenjske Toplice & Ljubljana 🛈Glavni trg 11; www.visit novomesto.si

Located on the banks of the Krka river, Novo Mesto is the largest city in southeastern Slovenia and the capital of Dolenjska region. Although its name literally means New Town, historical evidence suggests that a settlement has occupied this spot since prehistory. Today's city was founded in 1365 by the Habsburg Archduke Rudolph IV (1339–65), who originally christened it Rudolphswert. Novo Mesto blossomed into an important trading centre in the Middle Ages, and then into an industrial centre.

The modernity of the city's outskirts has not affected its historic centre. The oldest site in Novo Mesto is the Church of St Nicholas (Cerkev sv Nikolaja), built at the highest point on the river promontory. It features an altarpiece by the Venetian Renaissance artist Tintoretto (1518–94), as well as Slovenia's only Gothic crypt, built to prop up the presbytery and now a repository for bishops' tombstones.

The grand attraction of the town, however, is the Dolenjska Museum (Dolenjski muzej) beyond the church, which holds some of the richest ancient archaeological exhibits in the country. Particularly outstanding are the grave finds of Celtic Hallstatt tribes of the late Iron Age, notably the armour of a high-ranking warrior, as well as exceptional situlae (bronze cremation urns) forged with vivacious images of warriors and hunters. An adjacent building showcases exhibits of regional ethnography.

Glavni trg, the former merchant centre, is a picturesque cobbled thoroughfare with several cafés and, at the centre, the 1903 Town Hall (Rotovž). The Franciscan St Leonard's Church (Fračiškanskan cerkev sv Lenarta), a block behind the Town Hall, has a Secessionist and Neo-Gothic façade and houses illuminated manuscripts in the attached library; the tourist office can arrange visits.

At the end of Glavni trg is **Jakčev House** (Jakčev dom), a gallery of works by the artist Božidar Jakac who was born in this riverside quarter. Displays rotate, but include charming images of Novo Mesto and the Dolenjska countryside as well as lively sketches made when the artist travelled to Europe and America in the 1920s and 30s.

Dolenjska Museum

♿ 🏛Muzejska ulica 7 🕐Apr-Oct: 9am–6pm Tue-Sat, 2–6pm Sun; Nov-Mar: 9am-4pm Tue-Sat, 2-5pm Sun 🌐dolenjskimuzej.si

Jakčev House

♿ 🏛Sokolska ulica 1 📞(07) 373 1131 🕐10am-6pm Tue-Sat

↑ Charming painted houses in Novo Mesto, right on the bank of the Krka river

8 Črnomelj

D6 **33 km (21 miles)**
S of Novo Mesto **From
Ljubljana** **From Metlika
and Novo Mesto** **Trg
svobode 3; www.
belakrajina.si**

The administrative capital of
the Bela Krajina region is celebrated for a wonderful folk
festival that attracts dancers
and musicians from across
Slovenia, as well as for its pre-
Roman history. Jurjevanje is
the country's oldest folklore
festival, and is celebrated with
bonfires in late June every year.

Črnomelj's quaint **Town
Museum** (Mestna muzejska)
displays some superb finds
from Roman times through
to the Middle Ages, including
a stunning two-handed sword
recovered from the nearby
Lahinja river. The Church of
St Peter (Cerkev sv Petra),
located diagonally opposite
Črnomelj Castle (which now
houses a tourist information
bureau), is worth a visit for its
collection of Roman tomb-
stone fragments located near
the choir.

Town Museum

Ulica Mirana Jarca 3
8am–4pm Tue–Fri
muzej-crnomelj.si

9 Pleterje Monastery
Samostan Pleterje

E5 **17 km (11 miles)**
E of Novo Mesto; Drča 1,
Šentjernej **kartuzija-
pleterje.si**

The Carthusian order was
permitted by the Count of
Celje to found a monastery in
this remote location in 1407.
Today, white-cloaked monks
remain in the monastery
despite Turkish raids in the
16th century and the order's
dissolution by Emperor
Joseph II in 1784; the buildings
were reclaimed in 1899. The
monastery is screened by a
high wall and visitors have
access only to the Gothic
Church of the Holy Trinity
(Cerkev sv Trojice) – bare but
for a medieval rood screen –
and a shop that sells fruit
brandies, wines, honey and
beeswax candles made
by the monks.

In an attempt to deflect
attention from the monastery,
an **Open-Air Museum**
(Pleterje Skansen) was built
in an adjacent field. Historic
buildings from the region
were rebuilt here to recreate a
traditional farmstead, centred
around a snug 19th-century
cottage with a "black kitchen"
hung with smoke-cured

**INSIDER TIP
Pleterje Way**

For a different
perspective on the
Pleterje Monastery and
its surroundings, walk
the Pleterje Way, an
easy, 3-km- (2-mile-)
long circular footpath
that skirts the hills
above the complex.

meats and cabin-like
bedrooms with corn-sheaf
mattresses. A *toplar*, or
double hayrack, and a
small farmyard of animals
complete the picture.

Open-Air Museum

Drča 1, Šentjernej
**Apr–Nov: 10am–5pm daily;
Dec–Mar: 10am–4pm daily**
skansen.si

10 Metlika

E5 **27 km (17 miles)**
SE of Novo Mesto **From
Novo Mesto and Črnomelj**
**Metlika Castle, Trg
svobode 4; www.metlika-
turizem.si**

Set in lovely countryside, this
wine-producing town near the
Kolpa river is the most picturesque in the Bela Krajina
region. Given the historic
architecture in its town centre,
it is hard to believe the town
was frequently attacked and
occupied by Turkish forces in
the 15th and 16th centuries,
and gutted by fire in 1705.

During the Turkish raids,
Metlika Castle (Grad Metlika)
was a Renaissance fortress;
today's aristocratic manor is
a result of renovation in the
18th century. A wing of the
castle houses the **Bela Krajina
Museum** (Belokranjski muzej),
which has displays on the
region. An audiovisual slide-
show introduces the themes –
local history, notably Hallstatt
grave finds and Roman
remains excavated near

The simple exterior of the Church of St Peter,
a parish church in Črnomelj

One of the many thermal pools at the Balnea Wellness Centre in Dolenjske Toplice

Črnomelj; and rural lifestyles and crafts, including winemaking and displays of the white embroidered folk costume after which Bela Krajina (literally, White Carniola), according to one theory, is named. The cellars house a wine bar serving local wines. Next to the castle, the Slovenian Firefighting Museum (Slovenski gasilski muzej) holds a wonderful selection of helmets, uniforms and engines, honouring the fact that the country's first fire brigade was established here in Metlika in 1869.

The heart of the Old Town is Mestni trg, a pretty square with small, pastel-coloured houses. At the square's end, fronted by the Maltese crosses of the Teutonic Knights and with a fresco of the Last Judgment, is the Church of St Nicholas (Cerkev sv Nikolaja).

Located just over 2 km (1 mile) east of Metlika in Rosalnice are the Tri Fare (literally, Three Parishes) – a trio of Gothic pilgrimage churches set side by side and enclosed within a low wall. Historians speculate that the churches may have been built to cater to a mixed denomination of Croats, Slovenians and Greek Orthodox worshippers, or to cope with a surge in pilgrims in the early 1500s.

Both the largest and smallest of the churches, the Lady of Our Sorrows and Ecce Hommó respectively, contain fine Baroque frescoes. The churches are usually locked; it is best to consult the tourist office in Metlika for the keys.

Bela Krajina Museum
⊛ ⌂ Trg svobode 4 ◷ 9am-5pm Mon-Sat, 10am-2pm Sun 🌐 belokranjski-muzej.si

Dolenjske Toplice

🅐 D5 ⌂ 13 km (8 miles) SW of Novo Mesto 🚌 From Novo Mesto 🚹 Sokolski trg 4; www.visitdolenjska.eu

The oldest medicinal spa resort in Slovenia, Dolenjske Toplice lies at the foot of the Kočevski Rog plateau. Slovenian chronicler Janez Vajkard Valvasor *(p117)* recorded tourists coming to bathe in its thermal spring waters in the mid-1600s, when the Auersperg princes promoted its warm and mud baths. The small town prospered at the close of the 19th century as a fashionable health resort of the Austro-Hungarian Empire.

Today, Dolenjske Toplice remains popular with visitors who come for medicinal cures; the 36° C (96.8° F) calcium-rich water is said to work wonders for rheumatism. Recreational visitors come to the Balnea Wellness Centre, which has an impressive complex of pools, saunas and massage rooms. The surroundings, which include a lovely and ancient forest, are also very pleasant.

SPAS IN SOUTHEASTERN SLOVENIA

Slovenia has an unexpectedly large number of natural thermal spas, the majority of which are located in the eastern half of the country - in Štajerska (Lower Styria), Pomurje and Dolenjska (Lower Carniola). Set amid a fairy-tale-like landscape of castles and vineyards, many of these spas have an impressively long history; the baths at Dolenjske Toplice, which were built in the mid-17th century. Terme Čatež is the largest spa resort in Slovenia, with guests able to wander between 11 thermal springs and 12,000 sq m (129,000 sq ft) of outdoor pools.

EAT

Domačija Haler
This convivial roadside restaurant-pub offers a lengthy menu of grilled meats. There's also a decent range of beers from their own on-site brewery.

 E4 Olimje 6, Podčetrtek haler-sp.si

€€€

Gostišče Amon
Expect fine wine and first-rate food at this rustically designed spot, where the tables and chairs have been culled from old wine presses and barrels.

 E4 Olimje 24, Podčetrtek amon.si

€€€

Ošterija Debeluh
This beautifully decorated restaurant is renowned for its top-quality menu, which features delicately balanced meals such as roast duck with peaches.

 E5 Trg Izgnancev 7, Brežice debeluh.si

€€€

Gostilna Muller
Perched over the peaceful Lahinja river, this friendly restaurant is a popular venue among townsfolk. Its location near the Croatian border ensures that grilled meats dominate the locally sourced menu.

 D6 Ločka cesta 6, Črnomelj (07) 356 7200

€€€

↑ Rows of yellow-hued vines line the Bizeljsko-sremiška Wine Road at dawn

12
Bizeljsko-sremiška Wine Road
Bizeljsko-sremiški vinorodni okoliš

F4 51 km (32 miles) NE of Novo Mesto Cesta prvih borcev 22, Brežice; www.discoverbrezice.com

The lower Sava Valley area, north of Brežice, is known for excellent sparkling and blended white wines cultivated in sandy, mineral-rich soils. The greatest concentration of winemakers lies north of Brežice, around the villages of Stara vas, Brezovica and Bizeljsko. **Istenič** at Stara vas is one of Slovenia's premier sparkling wine producers and organizes cellar tours and tastings. A local attraction are the repnice cellars, cave-like sandstone cellars used by many winemakers. These were dug as natural refrigerators for farmers' crops, but their constant 6–8° C (43–47° F) temperatures and humidity proved ideal for laying down wines. Most of the repnice vineyards are in Brezovica. The cellars also give refuge to bee-eating birds, which can be seen nesting between May and July near Bizeljsko.

Istenič
 Stara vas 7 1–8pm Mon-Thu, 1–10pm Fri, noon–10pm Sat, 10am–8pm Sun; book in advance istenic.si

13
Gallery of Naive Artists
Galerija likovnih samorastnikov

D5 Goliev trg 1, Trebnje, 20 km (13 miles) NW of Novo Mesto From Novo Mesto From Novo Mesto & Ljubljana May-Sep: 10am-7pm Tue-Fri, 2–7pm Sat; Oct-Apr: 10am-6pm Tue-Fri, 2–6pm Sat galerijatrebnje.si

The otherwise anonymous town of Trebnje warrants a visit for its Gallery of Naive Artists, which was established here in 1971. Modelled after the famous Hlebine school in northern Croatia, the museum displays an outstanding collection of naive art that is principally from Slovenia and other countries of the former Yugoslavia, but also includes pieces from Africa and Asia. Characterized by sharp lines and bright clear colours, the art here depicts happy peasants, fairy-tale forests and bountiful fields. The unconventional compositions are influenced by Slovenian folk arts such as painted beehive panels and oil-on-glass votive art. Today, the collection numbers over 1,200 works, executed by more than 304 artists. The gallery also displays works by affiliated international artists.

14

Podsreda Castle
Grad Podsreda

A E4 **Q** Podsreda 45, 57 km (35 miles) NE of Novo Mesto **O** Mar–Nov: 10am–6pm Tue–Sun **W** kozjanski-park.si

With its sheer slab-sided walls perched on a high wooded spur above the valley, Podsreda Castle appears every bit the romantic castle. Originally erected in the 13th century and then owned by a succession of feudal dynasties, including the counts of Celje and Ptuj, this rectangular fortress was a near total ruin after World War II. Its impressive looks today are the result of three decades of renovation;

only the medieval kitchen looks as it did when the castle was built. Other rooms, which host an exhibition of glasswork, are bare and, in some cases, startlingly modern.

15

Olimje Monastery
Minoritski samostan Olimje

A E4 **Q** Olimje 82, 78 km (49 miles) NE of Novo Mesto **O** Pharmacy: Mar–late Oct: 10am–7pm daily; late Oct–Feb: 10am–5pm daily **W** olimje.net

Prettily located at the head of a valley near the Croatian border, Olimje Monastery is a squat Renaissance castle that was given to Pauline monks in the mid-17th century. The monks added a Baroque church to the original structure, in which they installed one of Slovenia's most extravagant religious artworks – an altar (1680)

which fills the choir with jet-black and gilt carving.

The church also features frescoes by the Pauline monk Ivan Ranger (1700–1753), a leading Baroque painter of Central Europe, which rise to a trompe l'oeil lantern. Contemporary frescoes adorn a side chapel with an altar dedicated to St Francis.

The former south tower, just off the cloisters, contains what is claimed to be Europe's third-oldest pharmacy. This low-vaulted circular room retains a low Baroque cabinet and frescoes that depict physicians from Christianity and antiquity as well as scenes of Christ healing. The pharmacy has a vestibule where the monks sell herbal cures. The chocolatier, located on one side of the monastery gardens, is also popular with visitors.

The broad Olimje Monastery, and *(inset)* its ornately frescoed interiors ↓

A DRIVING TOUR
KRKA VALLEY

Length 42 km (26 miles) **Stopping-off points** There are restaurants at every stop-off that serve traditional cuisine **Terrain** Single lane country roads

East of Novo Mesto, the Krka river snakes through a broad valley and passes a succession of large castles. These are a legacy of the Ottoman Turk expansion during the 16th century, when the Habsburg Emperor Ferdinand II established a military frontier (vojna krajina) to fight off raids from across the border. Modified later into palaces by feudal rulers, the strongholds on this route now house museums, galleries, spas and hotels. Take a full day to explore the rich Renaissance architecture dotted along this pretty valley, and reward yourself with a spa treat at Terme Čatež before a restful sleep at the charming Mokrice Castle.

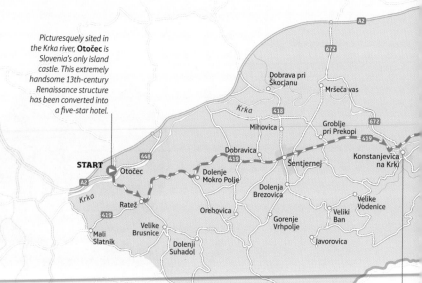

Picturesquely sited in the Krka river, **Otočec** *is Slovenia's only island castle. This extremely handsome 13th-century Renaissance structure has been converted into a five-star hotel.*

START

Otočec

Dobrava pri Škocjanu

Mršeča vas

Krka 418

Mihovica

Groblje pri Prekopi

Dobravica 419

Šentjernej

Konstanjevica na Krki

Dolenje Mokro Polje

Dolenja Brezovica

Velike Vodenice

Ratež

Orehovica

Gorenje Vrhpolje

Veliki Ban

Mali Slatnik

Velike Brusnice

Dolenji Suhadol

Javorovica

Konstanjevica na Krki, *a pretty village located on an island in the river, is home to a former Cistercian monastery.*

← An impeccable, charming room inside the castle at Otočec

↑ One of the inviting, relaxing indoor pools at Terme Čatež

Krka Valley

SOUTHEAST SLOVENIA

Locator Map

Located at the confluence of the Krka and Sava rivers, **Brežice** *centres around a Renaissance stronghold housing exquisite frescoes.*

Developed in the 1960s as a spa for people suffering from rheumatism, **Terme Čatež** *is today the largest and most popular resort in the country.*

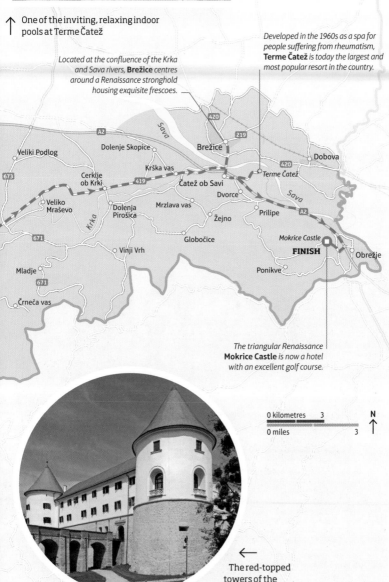

Veliki Podlog

A2

Dolenje Skopice

Sava

Brežice

420

219

420

Dobova

Krška vas

Cerklje ob Krki

419

Čatež ob Savi

Terme Čatež

673

Veliko Maševo

Dolenja Pirošica

Mrzlava vas

Dvorce

Sava

A2

Prilipe

671

Krka

Žejno

Vinji Vrh

Globočice

Mokrice Castle

FINISH

Obrežje

Mladje

671

Ponikve

Črneča vas

The triangular Renaissance **Mokrice Castle** *is now a hotel with an excellent golf course.*

0 kilometres 3
0 miles 3

N ↑

← The red-topped towers of the medieval Mokrice Castle

NEED TO KNOW

The Solkan railway bridge near Nova Gorica

BEFORE
YOU GO

Forward planning is essential to any successful trip. Be prepared for all eventualities by considering the following points before you travel.

AT A GLANCE

CURRENCY
Euro (EUR)

AVERAGE DAILY SPEND

SAVE	SPEND	SPLURGE
€35	€80	€150+

BOTTLED WATER	COFFEE	BEER	DINNER FOR TWO
€0.70	€2.00	€3.00	€35

ESSENTIAL PHRASES

Hello	Živijo
Goodbye	Nasvidenje
Please	Prosim
Thank you	Hvala
Do you speak English?	Govorite Angleško?
I don't understand	Ne Razumem

ELECTRICITY SUPPLY

Power sockets are type C and F, fitting two-pronged plugs. Standard voltage is 220–230v.

Passports and Visas

Citizens of the UK, EU, US, Canada, Australia and New Zealand do not need visas for tourist visits of up to 90 days; they can enter with just a valid passport or national ID. Always check the latest entry requirements on the Slovenian **Ministry of Foreign Affairs** website or contact the nearest Slovenian embassy before leaving.
Ministry of Foreign Affairs
W gov.si

Travel Safety Information

Visitors can get up-to-date travel safety information from the **UK Foreign and Commonwealth Office**, the **US Department of State**, and the **Australian Department of Foreign Affairs and Trade**.
Australia
W smartraveller.gov.au
UK
W gov.uk/foreign-travel-advice
US
W travel.state.gov

Customs Information

An individual is permitted to carry the following within the EU for personal use:
Tobacco products 800 cigarettes, 400 cigarillos, 200 cigars or 1 kg of smoking tobacco.
Alcohol 10 litres of alcoholic beverages above 22 per cent strength, 20 litres of alcoholic beverages below 22 per cent strength, 90 litres of wine (60 litres of which can be sparkling wine) and 110 litres of beer.
Cash If you plan to enter or leave the EU with €10,000 or more in cash (or the equivalent in other currencies), you must declare it to the customs authorities.
Limits vary if travelling outside the EU, so always check restrictions before travelling.

Insurance

It is wise to take out an insurance policy covering theft, loss of belongings, medical problems,

cancellations and delays. EU, EEA and Swiss residents with a valid **EHIC** (European Health Insurance Card) can claim free medical treatment in Slovenia. Visitors from other parts of the world must arrange private medical insurance. Note that you may have to pay upfront for medical treatment and claim it back from your insurance provider when home.
EHIC
gov.uk/european-health-insurance-card

Vaccinations

No inoculations are required, although you may wish to be vaccinated against tick-borne encephalitis if you are planning to spend time in the mountains or forested areas.

Money

Slovenia's currency is the euro. Major credit and debit cards are accepted in almost all hotels, shops, restaurants and petrol stations, while prepaid currency cards and American Express are accepted in some. Cash machines (ATMs) can be found everywhere, but it is best to change money at a bank or at one of the many *menjalnice* (bureaux de change) that can be found in larger towns and cities. You shouldn't have to pay commission at any of these places.

Booking Accommodation

Slovenia offers a wide range of accommodation, including five-star hotels, guesthouses, tourist farms and camping and caravan sites. Lodgings tend to fill up quickly in the summer, and in the ski resorts in winter (and prices are higher during both these periods), so it's worth booking ahead to secure both a place and a good deal. Browse the website of the **Slovenian Tourist Board** for a comprehensive list of accommodation.
Slovenian Tourist Board
slovenia.info

Travellers with Specific Needs

Slovenia still has some way to go to adapt to travellers with specific needs, and few hotels and restaurants are adequately equipped, although things are improving. Public transport is getting better too, with wheelchair facilities and specially adapted toilets on the InterCity

trains between Maribor and Piran, and an increasing number of stations with ramps. The website of the **Slovenian Disabled Association** has a list of disabled-friendly accommodation and facilities. The **Ljubljana by Wheelchair** app is another excellent resource.
Ljubljana by Wheelchair
ljubljanabywheelchair.com
Slovenian Disabled Association
zveza-paraplegikov.si

Language

Slovenian, a south Slavic tongue closely related to Serbian and Croatian, is not the easiest language to understand. However, the standard of English among younger Slovenes is excellent, and German is widely spoken by the older generation. Italian is widely spoken in the west (Primorska) and Hungarian in the northeast (Prekmurje). Attempting a few words in Slovenian will always be appreciated.

Closures

Sundays Most shops are open for limited hours, and public transport services are reduced.
Mondays Many, though not all, museums and tourist attractions are closed for the day. Some restaurants, especially high-end ones, are also closed.
Public holidays Schools, post offices and banks are closed.

PUBLIC HOLIDAYS	
1–2 Jan	New Year
8 Feb	Prešeren Day (Day of Slovene Culture)
Mar/Apr	Easter Sunday and Monday
27 Apr	Resistance Day
1–2 May	Labour Day
25 Jun	Slovenia Day
15 Aug	Assumption Day
31 Oct	Reformation Day
1 Nov	All Saints Day
25 Dec	Christmas Day
26 Dec	Independence and Unity Day

GETTING AROUND

Whether you are visiting for a short city break or relaxing rural retreat, discover how best to reach your destination and travel like a pro.

AT A GLANCE

PUBLIC TRANSPORT COSTS

LJUBLJANA

€1.30

Single journey
By bus

LJUBLJANA TO MARIBOR

€9–16

Single journey
By train

LJUBLJANA TO PIRAN

€12

Single journey
By bus

TOP TIP
Buy a pay-as-you-go Urbana card to pay for the funicular, buses and parking in Ljubljana.

SPEED LIMIT

MOTORWAY

130
km/h
(80 mph)

EXPRESS ROADS

110
km/h
(65 mph)

REGIONAL ROADS

90
km/h
(55 mph)

URBAN AREAS

50
km/h
(30 mph)

Arriving by Air

Slovenia has just one international airport – Jože Pučnik – located 23 km (14 miles) north of Ljubljana. Public bus 28 is the cheapest way to get into Ljubljana, and there are quicker, more expensive, shuttle buses and taxis. Alternatively, you can fly into the nearest airport in one of the neighbouring countries (Venice in Italy, or Graz or Klagenfurt in Austria) and continue from there by car or bus. **GoOpti** offers comfortable minibus transfers into Slovenia from all three of these airports, although these should be booked in advance.
GoOpti
W goopti.com

Train Travel

International Train Travel

Scheduled services link Slovenia to cities across Europe. A daily direct EuroCity service connects Vienna to Ljubljana, and there are two direct daytime services and an overnight sleeper every day from Munich to Ljubljana. There are several daily trains from Zagreb to Ljubljana. Daily direct services run from Trieste to Ljubljana, with connections from Venice. There is also a daily direct train from Budapest in Hungary. **The Man in Seat 61** is an excellent planning resource. Eurail and Interrail sell passes (to European non-residents and residents respectively) for trips lasting from five days up to three months.
Eurail
W eurail.com
Interrail
W interrail.eu
The Man in Seat 61
W seat61.com

Domestic Train Travel

The national railway operator, **Slovenian Railways** (Slovenske železnice), runs a clean, efficient service, with about 1,230 km (764 miles) of track that snake out from the capital to most areas of the country. Unusually, trains are often a little cheaper than buses. Top of the range are the ICS (InterCity Slovenia) trains that run

GETTING TO AND FROM THE AIRPORT

Airport	Distance to City	Transport	Journey Time	Fare
Jože Pučnik	23 km (14 miles)	Public bus	45 mins	€4.20
		Shuttle bus	30 mins	€10
		Taxi	30 mins	€25

between Maribor and Ljubljana (and in summer between Maribor and Koper via Ljubljana); these trains are wheelchair accessible and have air-conditioning and a buffet car. Next are the IC (InterCity) trains covering other long-distance destinations. In the next bracket are Regional (RG or LP) trains, which stop at every station on the line. Prices are calculated based on distance covered, with a return ticket costing exactly double that of a single.

Slovenian Railways
W slo-zeleznice.si

Special Train Services

Two other train services are worth mentioning. Slovenian Railways operates a car shuttle train between Bohinjska Bistrica (near Lake Bohinj) and Most na Soči via a tunnel, thereby saving a long ascent over Soriška Planina. A heritage steam locomotive known as the **Museum Train** operates between May and early November and takes in some spectacular scenery between Jesenice and Nova Gorica.

Museum Train
W abc-tourism.si

Bus Travel

International Bus Travel

Slovenia has good overland conenctions to its four neighbours: Austria, Croatia, Hungary and Italy. International bus travel can be cheaper than using high-speed trains, especially if booked at short notice, but the journeys are likely to be longer and less comfortable. Most international buses arrive and depart from Ljubljana bus station, although Maribor also has good links to Vienna, Zagreb and Belgrade. Seasonally, many Slovenian coastal cities offer direct routes to the Croatian coast and to Italy. **Flixbus** runs many services across Europe, while other major companies include **Arriva**, **Eurolines**, and **Avtobusna Postaja, Ljubljana**.

Arriva
W arriva.si
Avtobusna Postaja, Ljublana
W ap-ljubljana.si
Eurolines
W eurolines.eu
Flixbus
W flixbus.de

Domestic Bus Travel

An array of regional private companies operates the bus network within Slovenia. Buses are generally clean, punctual and rarely crowded – except for Friday evenings and weekends during the holidays. Although slightly more expensive than trains, they are able to reach many more destinations than the rail network. However, schedules are dramatically reduced at week-ends, and in many places are non-existent on Sundays. At larger stations such as Ljubljana and Maribor, you can buy your tickets hours, or days, in advance. Otherwise, buy your tickets from the counter or simply pay the driver. As with the trains, fares are priced according to distance travelled. For up-to-date information on times and prices, consult the **Ljubljana Bus Station** website.

Ljubljana Bus Station
W ap-ljubljana.si

Boats and Ferries

Between May and September, **Venezia Lines** operates a catamaran service every Saturday between Venice and Piran, a journey that takes two and a half hours. Over the same months **Liberty Lines** operates daily return trips by hydrofoil between Trieste, in Italy, and Piran, a journey of just 40 minutes.

Liberty Lines
W libertylines.it
Venezia Lines
W veneziailnes.com

Taxis

In Ljubljana and most other towns in Slovenia, you can usually find a taxi rank where you can wait for a cab, although it's much cheaper to phone ahead and book in advance. Taxis are very reasonably priced; expect to pay a starting fee of around €0.80–1.50, then a similar amount per kilometre. However, always try to confirm the fare to your destination before travelling. Tipping taxi drivers is customary but not obligatory – rounding up to the nearest euro will suffice. In Ljubljana, **Laguna Taxis** and **Rumeni Taxis** can be booked by phone.

Laguna Taxis
Ⓦ taxi-laguna.com
Rumeni Taxis
Ⓦ rumenitaxi.com

Driving

Touring by car remains by far the most enjoyable way to see Slovenia, thanks to the excellent condition of the roads, the relative lack of traffic and the short distances between destinations – for example, it takes just three hours to traverse the 280 km (174 miles) from the Adriatic coast to the Hungarian border. Moreover, a car allows you to reach those more remote parts of the country that public transport cannot. The scenery is consistently stunning, so many a stop or diversion is guaranteed. Note, though, that some high mountain passes – such as the magnificent Vršič Pass – are often closed in winter due to heavy snowfall.

The country's two main motorways are the A1, which runs east–west from Šentilj on the

ROAD JOURNEY PLANNER

Plotting the main driving routes, this map is intended as a handy reference for travelling between Slovenia's main towns and cities by car. The journey times given below reflect the fastest and most direct routes available.

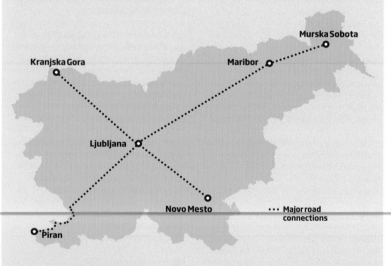

Ljubljana to Kranjska Gora	1.5 hrs
Ljubljana to Maribor	1.5 hrs
Ljubljana to Murska Sobota	2 hrs
Ljubljana to Novo Mesto	1 hr
Ljubljana to Piran	1.5 hrs
Murska Sobota to Kranjska Gora	3 hrs
Piran to Murka Sobota	3 hrs

Austrian border to Koper, and the A2, which runs northeast–southwest from the Karavanke Tunnel on the Austrian border to Obrežje on the Croatian border.

For any aspect of driving in Slovenia, contact the **Automobile Association of Slovenia** (AMZS). If your car breaks down, call the AMZS information-assistance service on their 24-hour emergency number 1987.
Automobile Association of Slovenia
🚾 amzs.si

Car Rental

To rent a car, you must be over 21, have held a full driver's licence for at least two years and have a credit card. You'll almost certainly get better rates by booking online in advance, while long-term hiring generally results in more favourable daily rates. The fee usually includes unlimited mileage (although do check this) as well as passenger indemnity insurance and coverage for third party, fire and theft, but not damage to the vehicle. Most major rental agencies have an outlet at Ljubljana airport, as well as in some of the major towns and cities such as Maribor. However, you may find that local companies, such as **ABC Rent-a-Car**, offer better deals. If you plan to cross into neighbouring countries, check with your car hire company first as this may incur a small premium.
ABC Rent-a-Car
🚾 europcar.si

Rules of the Road

If you are bringing in your own car, you will be required to bring the vehicle's registration documents and a valid certificate of third-party insurance.

Driving is on the right and overtaking is on the left; yield to traffic from the right. Seatbelts are compulsory for all passengers, dipped headlights must be used at all times and on all roads, and drivers are forbidden from using mobile phones. Carrying a reflective breakdown-warning triangle is mandatory, as is a reflective vest, a spare set of bulbs and a first-aid kit. Between mid-November and mid-March cars must be fitted with winter tyres or snow chains must be carried. To travel on motorways and expressways, you must purchase a *vinjeta* (vignette), which can be obtained at larger border crossings, petrol stations and post offices. They cost €15 for one week and €30 for a month; note that these are usually supplied if you are renting a car.

Traffic police are frequently on patrol, typically at the approaches to towns and villages. Violations are subject to fines ranging anywhere between €40 and €1,200, which must be paid at a bank or a post office. The maximum blood alcohol limit is currently 0.05 per cent; this is strictly enforced and there are severe penalties for exceeding it. All accidents should be reported to the police immediately on 113.

Parking

Parking is a problem in most cities, especially Ljubljana. Although the capital has dedicated car parks (follow the blue "P" signss), in Slovenia's towns most parking is on the streets, generally on roads on the periphery of pedestrianized areas and defined by a white line. Parking here is typically restricted to two hours and is on a pay-and-display basis, with costs being higher nearer the centre; parking costs along the coast are significantly higher too. Parking in small towns and villages is free and easy to find.

Cycling

Cycling is a hugely popular pastime in a nation where the outdoors is everything and which places such importance on the environment. Slovenia's small size and wonderfully varied topography makes it a joy to get around by bike. There are tough mountain climbs all over the country, although the terrain generally gets flatter the further east you go. There are several well-marked trails throughout Slovenia, while most cities have dedicated cycle lanes.

Note that in cities cycling is prohibited in pedestrianized areas. Apart from that, cycling is permitted on all roads except motorways and expressways. Bikes can be taken on most trains, although usually for a small fee, while some buses might allow you to store your bike in the luggage compartment.

Bike hire is widely available, from bike-sharing schemes, such as **Bicikelj** in Ljubljana, to rental outlets in all tourist hubs. An excellent outfit in Bled is **Helia**, who also offer cycling tours, while in Koroska there's **Bike Nomad**, who also do tours and even have their own dedicated bike hotel.
Bicikelj
🚾 biciklelj.si
Bike Nomad
🚾 bikenomad.com
Helia
🚾 rentabike.si

Hitchhiking

Hitchhiking is a common way for both tourists and backpackers to get around on a budget, especially in some of the more remote areas where there is no public transport; indeed, locals are usually very accommodating when it comes to giving lifts. You'll often find students on the outskirts of Ljubljana on Friday evenings seeking a ride. However, always consider your own safety before entering an unknown vehicle.

PRACTICAL
INFORMATION

A little local know-how goes a long way in Slovenia. Here you will find all the essential advice and information you will need during your stay.

AT A GLANCE

EMERGENCY NUMBERS

GENERAL EMERGENCY	POLICE
112	**113**

TIME ZONE

CET/CEST. Central European Summer Time (CEST) runs from the last Sunday in March to the last Sunday in October. Slovenia is 1 hour ahead of GMT, 6 hours ahead of EST and 10 hours behind AEST.

TAP WATER

Unless stated otherwise, tap water in Slovenia is generally considered safe to drink.

TIPPING

Waiter	10 per cent
Taxi Driver	Round up to the nearest euro

Personal Security

Slovenia is one of the safest countries in Europe, with violent crime almost non-existent; even petty theft is rare. However, it is wise to take the usual precautions: be careful where you walk at night, lock your car at all times and keep valuables out of sight. In the unlikely event of anything being stolen, report the crime to the **police**, who are generally courteous and have a good command of English. Get a copy of the crime report in order to claim on your insurance. Contact your embassy or consulate in Ljubljana if you have your passport stolen, in the event of a serious crime or accident or if you are arrested or need legal advice.

Police
w policija.si/eng

Health

Slovenia's public health services have very high standards and, accidents aside, the only real concerns for visitors are likely to be the possibility of tick-borne encephalitis and climate-related issues. If walking or climbing in the mountains, be sure to bring appropriate clothing, equipment and adequate provisions, and always keep a watchful eye on the weather, which can turn at a moment's notice. Summers can be extremely hot, so be sure to bring a high factor sun cream.

All towns and villages have at least one pharmacy *(lekarna)*. These usually have English-speaking staff and are open between 7am and 7 or 8pm; in cities and larger towns there should also be a duty pharmacy that is open 24 hours. EU citizens with a valid EHIC *(p221)* are eligible for free emergency medical treatment.

Smoking, Alcohol and Drugs

A smoking ban is enforced in all public places, including hotels, bars and restaurants. The legal blood alcohol limit for drivers is 0.05 per cent, and this is strictly enforced *(p225)*. The possession of illegal drugs is prohibited and could result in a prison sentence.

ID

There is no formal requirement for visitors to carry ID, although you may be asked to provide some form of identification if you're stopped while driving. It is therefore wise to carry some documents or at least a copy of your passport at all times.

Local Customs

On initial meetings, greet strangers with a firm handshake and maintain eye contact while doing so. If invited to visit a Slovenian home bring flowers or a bottle of wine, and don't forget to take your shoes off. Finally, the Slovene expression for "cheers!" is "Na zdravje!", which means "to your health".

LGBT+ Safety

While smaller towns and rural areas can be relatively conservative, Slovenia is a generally welcoming place and LGBT+ travellers should not face any issues. The focus of the LGBT+ scene is Ljubljana, which hosts a number of events, including the annual Gay Pride Parade in June and the Festival of Gay and Lesbian Film in December, the oldest such festival in Europe. The capital also has a number of gay bars.

Visiting Churches and Cathedrals

Always dress respectfully when visiting places of worship: cover your torso and upper arms, and ensure that shorts and skirts cover your knees.

Mobile Phones and Wi-Fi

Visitors travelling to Slovenia with EU tariffs will be able to use their devices without being affected by data roaming charges, but travellers coming from outside the EU should always check with their provider first; if international roaming charges are high it may be cheaper to buy a local SIM card in Slovenia. Almost all accommodation providers have Wi-Fi, as do most bars, cafés and restaurants, although you will be expected to make a purchase. There are also an increasing number of Wi-Fi hotspots, particularly in the cities and larger towns.

Post

The Slovenian postal service is well-run and efficient. Post offices are usually open from 8 or 9am to 5 or 6pm Monday to Friday, and until noon on Saturdays. Stamps (znamke) are available at post offices and newsstands. Allow four to five days for post to reach the UK and at least six days for the US.

Taxes and Refunds

Standard VAT is 22 per cent, with a reduced rate on accommodation, food and museums. Non-EU residents are entitled to a VAT refund on purchases totalling more than €50 (excluding alcohol and tobacco), as long as they take the goods out of the EU within three months. To make the claim, fill in a DDV-VP form and have it stamped by customs at the border or at the airport.

Discount Cards

Slovenia-specific discount cards are few and far between, but both the **ISIC** (International Student Identity Card) and **IYTC** (International Youth Travel Card) offer good discounts on transport, museums and other sights. The **Ljubljana Tourist Card** offers, among other things, free city-wide transport, free admission to more than 20 attractions, and a free guided walking tour.

ISIC
w isic.org
IYTC
w statravel.co.uk/youth-identity-card.htm
Ljubljana Tourist Card
w visitljubljana.com

WEBSITES AND APPS

I Feel Slovenia
www.slovenia.info is Slovenia's official tourism website.

Visit Ljubljana
Browse Ljubljana's official tourism website at www.visitljubljana.com.

LJ Bus
Not a route planner, this simple but useful Android app simply tracks the arrival times of Ljubljana's buses.

INDEX

Index

Page numbers in **bold** refer to main entries

PHRASE BOOK

PRONUNCIATION

c – "ts" as in rats
č – "chi" as in church
g – "g" is a hard g as in get
j – "y" as in yes
š – sh
ž – shown here as "zh", sounds like the "J" in the
French name, Jacques

EMERGENCIES

Help!	Pomóč!	pomochi
Stop!	Stóp!	stop
Call a doctor!	Poklíčite zdravníka!	poklichiite zdrawnika
Call an ambulance!	Poklíčite rešílca!	poklichiite reshilca
Call the police!	Poklíčite policíjo!	poklichiite policiyo
Call the fire brigade!	Poklíčite gasílce!	poklichiite gasilce
Where is the nearest telephone?	Kjé je najblížji telefón?	kye ye nayblizhyi telefon
Where is the nearest hospital?	Kjé je najblížja bólnica?	kye ye nayblizhya bolnitsa

COMMUNICATION ESSENTIALS

Yes	Dà	da
No	Nè	ne
Please	Prósim	prosim
Thank you	Hvála	hvala
Excuse me	Oprostíte	oprostite
Hello	Živio	zhivyo
Goodbye	Nasvídenje	nasvidenye
Good night	Láhkó nóč	lahko nochi
Morning	Jútro	Yutro
Afternoon	Popóldan	popoldan
Evening	Večér	vechier
Yesterday	Včéraj	vchieray
Today	Dánes	danes
Tomorrow	Jútri	yutri
Here	Túkaj	tukay
There	Tàm	tam
What?	Káj?	kay
When?	Kdáj?	kday
Why?	Zakáj?	zakay
Where?	Kjé?	kye

USEFUL PHRASES

How are you?	Kakó ste?	kako ste
Very well, thank you	Zeló dôbró, hvála	zelo dobro, hvala
Pleased to meet you	Me veselí	me veseli
See you soon	Kmálu se vídimo	kmalu se vidimo
That's fine	Odlíčno	odlichno
Where is/are...?	Kjé je/so...?	kye ye/so
How far is it to...?	Kakó dáleč je do...?	kako dalechi je do
How can I get to...?	Kakó láhko prídem do...?	kako lahko pridem do
Do you speak English?	Govoríte angléško?	govorite angleshko
I don't understand	Nè razúmem	ne razumem
Could you speak more slowly please?	Láhko govoríte počásneje?	lahko govorite pochiasneye
I'm sorry	Se opravíčujem	se opravichiuyem

USEFUL WORDS

big	vêlik	velik
small	májhen	mayhen
hot	vròč	vroch
cold	hláden	hladen
good	dóber	dober
bad	slab	slab
enough	dovòlj	dovolj
open	odpŕt	odprt
closed	zapŕt	zaprt
left	lévo	levo
right	désno	desno
straight on	narávnost	naravnost
near	blízu	blizu
far	dáleč	dalechi
up	gôr	gor
down	dól	dol
early	zgódaj	zgoday
late	pôzno	pozno
entrance	vhòd	vhod
exit	izhòd	izhod
toilet	straníšče	stranishchie
restaurant	restavrácija	restavratsiya

SHOPPING

How much does this cost?	Kóliko stáne to?	koliko stane to
I would like...	Želím...	zhelim
Do you have...?	Ali imáte...?	ali imate
I'm just looking	Samó glédam	samo gledam
Do you take credit cards?	Jêmljete kreditne kártice?	yemlyete kreditne kartitse
What time do you open?	Kdáj odpréte?	kday odprete
What time do you close?	Kdáj zapréte?	kday zaprete
This one	To	to
That one	Tísto	tisto
expensive	drágo	drago
cheap	pocéni	potseni
size (clothes)	velikóst (oblačíla)	velikost (oblachiila)
size (shoes)	velikóst (čévlji)	velikost (chievlyi)
white	béla	bela
black	čŕna	chirna
red	rdêča	rdechia
yellow	ruména	rumena
green	zeléna	zelena
blue	ódra	modra
bakery	pekárna	pekarna
bank	bánka	banka
bookshop	knjigárna	knyigarna
butcher's	pri mesárju	pri mesaryu
chemist's	v lekárni	v lekarni
market	tržníca	trzhnitsa
hairdresser's	pri frizêrju	pri frizeryu
newsagent's/ tobacconist	raznášalec časopísa/ trafikánt (trafikántka)	raznashalec chiasopisa/ trafikant (trafikantka)
post office	pôšta	poshta
shoe shop	trgovína za čévlje	trgovina za chievlye
supermarket	súpermárket	supermarket
travel agent	potoválni posrédnik	potovalni posrednik

SIGHTSEEING

art gallery	galerija z umetnínami	galeriya z umetninami
bus station	ávtobusna postája	avtobusna postaya
castle	grad	grad
cathedral	katedrála	katedrala
church	cérkev	cerkev
closed for holiday	zapŕto za práznike	zaprto za praznike
forest	gòzd	gozd
garden	vŕt	vrt
island	ôtok	otok
lake	jézero	yezero
mountain	gôra	gora
museum	muzêj	muzey
railway station	žéléžniška postája	zheleznishka postaya

tourist information centre	cénter za turístične informácije	center za turistichne informatsiye
waterfall	slap	slap

STAYING IN A HOTEL

Do you have a vacant room?	Imáte prosto sôbo?	imate prosto sobo
double room	Dvopósteljna sôba	dvopostelyna soba
single room	Enopósteljna sôba	enopostelyna soba
Is breakfast included?	Je zájtrk vkljúčen?	Je zaytrk vklyuchien
porter	portir	portir
key	kljúč	klyuchi
I have a reservation	Imám rezervácijo	imam rezervatsiyo

EATING OUT

Have you got a table for...?	Imáte mízo za...?	Imate mizo za
I want to reserve a table	Želím rezervírati mízo	zhelim rezervirati mizo
The bill please	Račún, prósim	rachiun prosim
I am a vegetarian	Sèm vegeterijánec/ vegetarijánka	sem vegetariyanets/ vegetariyanka
waiter/ waitress	natákar/ natákarica	natakar/ natakaritsa
menu	meni	meni
wine list	vínska kárta	vinska karta
glass	kozárec	kozarets
bottle	stekleníca	steklenitsa
knife	nòž	nozh
fork	vílica	vilitsa
spoon	žlíca	zhlitsa
breakfast	zájtrk	zaytrk
lunch	kosílo	kosilo
dinner	večérja	vechierya
main course	glávna jéd	glavna yed
starters	prèdjédi	predyedi
dessert	sladíca	sladitsa

MENU DECODER

krùh	kruh	bread
sól	sol	salt
pôper	poper	pepper
pásta	pasta	pasta
soláta	solata	salad
krompír	krompir	potatoes
krúhovi cmòki	kruhovi tsmoki	potato dumplings
zélje	zelye	cabbage
rèpa	repa	turnip
góbe	gobe	mushrooms
jábolka	yabolka	apples
hrúške	hrushke	pears
slíve	slive	plums
svinjína	svinyina	pork
klobáse	klobase	sausages
šúnka	shunka	ham
ájdova káša	aydova kasha	buckwheat porridge
njoki	nyoki	gnocchi
rižóta	rizhota	risotto
gólaž	golazh	goulash
telétina	teletina	veal
govédina	govedina	beef
divjáčina	divjachiina	venison
fazán	fazan	pheasant
zájec	zajets	rabbit
postŕv	postrv	trout
máslo	maslo	butter
piščánec	pishchianets	chicken
ríž	rizh	rice
ravióli (slovenske vrste)	ravioli	ravioli (the Slovene type)
mesné króglice	mesne kroglitse	meatballs

dúnajski zrézek	dunajski zrezek	wiener schnitzel
čevápčiči	chievapchiichii	čevapčiči
dágnje	dagnje	mussels
môrski rákci	morski raktsi	shrimp
kalamári	kalamari	squid
štrúklji	struklyi	štruklji
potíca	potitsa	potica
gibánica	gibanitsa	gibanica
zavítek	zavitek	zavitek
sladoléd	sladoled	ice cream
popárjeno	poparyeno	steamed
zavréto	zavreto	boiled
ocvrto	otsvrto	fried
zapéčeno	zapechieno	roasted

DRINKS

bélo víno	belo vino	white wine
čáj	tsay	tea
rdèče víno	rdeshie vino	red wine
gazírana minerálna vôda	gazirana mineralna voda	sparkling mineral water
negazírana minerálna vôda	negazirana mineralna voda	still mineral water
kava	káva	coffee
žgana pijača	zhgana peeyatsa	spirit
voda	vôda	water

NUMBERS

0	nìč	nichi
1	êna	ena
2	dve	dve
3	tri	tri
4	štíri	shtiri
5	pét	pet
6	šést	shest
7	sédem	sedem
8	ósem	osem
9	devét	devet
10	desét	deset
11	enájst	enayst
12	dvánajst	dvanayst
13	trínajst	trinayst
14	štírinajst	shtirinayst
15	pétnajst	petnayst
16	šéstnajst	shestnayst
17	sédemnajst	sedemnayst
18	ósemnajst	osemnayst
19	devétnajst	devetnayst
20	dvájset	dvayset
21	ênaindvájset	enaindvayset
22	dvaindvájset	dvaindvayset
30	trídeset	trideset
31	ênaintrídeset	enaintrideset
40	štírideset	shtirideset
50	pétdeset	petdeset
60	šéstdeset	shestdeset
70	sédemdeset	sedemdeset
80	ósemdeset	osemdeset
90	devétdese	devetdeset
100	stó	sto
101	stoena	stoena
102	stodve	stodve
200	dvesto	dvesto
500	petsto	petsto
700	sedemsto	sedemsto
900	devetsto	devetsto
1,000	tisoč	tisochi
1,001	tisočena	tisochiena

TIME

One minute	Ena minuta	êna minúta
One hour	Ena ura	êna úra
Half an hour	Pol ure	pól úre
Monday	Ponedeljek	ponedéljek
Tuesday	Torek	tôrek
Wednesday	Sreda	sréda
Thursday	Četŕtek	chietrtek
Friday	Pétek	petek
Saturday	Sobóta	sobota
Sunday	Nedélja	nedelya

ACKNOWLEDGMENTS

The publisher would like to thank the following for their kind permission to reproduce their photographs:

Key: a-above; b-below/bottom; c-centre; f-far; l-left; r-right; t-top

123RF.com: Zvonimir Atletic 72bl; Iakov Filimonov 119br; Vladislav Gajic 93crb; Tanja Gorjan 177tr; Kasto 99tr, 173b; Leonid Pilnik 215b; Piotrvbero 174–5t, 210tl, 212bl.

4Corners: David Bebber 134br; Franco Cogoli 4; Johanna Huber 137bc; Sebastian Wasek 162–3b; Jan Wlodarczyk 18t, 135br, 150–51.

akg-images: 53cb; Erich Lessing 53tl.

Alamy Stock Photo: Active Museum / Collection 43br; agefotostock / F. J. Fdez. Bordonada 44–5b, / J.D. Dallet 210–11b; Peter Alexander / Designed by Franc Popek 55cra; Archivah 119tr; ART Collection 54cr, 54clb; Art Collection 4 53tr; Roman Babakin 49cla; Erin Babnik 194tl; Pat Behnke 216bl; Tibor Bognar 70cl; Cavan / Aurora Photos / Menno Boermans 11t, 27cla, 31br, 138br, 144bl; Classic Image 10clb, 172tl, 172tr; Roger Cracknell 01 / classic 87br; Matjaz Corel 26–7ca, 40–41t, 120t; Danita Delimont; Agent / Walter Bibikow 174bl, / Lisa S. Engelbrecht 83br; East Images 123bl, 201b, 217bl; EBstock 146bl; Europe 24–5t, 73cl; Greg Balfour Evans 26–7t, 41cl, 104–5b; eye35 62c, 66–7, 102–3t; eye35 stock 42br, 75t, 84bl; eye35.pix 26t; FLHC 37 55cb; FLHC9 117cra; Gaertner 130t; Olga Gajewska 140tr; Janos Gaspar 29tr; Marius Graf 11cr; Guy Edwardes Photography 36bl; Hackenberg-Photo-Cologne 201crb; Peter Horree 54br; Chris Howes / Wild Places Photography 48–9b; Image Professionals GmbH / Don Fuchs 50cl; imageBROKER / Iris Kürschner 33br; Tjasa Janovljak 98tl; Jon Arnold Images Ltd / Steve Outram 54tl; Matej Kastelic 114t; Boštjan Kepic 37bl; Keystone Press / USA 56clb; Gunter Kirsch 20crb, 71tr, 96br; Matic Štojs Lomovšek 122–3t; Nino Marcutti 149; mauritius images GmbH / ClickAlps 19t, 182–3; Mehdi33300 203tr; Ian Middleton 78tr, 102bl, 121br; Mikel Bilbao Gorostiaga- Travels 12clb; 37crb, 52clb, 98b; Mint Images Limited / Spaces Images 80bl; MITO images GmbH / Robert Niedring 30–31b; Tuul and Bruno Morandi 10–11b; Serge Mouraret 100t; Juan Carlos Muñoz 176b; Nature Picture Library / Alex Hyde 45cla, / Juan Carlos Munoz 179b; Ivan Nesterov 57t; Old Images 52t; Pictorial Press Ltd 56tl; PjrTravel 33cl; Bojan Podvornik 109br; Uros Poteko 74br; Robert Preston 24cra; Prisma by Dukas Presseagentur GmbH / Van der Meer Rene 76–7t; Realy Easy Star / Toni Spagone 13br, 34–5t, 81t, 82–3t, 86cla, 97t, 169t, 169cl, 170–71b, 196t, 213t, 217tl, / Tullio Valente 165br; REDA &CO srl / Michele Bella 20cr, 101ca; RichardBakerSlovenia 192crb; Robertharding / Neale Clark 20t, / Matthew Williams-Ellis 161br; RooM the Agency / coberschneider 157tr; Goran Šafarek 28cra; Adrian Sherratt 31tr; Matic Štojs 47crb, 50cr, 51tr, 168bl, 194–5b; Sergey Strelkov 28cla; Superclic 215crb; Travel Pictures / Dallas and John Heaton 38–9t; Samo Trebizan 144–5t; VPC Photo 64b, 106l, 110tl; Ken Welsh 164–5t; Westend61 GmbH / Daniel Simon 202bl; Jan Wlodarczyk 13t; Xinhua / Luka Dakskobler 51cla, 147tr; Zoonar GmbH / Candy Rothkegel 190tl.

AWL Images: Marco Bottigelli 27tr, 28–9t; ClickAlps 24tl; Alan Copson 22br; Michele Falzone 133clb; Moreno Geremetta 28tl; Tom Mackie 2–3, 8cla, 10ca; PhotoFVG 160–61.

Bridgeman Images: © Archives Charmet 53br.

City of Women: Nada Žgank 50crb.

Depositphotos Inc: anze.bizjan 20bl; csakisti 6–7; erikzunec 179cra; kasto 51crb.

Dorling Kindersley: 116br; Linda Whitwam 93tl, 93ca, 93cra, 95cra, 95c, 95bl, 95br, 157tl.

Dreamstime.com: Anderm 200tl; Leonid Andronov 158–9t; Bereczki Barna 133br; Vojko Berk 192b; Blasch 35br; Boarding1now 57bc; Sinisa Botas 142tl; Julia Burlachenko 22t, 156–7b; Mauro Carli 186t; Dinosmichail 34bl; Marko Embreus 193tl; Erix2005 12–13b, 78–9b, 171tr; Zdenek Fiamoli 40br; Jure Gasparic 142–3b; Jamdotsi 8cl; Gregor Jeric 138–9t; Jessamine 181tl; Joyfull 188–9t; Kasto80 16c, 30tl, 58–9, 101br; Kuhar 32bl; Dejan Kuralt 118tr; Svetlana Kurochkina 132–3t; Vadim Lerner 209br; Majorosl66 166t; Martinslezacek 165cl; Alberto Masnovo 136b; Sergey Novikov 77bl; Elena Odareeva 140–41b; OneWalker 124–5; Sergiy Palamarchuk 39cla; Pawel383 52br; Photosampler 35cla; Rosshelen 22clb, 32–3t, 51cr; Rsfotography 109tl; Andrej Safaric 180bl, 197b; Sonsam 110–11b; Matic Štojs 208–9t; Daniela Simona Temneanu 11br; Andreja Tominac 13cr, 50cra, 51clb; Urospoteko 46–7t, 118tl, 214tr; Dušan Zidar 29cla; Erik Zunec 178tl; Rudmer Zwerver 85br.

Penguin
Random
House

Main Contributors Rudolf Abraham,
Darren Longley, Jonathan Bousfield,
James Stewart
Senior Editor Alison McGill
Senior Designers Sarah Snelling, Ben Hinks
Project Editor Zoë Rutland
Project Art Editors Van Anh Le, Meghna
Baruah, Ankita Sharma, Vinita Venugopal
Designer Nell Wood
Factchecker Darren Longley
Editors Rachel Laidler, Rada Radojicic,
Lucy Sara-Kelly, Lucy Sienkowska,
Rachel Thompson, Yvonne Thouroude,
Ankita Awasthi Tröger, Danielle Watt
Proofreader Susanne Hillen
Indexer Helen Peters
Senior Picture Researcher Ellen Root
Picture Research Åsa Westerlund,
Sumita Khatwani, Rituraj Singh, Vagisha Pushp
Illustrators Chinglemba Chingtham,
Sanjeev Kumar, Arun Pottirayil,
Shruti Soharia Singh
Senior Cartographic Editor Casper Morris
Cartography Ashif, Subhashree Bharati,
Simonetta Giori
Jacket Designers Sarah Snelling, Bess Daly
Jacket Picture Research Susie Watters
Senior DTP Designer Jason Little
DTP Coordinators George Nimmo, Rohit Rojal
Technical Prepress Manager Tom Morse
Image Retouching Steve Crozier
Production Controller Samantha Cross
Managing Editor Hollie Teague
Managing Art Editor Bess Daly
Art Director Maxine Pedliham
Publishing Director Georgina Dee

First edition 2012

Published in Great Britain by Dorling Kindersley Limited,
80 Strand, London, WC2R 0RL

Published in the United States by DK Publishing,
1450 Broadway, Suite 801, New York, NY 10018

Copyright © 2012, 2020 Dorling Kindersley Limited
A Penguin Random House Company
20 21 22 23 10 9 8 7 6 5 4 3 2 1

All rights reserved.

A CIP catalog record for this book
is available from the British Library.

ISSN: 1542 1554
ISBN: 978 0 2414 1132 2

Printed and bound in China.

www.dk.com